# THIS DAY IN ST. LOUIS HISTORY

The Remarkable, the Outrageous, the Spectacular, and Everything in Between

Joe Sonderman

REEDY PRESS

Final piece of Gateway Arch placed.
*Missouri Historical Society, St. Louis*

Reedy Press
PO Box 5131
St. Louis, MO 63139
reedypress.com

Design: Richard Roden

Library of Congress Control Number: On File

ISBN: 9781681065113

Printed in the United States

24 25 26 27 28  5 4 3 2 1

# CONTENTS

# INTRODUCTION

**Hazelwood West, 1980.** I just thought I would answer the old St. Louis question right off the bat because the truth is, I really started working on this book back then. When I was a student, I used to be interested in the "Through the Years" feature in the old *St. Louis Globe-Democrat*. It consisted of brief excerpts from articles on that date in history. I clipped a few of those articles and forgot about them until I was working at KLOU, 103.3 FM, in the late 1980s and early 1990s.

I had a fascination for all things '50s and '60s, which led me to research newspaper articles for history and trivia. In those pre-Internet days, that meant hours at the city library poring over old microfilm, which brought me back to those old "Through the Years" columns. Eventually, I compiled a list of dates into a primitive database that became the *Day in History* feature on the air and ultimately to a project that came out in 2002 called *St. Louis 365*.

The real impetus for this work came about once I started a Facebook page called *Vintage St. Louis* and began posting these snippets every day. The interaction with readers prompted me to do additional research, make corrections to what I had posted, and update the page with the latest historic events.

So a list of a few dates clipped from the *St. Louis Globe-Democrat* grew into a collection of 10, sometimes 15 or more, items per day, posted on a site with thousands of followers. The hard part was narrowing them down to the most interesting items for this book. So what we have here is what I thought to be an interesting cross section of St. Louis history and trivia. It ranges from the important events to the trivial and pop-culture oriented.

The goal is not to present a serious historical work but to provide things you may not know about St. Louis history, personalities, historic buildings, institutions, roads, bridges, TV and radio, and sports. I hope you find it interesting, no matter where you went to high school.

1944 Browns versus Cardinals World Series at Sportsman's Park
Missouri Historical Society, St. Louis

South Side National Bank
*Missouri Historical Society, St. Louis*

## January 1, 1926

**The Shell Building at 13th and Locust opened.** At the time, Shell was known as the Roxana Petroleum Company. The name was changed in 1928, and the building served as the Shell Oil Company headquarters until 1940. Designed by architects James Jamieson and George Spearl, the rounded building is patterned after the Shell Oil Company's logo. During the 1930s, General James H. Doolittle, leader of the famous bombing raid on Tokyo during World War II, worked here and was in charge of the company's aviation department.

### Served as the Shell Oil Company HQ until 1940

*Courtesy Missouri Historical Society, St. Louis*

## January 3, 1836

**Anthony Edward Faust was born in Prussia.** He later moved to St. Louis and, in 1862, opened a small restaurant at Broadway and Chouteau, which he later relocated to Broadway and Elm. In 1878, the restaurant became the first building in St. Louis with electric lights. During the 1890s, Tony Faust's Oyster House, or "Tony's," was the place where the elite in St. Louis met. Faust's restaurant closed in 1916.

*Courtesy Missouri Historical Society, St. Louis*

## January 1, 1954

**In an unprecedented message read at New Year's masses, Archbishop Joseph Ritter forbade Catholics "under the penalty of sin" to see** *The French Line*, **which was playing at the Fox Theatre.** An 80-foot-tall likeness of the movie's star, Jane Russell, towered over the Fox to promote the film. Ritter urged Catholics to boycott the Fox, which he called "a palace of sin."

*Courtesy Wikipedia*

## January 2, 1929

**The first skyscraper on the south side was constructed for the South Side National Bank.** The opening of this 10-story Art Deco building was heralded as "The Dawn of a New Day for Grand and Gravois." It was nearly demolished and replaced by a Walgreens in the late 1990s, but instead the upper portion was converted to condominiums and the bank space became the Noble reception hall. *(facing page)*

## January 2, 2017

**St. Louis hosted the Bridgestone Winter Classic.** On a wet and dreary day, 46,556 fans came to Busch Stadium to see the Blues and the Blackhawks play outdoors in the 2017 Bridgestone NHL Winter Classic. The Blues won 4–1 with Vladimir Tarasenko scoring two goals in the third period.

*Courtesy author*

### January 3, 1988

**The Varsity Theater closed with a final showing of *The Rocky Horror Picture Show*.** The theater at 6610 Delmar opened in 1935. In March 1976, the Varsity was one of the first US theaters to run *Rocky Horror*, and by the spring of 1978, it was being shown as a midnight movie every weekend. After the theater closed, it was gutted and became a drugstore. Vintage Vinyl is now located there.

### January 4, 1884

**The mercury plunged to 26 degrees below zero, the lowest official reading ever recorded here.** That terrible night, 26 Sisters of Notre Dame died in a fire at their convent in Belleville.

### January 4, 1965

**Thomas Stearns Eliot died in his London apartment.** Born in St. Louis, the grandson of the founder of Washington University established himself as a poet with "The Love Song of J. Alfred Prufrock." His *Old Possum's Book of Practical Cats* is the basis for the play and the film *Cats*.

### January 5, 1914

**Aaron "Bunny" Lapin was born in St. Louis.** He invented whipped cream in an aerosol can (Reddi-wip) in 1947. It was first sold by Pevely Dairy milkmen in St. Louis in 1948 and gained national distribution in 1954.

### January 5, 1994

**The new Clark Bridge over the Mississippi River at Alton was dedicated.** Sometimes called the "Super Bridge" because of its revolutionary design, the 4,260-foot-long structure was the first to use dual continuous cable stays suspended from a single pylon to support the road deck.

*Courtesy Wikipedia*

### January 4, 1942

**Rogers Hornsby was elected to the Baseball Hall of Fame.** Considered the greatest right-handed hitter of all time, Hornsby led the National League in batting from 1920 to 1925 and again in 1928. His lifetime batting average of .358 is the highest in National League history and the third highest in major-league history. He managed the 1926 World Champion team and won MVP awards in 1925 and 1929.

## Considered the greatest right-handed hitter of all time

### January 5, 1905

**The *St. Louis Globe-Democrat* reported that Louisiana Purchase Exposition employees had discovered a new use for the hill in front of the Palace of Fine Arts.** Now cleared of trees, "Art Hill" made a perfect toboggan slope. The employees used discarded folding chairs as sleds.

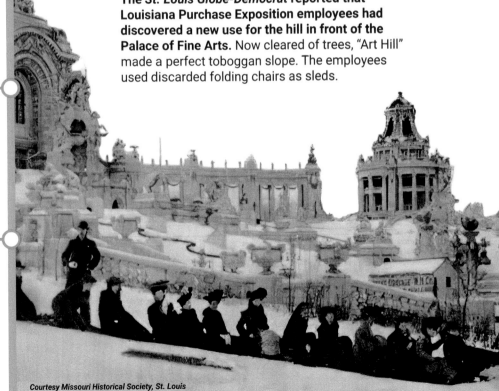

*Courtesy Missouri Historical Society, St. Louis*

## January 6, 1963

***Mutual of Omaha's Wild Kingdom* made its debut.** Saint Louis Zoo Director Marlin Perkins hosted the television show, which inspired the many familiar nature-show concepts we have today. Field correspondent Jim Fowler usually ended up facing the dangerous creatures. The show ran in prime time until 1971, when it went into syndication. Original episodes were produced for another 19 years.

*Courtesy Wikipedia*

*Courtesy Don Korte*

## January 7, 1985

**The great base burglar Lou Brock was elected to the Baseball Hall of Fame.** Brock came to the Cardinals in a trade with the Cubs for struggling pitcher Ernie Broglio in 1964 and then sparked the team to the 1964 World Championship. He was a vital part of the 1960s championship teams. He stole 938 bases in his career and 118 bases in 1974.

**The great base burglar Lou Brock was elected to the Baseball Hall of Fame.**

*Courtesy St. Louis Public Library–Lemens Collection*

## January 8, 1894

**William H. Danforth incorporated the Robinson-Danforth Commission Company with a capital investment of $12,000.** Danforth started out in a seasonal feed business but observed that "animals need to eat year-round," so he began mixing feed. The name of the firm was changed to Ralston Purina in 1902. While serving in World War I, Danforth noticed how eagerly the soldiers waited for "chow" and applied the name to his feeds.

## January 6, 1912

**The magnificent new Main Library on Olive opened.** Andrew Carnegie had donated $1 million for the library, with the stipulation that the city should provide $150,000 annually for maintenance. It was designed by pioneering architect Cass Gilbert. The library closed for a $70 million rehab in June 2010 and was rededicated on November 17, 2012.

## January 6, 1972

**Blues coach Al Arbour, along with players John Arbour, Phil Roberto, and Floyd Thompson, were hauled off to jail after a riot at the Spectrum in Philadelphia.** Several Blues players climbed into the stands to brawl with fans who had dumped a beer on the coach. Four fans were hurt.

## January 7, 1856

**Thousands flocked to the riverfront to see the Mississippi completely frozen over.** Some of the more hardy souls walked across, and saloonkeepers did a thriving business in the middle of the river, out of the reach of the law. Before it was narrowed and channeled, the Mississippi frequently froze over.

## January 7, 1913

**Cardinals great Johnny Mize was born in Demorest, Georgia.** He held the all-time single-season Cardinals record for home runs until Mark McGwire came along. The "Big Cat" stands at number two on the Redbird career batting average list with .312. A contract dispute led to Mize being dealt to the Giants in 1941. He was elected to the Hall of Fame in 1981.

*Courtesy Wikipedia*

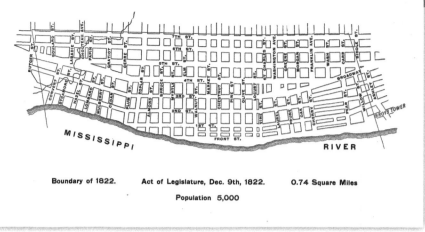

### St. Louis, Mo.

Boundary of 1822.   Act of Legislature, Dec. 9th, 1822.   0.74 Square Miles

Population 5,000

*Courtesy Missouri Historical Society, St. Louis*

## January 8, 1952

**Frankie Baker died in a Portland, Oregon, mental institution.** She claimed to be the former teenage prostitute who shot her lover "Johnny" at 212 Targee Street on October 15, 1899. The shooting was immortalized in the song "Frankie and Johnny." When the song became the basis for a motion picture, she sued, but she lost the case.

## January 8, 1953

**Bruce Sutter was born in Lancaster, Pennsylvania.** Whitey Herzog traded Ken Reitz, Ty Waller, and Leon Durham to Chicago for Sutter on December 9, 1980. His split-finger fastball baffled hitters and helped the Cardinals to the 1982 World Championship.

## January 9, 1978

**It snowed in St. Louis.** Now, that wasn't unusual except that it marked the start of 71 days in a row with snow on the ground here. That's the local record.

## January 10, 2001

**TWA filed for bankruptcy and reached a $500 million buyout agreement with American Airlines.** TWA CEO William Compton said the deal would "protect substantially all of our thousands of employees."

## January 10, 2006

**Former Cardinals reliever Bruce Sutter was named to the Baseball Hall of Fame.**

## January 11, 1963

**The first stainless-steel section to be used in the construction of the Gateway Arch was delivered.** Each sheet was 12 feet high, three feet wide, and 54 feet long. When three sheets were welded together, they would form a triangular section. One steel section on each leg was expected to go up each week.

## January 9, 1822

**The Missouri Legislature approved the incorporation of St. Louis as a city.** The measure was not to take effect until voted on by the inhabitants. Voters approved it on March 3, 1823, and the first election of officers took place on April 7, 1823. At the time, St. Louis had a population of about 5,000. St. Louis had been incorporated as a town in 1809.

## January 10, 1962

**A dust fire led to an explosion and a huge blaze at the landmark Purina Chow plant at Checkerboard Square.** The fire burned out of control for over 20 hours. Two workers died, 41 were hurt, and a fire captain died of a heart attack. It was seven below zero that day.

*Courtesy State Historical Society of Missouri*

## January 11, 1822

**The Great Seal of Missouri was adopted by the General Assembly.** Designed by Judge Robert William Wells, who was also a congressman, the center contains the seal of the US on the right and state symbols on the left. The bears represent strength and bravery, and the crescent moon represents newness and growth. The state motto on the scroll is "Salus Populi Suprema Lex Esto." The Latin meaning is "Let the welfare of the people be the supreme law."

## January 12, 2007

**Police found kidnapped teens Ben Ownby and Shawn Hornbeck safe in a Kirkwood apartment.** Shawn had disappeared in Richwoods, Missouri, on October 6, 2002. Ben had been kidnapped on January 8, 2007, in Beaufort, Missouri. The suspect was identified as Michael Devlin, the manager of a pizza restaurant. Investigators hailed 15-year-old Mitchell Hults as a hero for giving the police an accurate description of the truck used to take Ben. The national media dubbed the case "The Missouri Miracle."

### The Missouri Miracle

## January 13, 1950

Bob Forsch
*Courtesy Wikipedia, credit Johnmaxmena2*

**Robert Forsch was born in Sacramento, California.** Forsch pitched for the Redbirds from 1974 until 1988. He is the only Cardinals pitcher to toss two no-hitters. His brother Ken also threw a no-hitter for Houston, making them the only brothers in Major League history to hurl no-hitters. When he died in November 2011, Bob was third all time in victories among Cardinals pitchers.

Ken Forsch
*Courtesy Wikipedia*

## January 14, 1928

**The city of St. Louis formally acquired an airport.** Mayor Victor Miller signed a bill allowing for the leasing and eventual purchase of Albert Bond Lambert's flying field for 18 months. The mayor said work would begin at once to transform the field into "one of the finest airdromes in the world."

*Courtesy Missouri Historical Society, St. Louis*

## January 15, 1929

**Jacques Plante was born.** The Hall of Fame NHL goalie was the first to wear a mask during games. He played for the Blues late in his career, sharing the Vezina Trophy for best goaltender with teammate Glenn Hall in 1969. Plante died on February 27, 1986.

Jacques Plante
*Courtesy Missouri Historical Society, St. Louis*

## January 12, 1999

**The man behind the "Monday Night Miracle" lost his battle with cancer.** Former Blues player Doug Wickenheiser was 37. Number 14 is best remembered for his overtime goal that clinched the dramatic come-from-behind win in Game Six of the 1986 Campbell Conference Finals.

## January 13, 1951

**The $11 million Veterans Bridge across the Mississippi opened.** At the time, the bridge was the sixth-largest cantilever-type bridge in the country. It carried Route 66 traffic from 1955 until 1967 and was renamed to honor Dr. Martin Luther King Jr. in 1972.

## January 14, 1898

**Five Tennessee and Mississippi businessmen opened a wholesale house that would develop into the largest shoe manufacturing company in the world.** John Roberts, Jackson Johnson, Edgar Rand, Oscar Johnson, and Eugene Roberts founded International Shoe. The former headquarters building is now a hotel.

## January 15, 1981

**Cardinals great Bob Gibson was elected to the Baseball Hall of Fame in his first year of eligibility.** Gibson was a five-time 20-game winner with 3,117 career strikeouts. His 1.12 ERA in 1968 was the lowest ever by a Major Leaguer. He fanned 200 or more batters in a season nine times and had two seasons with 13 shutouts.

*Courtesy Getty Images*

# JANUARY

**January 15, 1988**

**Big Red owner Bill Bidwill formally announced that the team was moving to Phoenix.** During the previous season, Bidwill made it clear that the team was headed either to Jacksonville, to Baltimore, or to the desert. During that last season, Bidwill was threatened so often that he stopped attending games. Bidwill tearfully described his feelings as "mixed."

**January 16, 1980**

**José Alberto Pujols Alcántara was born in the Dominican Republic.** He would go on to play 22 seasons in the Major Leagues for the Cardinals, the Los Angeles Angels, and the Los Angeles Dodgers. Pujols would win three MVP awards and a Rookie of the Year Award and would play on two World Championship teams while hitting 703 career home runs.

**January 17, 1952**

**Darrell Porter was born in Joplin.** He played for Milwaukee and Kansas City and publicly announced he had overcome a drug and alcohol problem before signing with the Cardinals in 1981. Porter dominated the 1982 postseason, batting .556 in the NLCS and being named MVP of the World Series. He was found dead of an apparent heart attack in a suburban Kansas City park in 2002.

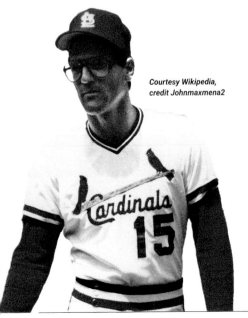

*Courtesy Wikipedia, credit Johnmaxmena2*

*Courtesy Heinrich Klaffs*

**January 16, 1991**

**Ike & Tina Turner were inducted into the Rock & Roll Hall of Fame.**

*Courtesy Wikipedia*

*Courtesy Wikipedia, credit Jamal Farmer*

**January 17, 1995**

**Los Angeles Rams owner Georgia Frontiere announced her team was moving to St. Louis, ending the city's long quest to replace the Cardinals.** Frontiere was born in St. Louis. She took over the team in 1979, when husband Carroll Rosenbloom accidentally drowned while swimming in the ocean off the coast of Golden Beach, Florida.

## The Rams are moving to St. Louis!

**January 18, 1992**

**The landmark Southtown Famous-Barr at Chippewa and Kingshighway closed.** It was torn down in 1995, and plans called for construction of a Venture store. But Venture folded, and the site remained vacant as plans for a big-box retailer fell through and neighbors fought a proposal for a Kmart on the site. A Walgreens on the corner and a strip mall on the rest of the site opened in 2005.

*Courtesy Missouri State Archives*

## January 19, 2013

**Stan Musial died at the age of 92.** "The Man" played his entire 22-year career with the Cardinals. After the 1963 season, Musial retired with a .331 career batting average and as the National League's career leader in RBIs, games played, runs scored, hits, and doubles. In 1969, he was elected to the National Baseball Hall of Fame.

*Courtesy Wikipedia*

*Courtesy author*

## January 20, 1917

**The first free bridge over the Mississippi River at St. Louis opened.** The Municipal Bridge, renamed in honor of General Douglas MacArthur in 1942, carried Route 66 traffic from 1929 to 1935, and City 66 from 1936 to 1955. The bridge's very high and narrow approaches from the east and sudden jog at the west end resulted in many accidents.

*Courtesy Missouri State Archives*

## January 21, 1845

**Edward Mallinckrodt was born in St. Louis.** He studied chemistry in Germany with his brother Otto. In 1867, Edward and his brothers Gustave and Otto established G. Mallinckrodt and Company on the family farm in North St. Louis. The firm became the first to manufacture fine chemicals west of the Mississippi. Mallinckrodt was manufacturing 400 chemicals by the turn of the century.

*Edward Mallinckrodt*
*Courtesy Missouri Historical Society, St. Louis*

## January 19, 1807

**Robert E. Lee was born in Stratford, Virginia.** As a lieutenant in the Corps of Engineers in 1838, he designed a system of dikes that kept the Mississippi from silting up and threatening the harbor at St. Louis. Lee met another former St. Louisan on April 9, 1865, at Appomattox Court House, Virginia, when he surrendered to General Ulysses S. Grant.

## January 19, 1975

**Thomas Hart Benton died at the age of 85.** His most famous work is a 13-panel mural in the Missouri capitol, *Social History of Missouri*. Benton's murals caused a scandal when they were unveiled because the scenes included images of criminals, crooked politicians, slavery, religious persecution, and other controversial social issues.

*Courtesy Wikipedia*

## January 20, 1958

**Radio station KWK finished its "Record-Breaking Week."** During the week, disc jockeys gave every rock and roll record in the library a farewell spin and then smashed it to bits on the air. Station manager Robert Convey called it "a simple weeding out of undesirable music." In response, Danny & the Juniors were inspired to record "Rock and Roll Is Here to Stay."

*Courtesy Wikipedia*

## January 21, 1953

**Dizzy Dean was inducted into the Baseball Hall of Fame.** One of the few pitchers to win 30 or more games in a season during the modern era, he was the National League MVP in 1934 while leading the Cardinals' Gashouse Gang to the World Championship. He is also remembered for mangling words as a broadcaster.

## January 22, 1959

**Linda Blair was born in St. Louis.** Raised in Connecticut, Linda is best known for playing Regan in the 1973 film *The Exorcist*. The role earned her Golden Globe and People's Choice Awards for Best Supporting Actress as well as an Academy Award nomination. The film was based on an incident that occurred in St. Louis.

## January 23, 1975

**Construction of the 35-story, 484-foot-tall Mercantile Tower was completed in downtown St. Louis.** At the time, it was the tallest building in the city. Now known as One US Bank Plaza, it has been topped by the Eagleton Courthouse (557 feet), One AT&T Center (formerly SBC Center, 588 feet), and the Metropolitan Square Building (42 stories, 593 feet).

## January 23, 2000

**Ricky Proehl assured himself a place in St. Louis sports history.** With 4:44 left in the NFC Championship Game, the wide receiver made "The Catch." His one-handed, leaping 30-yard touchdown grab gave the Rams an 11–6 win over Tampa Bay and earned St. Louis its first trip to the Super Bowl.

## January 22, 1968

**Joe Medwick was named to the Baseball Hall of Fame.** "Muscles" Medwick patrolled the outfield for the Cardinals from 1932 to 1940 and again in 1947 and 1948. In 1937 he led the National League in batting average and RBIs while tying for the lead in home runs.

*Courtesy Wikipedia*

*Courtesy Wikipedia*

## January 23, 1986

**Chuck Berry was among the first group of performers to be inducted into the Rock & Roll Hall of Fame.** Keith Richards of the Rolling Stones inducted Berry that night. Richards said, "It's hard for me to induct Chuck Berry, because I lifted every lick he ever played!"

## January 24, 1883

**The Anheuser-Busch Brewing Association took over the rights to sell Budweiser in the US.** They acquired the rights from Carl Conrad, who had been bottling and selling the beer made by his friend Adolphus Busch. "Budweiser" is actually a centuries-old traditional name for beers made in the style of the breweries of the Bohemian town of Ceske Budovice, or "Budweis" in German. At one time, several other breweries, including Miller and Schlitz, made Budweisers.

*Courtesy Missouri Historical Society, St. Louis*

## January 25, 1991

**Brett Hull of the St. Louis Blues became the fifth player in NHL history to score 50 goals in 50 or fewer games.** Hull scored his 50th in the Blues 49th game of the year, a 9–4 rout of the Detroit Red Wings.

*Fifth player in NHL history to score 50 goals in 50 or fewer games*

## January 26, 1961

**Wayne Gretzky was born in Brantford, Ontario.** "The Great One" came to the Blues on February 27, 1996, in a trade for Patrice Tardif, Roman Vopat, and Craig Johnson. He racked up 37 points in 31 games for the Blues but was uncomfortable under coach Mike Keenan. He signed with the New York Rangers as a free agent in July of 1996.

Brett Hull (left) and Wayne Gretzky (right)
*Courtesy Getty Images*

## January 27, 1999

**More than 100,000 attended a Mass led by Pope John Paul II at the Trans World Dome.** He urged wayward Catholics to return to the faith. The pope then wrapped up his 30-hour visit with a service at the Cathedral Basilica, attended by Vice President Al Gore. He also met with civil rights leader Rosa Parks. John Paul II boarded a plane dubbed "Shepherd One" by TWA for the trip back to Rome.

*Courtesy Wikipedia, credit Zkoty1953*

## January 24, 1968

**The St. Louis Symphony Orchestra played its first concert at its new home, Powell Hall.** The hall is named for shoe manufacturing executive Walter S. Powell, whose widow, Helen Lamb Powell, donated $1 million for the hall. The building was originally known as the St. Louis Theatre. The last movie shown there was *The Sound of Music*.

## January 25, 1978

**The temperature dipped below 32 degrees.** That's not normally worth noting in January, but this time, the mercury would not rise above the freezing mark until February 23. That's a string of 30 consecutive freezing days, the longest recorded in St. Louis history.

*Courtesy Pixabay*

## January 26, 1999

**President Bill Clinton met Pope John Paul II as the pontiff arrived at Lambert Field in St. Louis.** Dire predictions of gridlock on the streets never materialized. Downtown parking lot owners were actually grumbling over the number of empty spaces. More than 20,000 youths cheered the pope at a service at Kiel Center, and backstage, John Paul II met Mark McGwire. It was 54 degrees that day, which added to the legend of the "Pink Sisters." The nuns had prayed for good weather for the visit.

*Courtesy Wikipedia*

## January 27, 2002

**The Rams booked a trip to the Big Easy after beating the Philadelphia Eagles 29–24 to take the NFC Championship.** Donovan McNabb's touchdown run with three minutes to go and a three-and-out by the Rams gave the Eagles a shot. But with a minute to go, McNabb was picked off by Aeneas Williams, sending the Rams to their ill-fated showdown with the New England Patriots.

## January 28, 1891

**Bill Doak was born in Pittsburgh.** He pitched for the Cardinals for 11 seasons and still ranks second behind Bob Gibson with 32 shutouts as a Cardinal. When the spitball was banned in 1920, "Spittin' Bill" was one of 17 pitchers allowed to continue throwing the pitch. But he is best remembered for designing a glove with laced webbing between the first finger and the thumb. The Rawlings "Bill Doak Model" is still the standard today.

## January 29, 1904

**The *St. Louis Post-Dispatch* reported that the Palace of Fine Arts at the St. Louis World's Fair would remain after the fair.** The report said the 348-by-166-foot central pavilion of Bedford cut stone would be converted into a permanent museum of fine arts on the order of the Field Museum in Chicago.

*Courtesy Patrick Murphy*

## January 30, 1821

**The town of Alton, Illinois, was incorporated.** Colonel Rufus Easton laid out the town and named it after his son Alton. Colonel Easton was the first postmaster general of St. Louis and a former Missouri Territorial delegate to Congress. He saw Alton as an ideal site to establish a ferry. Langdon, George, Easton, and Alby Streets are named for his sons and daughter.

*Courtesy author*

## January 28, 1981

**Former hostage Marine Sergeant Rocky Sickmann arrived aboard an Ozark Airlines plane to a wild welcome at Lambert Field.** A motorcade took him home to Krakow, Missouri. Sickmann spent 444 days as one of 52 Americans held hostage in Iran. He went on to work for Anheuser-Busch for 34 years.

*Courtesy Wikipedia*

## January 29, 1959

**The *Great St. Louis Bank Robbery* made its world premiere at Loew's Orpheum Theatre.** The film starred Steve McQueen, who had played his first major role in *The Blob* a year earlier. Charles Guggenheim and John Stix directed the film. The movie told the story of the April 1953 holdup and shoot-out at Southwest Bank. It featured 24 St. Louis police officers, many of whom had been on the scene on that violent day.

## January 30, 2000

**The Rams brought St. Louis its first Super Bowl title with a 23–16 win over the Tennessee Titans in Super Bowl XXXIV at the Georgia Dome in Atlanta.** Kurt Warner, who was named the game's most valuable player, was 24 of 45 for a Super Bowl–record 414 yards and two touchdowns. Isaac Bruce had six catches for 162 yards. Rams linebacker Mike Jones tackled Titans receiver Kevin Dyson at the one-yard line as time ran out to preserve the win.

*Courtesy Wikipedia, credit Baer Tirkel*

## The Rams brought St. Louis its first Super Bowl title with a 23–16 win over the Tennessee Titans.

## January 31, 1982

**The Missouri National Guard was called out in the aftermath of the worst snowstorm in St. Louis in 70 years.** At least 10 people were dead. Exactly nine months later, nurses at St. John's Mercy Medical Center said they noticed a marked increase in births due to the blizzard. The babies began arriving on schedule between October 23 and November 14.

*Courtesy Missouri Historical Society, St. Louis*

### January 30, 1982

**At about 3:30 on this Saturday afternoon, forecasters issued a winter storm watch.** That meant four or more inches of snow was expected. By suppertime, heavy snow was falling, and a violent snowstorm had developed. Officially, 13.9 inches of snow fell at Lambert Field by the next day, but unofficial totals were closer to 22 inches.

### January 31, 1929

**The Fox Theatre was dedicated.** Governor Henry Caulfield and Mayor Victor Miller attended the showing of *Street Angel* starring Janet Gaynor. William Fox had turned a $1,600 investment in a single Brooklyn theater into an empire of 305 nationwide by 1929. A few months after the Fox opened, he took over the Loew's Corporation, adding 500 more theaters and MGM Studios. But the expense of converting his theaters to sound in the midst of the Great Depression bankrupted him in 1936.

*Courtesy Missouri Historical Society, St. Louis*

### January 31, 2000

**About 100,000 people braved the cold and lined the route downtown for a parade honoring the Super Bowl Champion Rams.** Players rode in the back of pickup trucks while shaking hands with the crowd and waving. The Budweiser Clydesdales led Coach Dick Vermeil through the parade.

## February 1, 2000

**Less than 48 hours after his team won the Super Bowl, Rams Coach Dick Vermeil announced his retirement.** The Rams named offensive coordinator Mike Martz as the 21st head coach of the Rams the following day.

## February 2, 1863

**A young writer from Missouri used his new pen name for the first time, in three dispatches for the Virginia City, Nevada, *Territorial Enterprise*.** Samuel Clemens heard the term "Mark Twain" during his days as a steamboat pilot in St. Louis. The term signified a depth of two fathoms, safe for a steamboat.

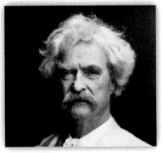

*Courtesy Wikipedia*

## February 2, 1876

**The St. Louis Brown Stockings were among the eight teams to sign on when the National Baseball League was founded.** The other seven cities were Boston, Chicago, New York, Cincinnati, Philadelphia, Louisville, and Hartford. This first Brown Stockings club folded after the 1877 season.

## February 3, 1902

**Seven city firemen were killed in a fire at the five-story building housing the American Tent and Awning Company at Third and Chestnut.** First Assistant Chief August Thierry was among the dead. The wall of the building collapsed on the firefighters just as they were satisfied the blaze was under control.

*Courtesy Wikipedia*

## February 1, 1869

**Kerry Mills was born in Philadelphia.** One night in 1904, the New York composer ordered a popular drink known as a "Louis." The bartender's name was also Louis, so he said, "Give me another Louis, Louis." His friend, lyricist Andrew B. Sterling, chuckled at the repetition. Sterling soon penned a song about a wife who left her husband Louis to go to the World's Fair and asked him to "Meet Me in St. Louis, Louis." (Louis was pronounced "Louie" in the song.) Mills wrote the music.

## February 2, 1923

**Albert "Red" Schoendienst was born in Germantown, Illinois.** He became one of the top second basemen in the National League despite suffering from double vision from an injury as a teenager and playing for years with tuberculosis. He managed the Cardinals from 1965 to 1976, and again in 1980 and 1990. He was elected to the Baseball Hall of Fame in 1989. He died on June 6, 2018.

### One of the top second basemen in the National League

*Courtesy Wikipedia, credit John Mena*

## February 3, 1956

**Becky "The Queen of Carpet" Rothman was born in St. Louis.** Her parents owned Veterans Linoleum and Rug Company in East St. Louis. In 1988 she began appearing in zany TV commercials riding on a magic carpet, often with Wanda "Princess of Tile" Kilzer, to promote Becky's Carpet & Tile Superstores. The carpet stores closed during the recession in June 2012. Rothman passed away on May 28, 2023.

*Courtesy Pixabay*

## February 4, 1902

**Charles Lindbergh was born in Detroit.** He spent his childhood in Little Falls, Minnesota, and in Washington, DC. While best remembered for his transatlantic flight, he also convinced the Guggenheim family to fund rocketry experiments by Robert Goddard and invented an artificial heart. Lindbergh was criticized for speaking out against voluntary US entry into World War II. But once war came, he flew 50 combat missions as a civilian advisor and developed new techniques that increased the capability of American fighter planes.

*Courtesy Missouri Historical Society, St. Louis*

## February 5, 1977

**A couple of rookies who would go on to great success made their debut for the Blues.** Future Hall of Famer Bernie Federko and the great Brian Sutter came to the Blues on the same day. Federko scored three goals in his first game, including the winner against Buffalo at the Arena.

Bernie Federko (top) and Brian Sutter (right)
*Courtesy Getty Images*

## February 6, 1988

**Barclay Plager died of cancer.** Number Eight was known as "The Spirit of the Blues" and was a four-time All-Star. Two of his brothers, Bobby and Billy, also played for the Blues. Barclay also coached the Blues for parts of four seasons and they retired his number in 1982.

Barclay Plager
*Courtesy Getty Images*

## February 4, 2017

**Kurt Warner was named to the NFL Hall of Fame.** After playing in the Arena Football League and NFL Europe, he played in one game for the Rams in 1998 and became the starting quarterback in 1999 after an injury to Trent Green. Warner went on to become the NFL MVP as the Rams capped the season with a 23–16 victory over the Tennessee Titans in Super Bowl XXXIV.

He recorded another MVP season two years later as the Rams returned to the Super Bowl and made a third Super Bowl appearance in 2008 with the Arizona Cardinals.

## February 5, 1830

**Fee Fee Road was declared an open public road.** One of the oldest roads in St. Louis County, Fee Fee is named for Nicholas "Fifi" Beaugenou. (Fifi denoted "son" or "junior" in French.) Beaugenou was one of the 30 men who helped Pierre Laclède begin construction on the trading post that became the city of St. Louis. He settled in what is now Bridgeton after his wife died.

## February 5, 1914

**Author William Burroughs was born at 4644 Pershing.** He was the grandson of the man who founded the Burroughs Adding Machine Company. Burroughs went to New York in his 30s and became a heroin addict before meeting future Beat Generation icons Jack Kerouac and Allen Ginsberg. Burroughs's most famous work, *Naked Lunch*, was published in 1959.

## February 6, 1837

**The Missouri Legislature approved a state road from St. Louis to Springfield, following the old Indian Osage Trail.** The road became known as the Springfield to St. Louis Road. During the Civil War, telegraph wires along its length gave it the name the Wire Road. Portions of it became MO 14 in 1922 and then US 66 in 1926. Interstate 44 follows the corridor today.

# FEBRUARY

**February 7, 1928**

**The city agreed to the generous offer by Albert Bond Lambert to sell the airfield he had developed at his own cost.** He sold the airport for $68,000, a fraction of its market value. The purchase was contingent on the passage of a bond issue to pay for improvements.

**February 8, 2014**

**On a bitterly cold day, the $695 million Stan Musial Veterans Memorial Bridge over the Mississippi River was dedicated.** It opened the next day. The 2,803-foot-long bridge is the third-longest cable-stayed span in the nation. Once the bridge opened, Interstate 70 was routed across the Musial and Interstate 44 was extended to the east over the old I-70 alignment downtown.

**February 9, 1951**

**The St. Louis Browns signed the great Satchel Paige to pitch for the coming season.** At the time, he was 46 years old. Paige relaxed in his own personal rocking chair on the sidelines when he was not on the mound. That year he would win 12 games and become the oldest player ever named to the All-Star team. He also threw a 12-inning complete game.

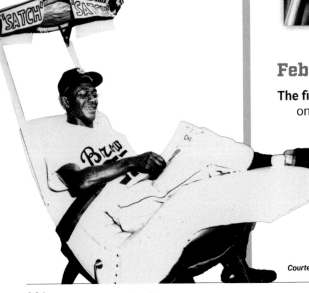

**February 7, 2008**

**Disgruntled resident Charles "Cookie" Thornton came to Kirkwood City Hall armed with a .44 magnum.** He shot and killed police Sgt. William Biggs outside, then burst into the council chamber, killing officer Tom Ballman, public works director Ken Yost, and council members Connie Carr and Michael Lynch. Mayor Mike Swoboda was also shot and died of his injuries on September 6. Police officers shot and killed Thornton.

*Courtesy author*

*Courtesy Wikipedia*

**February 8, 1947**

**The first television station in St. Louis signed on the air.** KSD was one of only seven television stations in the US at the time and the second west of the Mississippi. The call letters KSD stand for the initials of Joseph Pulitzer's grandmother, Kate Star Davis. The first broadcast lasted 90 minutes and featured news with KSD radio veteran Frank Eschen, ballroom dancers, a wrestler, and an appearance by Joe Garagiola.

*Courtesy Missouri Historical Society, St. Louis*

## February 9, 1966

**Demolition work began on a St. Louis landmark.** Three years earlier, a fire had destroyed most of the Forest Park Highlands Amusement

*Courtesy Missouri State Archives*

Park next to the Arena, sparing only the Comet roller coaster. The remnants of the Highlands were torn down to make room for Forest Park Community College.

*Courtesy Wikipedia*

*Courtesy Missouri Historical Society, St. Louis*

## February 10, 1959

**A tornado struck just after midnight and killed 21 people.** The twister knocked the Channel Two tower onto an apartment building on Oakview. It took out one of the twin towers of the Arena and took off a chunk of the roof. It bent the Ferris wheel at the Forest Park Highlands in half. The worst damage was in the area around Boyle and Olive. More than a thousand buildings were damaged, and more than 2,000 people were made homeless. The tornado was probably an F4 on today's Fujita scale.

## February 11, 1961

**Mr. and Mrs. Ed Ceries signed KSHE-FM on the air from the basement of their home at 1035 Westglen Lane in Crestwood.** The station called itself "The Lady of FM" (K*SHE*). The station offered drama and fine arts features, as well as classical and "time-tested" lighter music. There would be no rock and roll.

## February 10, 1843

**The city council accepted a gift of land from Mrs. Julia Cérre Soulard.** The city had to agree that the land would always be used for a public market. Julia's husband, Antoine, had surveyed the area for the Spanish government. After his death, she fought a long legal battle over her claim to the land. She also donated two lots to Bishop Rosati. St. Vincent DePaul Church would be built there in 1843.

## February 10, 2022

**Dick Vermeil was named to the Football Hall of Fame.** The Rams hired Vermeil as coach in 1997 to take over a team that had not posted a winning record in seven seasons. In his third season, the Rams went 13–3 and won Super Bowl XXXIV with "The Greatest Show on Turf." He retired 11 days after the win, but he returned to coaching with Kansas City before retiring for good in 2005.

*Courtesy Wikipedia*

## February 10, 1934

**August A. Busch Sr. scrawled a note, "Goodbye Mama and Precious Children," then shot himself at Grant's Farm.** He had been in intense pain due to heart trouble. St. Louis police called suicide "the Dutch Act," because so many German brewers had killed themselves. Besides the Lemp suicides, Otto Steifel of the Union Brewery had killed himself in 1920.

## February 11, 1901

**The *St. Louis Post-Dispatch* Weatherbird appeared for the first time.** It is the oldest continuous cartoon in American journalism. Staff artist Harry B. Martin drew the first Weatherbird, who at first had nothing to say. Six artists have drawn him, with Amadee Wohlschlaeger handling the duties from 1932 to 1981. Until recently, the bird appeared without a "bird line" only a handful of times, including after the deaths of Franklin Roosevelt, John F. Kennedy, Martin Luther King Jr., August Busch Jr., and Stan Musial, as well as after the *Challenger* disaster and after 9/11.

## February 12, 1926

**Joseph Henry Garagiola was born in St. Louis and grew up at 5446 Elizabeth Avenue on the Hill.** "Yogi" Berra lived across the street at 5447 Elizabeth. The Cardinals decided not to sign Berra, but they brought Garagiola to the big leagues in 1946. Garagiola joined Harry Caray and Jack Buck on the KMOX broadcasts beginning in 1955 and went on to broadcast for the Yankees and host the *Today* show. He died on March 23, 2016.

*Courtesy Wikipedia*

## February 12, 1952

**Michael McDonald was born.** He grew up in Ferguson and played with the Majestics and Jerry Jay and the Sheratons before joining Steely Dan. He joined the Doobie Brothers in 1977, writing and singing hits like "What a Fool Believes" and "Takin' It to the Streets." McDonald went solo in 1982. His duet with Patti LaBelle, "On My Own," reached number one in 1986.

*Courtesy Missouri Historical Society, St. Louis*

## February 12, 1964

**The new St. Louis flag created for the bicentennial was raised for the first time.** Designed by Professor Emeritus Theodore Sizer, Pursuivant of Arms at Yale University, it features two blue-and-white heraldic wavy bars to symbolize the confluence of the great rivers. The blue fleur-de-lis recognizes the French heritage of the city and its namesake. The golden disk is a "bezant," a Byzantine coin that symbolizes the Louisiana Purchase. The colors are for Spain (red and yellow/gold), Bourbon France (white and gold), Napoleonic and Republican France (blue, white, and red), and the United States (red, white, and blue).

**Designed by Professor Emeritus Theodore Sizer, Pursuivant of Arms at Yale University**

## February 13, 1904

**William Lemp killed himself at the family mansion at 3322 DeMenil Place.** The Lemp Brewery was by far the most successful in St. Louis at the time and William's father had introduced lager beer to St. Louis in 1838. Lemp sank into a depression after his son Frederick died of a heart issue in 1901. Prohibition would force the brewery out of business in 1919 and tragedy stalked the family. Elsa Lemp, the wealthiest heiress in St. Louis, killed herself in 1920. William Lemp Jr. shot himself to death in the mansion in 1922. In 1949, his brother Charles also committed suicide in the mansion.

*Courtesy Missouri Historical Society, St. Louis*

Courtesy Missouri Historical Society, St. Louis

## February 14, 1764

**According to most sources, 14-year-old Auguste Chouteau and 30 men under his direction arrived on the west bank of the Mississippi, a few miles below the confluence with the Missouri.** His stepfather, Pierre Laclède, had chosen the site a year earlier for a trading post and settlement that he said "might become hereafter one of the finest cities in America." The next day, the workers began clearing the site that grew into the city of St. Louis. It was a French community, established without legal authority on Spanish soil, with the British Empire, enemies of the French, just across the river.

**14-year-old Auguste Chouteau and his stepfather, Pierre Laclède, began clearing the site that grew into the city of St. Louis.**

Courtesy author

## February 15, 1970

**A reproduction steamboat named for Robert E. Lee arrived on the riverfront to become a floating restaurant.** The *Robert E. Lee* was damaged by the Flood of 1993 and then reopened and closed twice before being moved to Kimmswick for a brief, ill-fated venture. Moored at a repair yard north of downtown, the *Robert E. Lee* burned in March 2010.

## February 16, 1921

**Cardinals president Branch Rickey was speaking at the Presbyterian Church in Ferguson when the table decorations featuring a pair of redbirds perched on a branch caught his eye.** Allie May Schmidt had made the decorations. Her father, a graphic designer, modified the design by putting the birds on a baseball bat. Some variation of the logo has appeared on Cardinals uniforms ever since, except during the 1956 season.

Courtesy Missouri Historical Society, St. Louis

### February 14, 1922

**The first public radio broadcast in St. Louis was made over KSD, "the wireless service of the *Post-Dispatch*."** The station presented an address by Walter P. Upson of the Washington University Electrical Engineering Department. No one had bothered to get a license, so the station had to wait until June 26, 1922, to officially sign on.

### February 15, 1871

**The *St. Louis Globe-Democrat* reported that President Grant had nominated James Milton Turner to become ambassador to Liberia.** He became just the second African American diplomat. Turner was born into slavery in St. Louis County and was educated in secret schools for Blacks. After the Civil War he worked with the Freedmen's Bureau and the State Department of Education to establish schools for Blacks, including Lincoln University.

### February 16, 1846

**This is believed to be the date that William B. Ferguson and his wife arrived in an area north of St. Louis to build homes.** Ferguson bought 107 acres, and in 1855, he offered nine of them to the North Missouri Railroad (later the Wabash) for a station under the condition that the station be named Ferguson.

### February 16, 1959

**A wrecking ball smacked into a tenement at 3519 Laclede, the first structure cleared in the Mill Creek Valley redevelopment.** Running from 20th Street to Grand and from Olive to the railroad yards to the south, the 465-acre site was home to a large African American population. About 5,000 families would be displaced. The clearance would be so extensive that the area was referred to as "Hiroshima Flats."

Courtesy Wikipedia, credit bradleypjohnson

# FEBRUARY

*Courtesy author*

## February 17, 1961

**The new Stan Musial and Biggie's restaurant at 5130 Oakland Avenue opened.** The original Stan Musial and Biggie's was once the 66 Café at 6435 Chippewa. The Redbird slugger joined his friend Julius "Biggie" Garagnani as partners at that location, then known as Biggie's, in 1949. Stan Musial and Biggie's served its last customers on New Year's Eve of 1986, and the site is now part of the St. Louis Science Center complex.

## February 18, 1859

**The city of Pacific was incorporated by the Missouri General Assembly.** The town was originally named Franklin, but the name was changed because of the constant mix-ups in the mail between Franklin and New Franklin. The name Pacific was chosen to honor the new Pacific Railroad.

## February 18, 1998

**Harry Caray died a few days after collapsing at a Palm Springs restaurant.** After he was fired from the Cardinals job in 1969, Caray broadcast for the A's and White Sox before moving to Wrigley Field in 1982. He became beloved nationwide for his broadcasts on WGN-TV and for his renditions of "Take Me Out to the Ball Game" during the seventh-inning stretch. Caray was inducted into the broadcasters wing of the Baseball Hall of Fame in 1989.

## February 19, 1859

**The village of Illinoistown was incorporated.** In 1861, a hotly contested election was held to choose a new name. Most preferred "Illinois City." A group favoring the name East St. Louis spread money and whiskey around a railroad construction site, winning the crucial votes from the workers.

## February 17, 1928

**Ted Drewes Jr. was born.** His father was a prominent St. Louis tennis player who started selling frozen custard in Florida and opened his first St. Louis stand on Natural Bridge in 1930. The iconic Route 66 location opened in 1941. In 1959, Ted Drewes Jr. invented the concrete, a shake so thick it could be turned upside down.

## February 18, 1930

**The first flight by a cow in an airplane took place as part of the St. Louis Air Exposition.** A Guernsey named Elm Farm Ollie made the 72-mile flight from Bismarck, Missouri, to St. Louis. Elsworth W. Bunce of Milwaukee became the first man to milk a cow in flight. The milk was sealed in paper containers and dropped by parachute. The event is marked each year as Elm Farm Ollie Day at the Mt. Horeb Mustard Museum in Middleton, Wisconsin.

*Courtesy Pixabay*

*Courtesy City of St. Peters*

## February 19, 1910

**The village of St. Peters was incorporated.** The town trustees laid out a set of ordinances, including a five-mph speed limit for automobiles. They also made it a misdemeanor to ride a horse or drive a carriage through town "faster than a moderate trot." The population stood at 269. By 1960, only 404 people lived there.

*Courtesy Missouri Historical Society, St. Louis*

## February 20, 1953

**Anheuser-Busch bought the Cardinals from Fred Saigh, who turned down offers of more money from out-of-town interests.** Browns owner Bill Veeck had planned to stay in St. Louis but decided to leave when he heard the news. The purchase boosted Anheuser-Busch, which was only the third-largest brewery at the time. Griesedieck Brothers lost rights to the Cardinals baseball broadcasts.

*Courtesy Wikipedia*

## February 21, 1871

**Henry Kiel was born in St. Louis.** He was the 32nd mayor of St. Louis, in office from 1913 to 1925. During his administration, the Muny was constructed and the city passed a bond issue that changed the face of the city with projects such as the Soldiers Memorial and the Municipal Auditorium. Kiel's construction firm built the auditorium that would bear his name.

During his administration, the Muny was constructed, as well as other projects such as the Soldiers Memorial and the Municipal Auditorium.

### February 19, 1948

**Eero Saarinen was chosen as the winner of a design competition for the proposed riverfront memorial.** The Finnish-born architect's design called for a 630-foot-tall arch of steel. Saarinen said he wanted a monument that would "have lasting significance and would be a landmark of our time." Saarinen also designed the GM Technical Center near Detroit, the TWA Terminal in New York City, and Dulles International Airport near Washington, DC.

### February 20, 1865

**The state granted the town charter of Kirkwood.** An association of businessmen who wanted to escape the crowded city ravaged by fire and cholera planned the community. In 1853, they bought land along the proposed Pacific railroad and began promoting their development, the first planned suburb west of the Mississippi. The town was named for James Pugh Kirkwood, chief engineer of the Pacific Railroad.

### February 21, 1836

**William Lemp Sr. was born in Germany.** His father, Adam, founded the Western Brewery. When his father died, William took over and built a new Lemp brewery on Cherokee Street. The new brewery was built over a maze of caves that were used to "lager" or age the beer. By 1875, the Lemp Brewery was the largest in the city. Sadly, William Lemp killed himself on February 13, 1904.

*Courtesy Wikipedia, credit Lambtron*

# FEBRUARY

## February 22, 1788

**Ralph Clayton was born in Virginia.** In 1820 he bought about 630 acres of land in St. Louis County from John McKnight for $9 per acre. In 1831, the farmer, tanner, and shoemaker married Rosanna McCausland, whose family lived nearby. When the county separated from the city in 1876, Clayton donated 100 acres for the new county seat. His only condition was that the town be named for him.

## February 22, 1854

**The Reverend William Greenleaf Eliot organized the board of directors under the charter of Eliot Seminary.** At that meeting, they chose to name their school Washington University.

## February 22, 1937

**Homer G. Phillips Hospital on Whittier was dedicated.** At the time, it was the largest and best health care facility in the nation dedicated to the care of African Americans but it closed amid controversy in 1979. The renovated hospital reopened as the Homer G. Phillips Dignity House/Senior Living Community in 2003.

*Courtesy Missouri Historical Society, St. Louis*

**Attorney Homer Phillips fought for better health care for African Americans. He was murdered in 1931.**

## February 23, 1834

**Johann George Aff was born in Germany.** Fleeing a failed revolt, he settled in South St. Louis County in 1859. He farmed property on Weber Road and later built a store near Gravois and Tesson Ferry. The area around the store became known as Aff's Town, later shortened to Affton.

## February 22, 1918

**"The Alton Giant" was born.** Robert Pershing Wadlow weighed a normal eight pounds, six ounces at birth. But he weighed 30 pounds by six months and 62 pounds at 18 months. He was 6' 2" and weighed 195 pounds by the time he was eight years old. He reached a height of 8' 11.1" before his death in 1940 and was recognized as the tallest man who ever lived by the *Guinness Book of World Records*. His extraordinary growth was due to an overactive pituitary gland, a condition that is treatable today.

**He reached a height of nearly nine feet before his death in 1940.**

*Courtesy Flickr, UpNorth Memories, Don Harrison. (Image colorized)*

## February 23, 1819

**Edwardsville, Illinois, was chartered by the state.** The community founded in 1805 was named after Ninian Edwards, the first governor of the Illinois Territory. He became the new state's senator in 1819 and later was appointed minister to Mexico. Edwards served as governor of the state from 1827 to 1830 and died of cholera in Belleville in 1833. Edwards County is also named in his honor.

*Courtesy Wikipedia, credit pasa47*

## February 24, 1829

**Auguste Chouteau died at the age of 80.**
When he was just 14, he led the men who began building a trading post and settlement at a site selected by his stepfather, Pierre Laclède, a year earlier. Chouteau helped build the settlement into an important commercial city. He became the first board of trustees chairman when the village of St. Louis was incorporated in 1809.

*Courtesy Missouri Historical Society, St. Louis*

## February 25, 1972

**The Cardinals made the worst trade in franchise history.** They sent Steve Carlton to the Phillies for Rick Wise. Gussie Busch had ordered Carlton traded after a contract dispute. The next season, Carlton won 27 games for the last-place Phillies and picked up the first of his four Cy Young Awards. Wise did win 16 games in 1972 and 1973, but was traded to Boston after the 1973 season.

*Courtesy Wikipedia*

## February 26, 1973

**Marshall Faulk was born in New Orleans.** He grew up in the Desire Street Projects and appeared headed for a troubled life. But Carver High School football coach Wayne Reese took him under his wing. Faulk sold popcorn at the Superdome before becoming a college star at San Diego State. The Indianapolis Colts drafted him in 1994 and traded him to the Rams on April 1, 1999.

*Courtesy Getty Images*

## February 24, 1918

**Private David Hickey became the first St. Louisan to die in World War I.** The former *St. Louis Post-Dispatch* mailroom worker was killed in the Battle of the Toul Sector. The Soldiers Memorial lists 1,075 names of St. Louisans who died in the "War to End All Wars." Hickey Park on North Broadway was dedicated in his honor on April 10, 1941.

## February 24, 1968

**Garry Unger's amazing record-breaking consecutive games streak began as he took to the ice as a rookie with the Toronto Maple Leafs.** He would start the next 914 consecutive games, including 662 straight with the Blues. Doug Jarvis broke his "Iron Man" record in 1986 and Jarvis's streak ultimately ended at 964 games. Unger did have another impressive streak as he appeared in seven consecutive All-Star games.

## February 25, 1966

**CBS Television aired the documentary *16 in Webster Groves* (a documentary about modern teenagers).** At first, Webster Groves residents were thrilled to have been chosen. But the documentary made the teens look shallow and materialistic, and some of the parents looked even worse.

## February 25, 1976

**Reporters and some of the workers who built it took the first rides on the brand-new roller coaster at Six Flags over Mid-America.** The Screaming Eagle reached speeds of 62 mph on a 3,872-foot course.

## February 26, 1887

**Grover Cleveland Alexander was born in Elba, Nebraska.** The Cards obtained the aging pitcher on waivers from the Cubs in 1926. He won several important games down the stretch to lead the Cardinals to their first pennant. He won two games in the World Series. Nursing a hangover, "Old Pete" was called in to face slugger Tony Lazzeri with the bases loaded in the seventh inning of Game Seven. He struck out Lazzeri, and the Cards went on to win the game.

# FEBRUARY

Courtesy Wikipedia

## February 27, 1843

**The town of Bridgeton was officially incorporated.** The French called it "Marais des Liards," which means "cottonwood swamp." The Spanish called it "Villa a Robert." The Americans called it Owen's Station, then Bridgeton. Airport expansion beginning in 2001 decimated Bridgeton, with the clearance of nearly 2,000 homes and 75 businesses to make way for the new runway.

## February 27, 1996

**The Blues traded Patrice Tardif, Roman Vopat, Craig Johnson, and a draft pick to the Kings for "the Great One," Wayne Gretzky.** In 31 games, he would score 10 goals and tack on 27 assists. But Gretzky clashed with Coach Mike Keenan, and he signed a contract with the New York Rangers on July 22, 1996. *(facing page)*

## February 28, 1989

**Red Schoendienst was elected to the Baseball Hall of Fame by the Veterans Committee.** He played for 19 years with the Cardinals, from 1945 to 1956 and 1961 to 1963. Schoendienst was a 10-time All-Star; he managed the Cardinals from 1965 to 1976; and is the second-longest-serving manager in Redbird history, behind only Tony La Russa.

## February 29, 1960

**The talk radio era opened as KMOX aired the first *At Your Service* program.** Jack Buck hosted the show with Mayor Raymond Tucker as the first guest. Eleanor Roosevelt also appeared on the first show. The idea of newsmakers taking calls from listeners was given little chance of succeeding. But Robert Hyland was so convinced that he ordered the station's record library given away.

## February 27, 1999

**It took less than 15 seconds for explosives to bring nearly 70 years of memories crashing down.** Thousands of people gathered hours before the 5:45 p.m. implosion reduced the Arena to a pile of rubble. The former home of the Blues opened in 1929 and hosted its last sporting event in 1994. The building was costing the city $50,000 per month to sit idle. Mayor Clarence Harmon said an office park on the site would create jobs and revenue.

Elliot See (left) and Charles Bassett (right)
Courtesy Wikipedia

## February 28, 1966

**US astronauts Elliot See and Charles Bassett died when their T-38 jet trainer crashed at Lambert Field.** They were coming here to train in a rendezvous simulator and inspect their Gemini Nine space capsule, under construction at McDonnell Douglas. Lost in the mist and fog, the plane crashed into the very building they were to have visited. The crash hurt 15 people, but 8,000 scrambled to safety.

## February 29, 1904

**John Leonard Roosevelt Martin was born in Temple, Oklahoma.** His aggressive play earned "Pepper" Martin another nickname, "the Wild Horse of the Osage." Martin batted .500 in the 1931 World Series and starred for the "Gashouse Gang" World Champions of 1934. He was also one of the most colorful characters in Redbird history. Martin formed the "Mississippi Mudcat Band" with other players and entertained fans with jug and washboard country music.

Martin (left) and Dizzy Dean (right)
Courtesy Missouri Historical Society, St. Louis

Brett Hull and Wayne Gretzky
*Getty Images*

Sports' primary color

**The Sporting News**

MARCH 11, 1996 / $2.50 ($2.95 Can.)

**BLUES BROTHERS**

Great move, golden opportunity

Top 40 countdown: NBA's Wild West
PURDUE basketball: Love boils over
Table hopping with DAVE KINDRED

## March 1, 1912

**Jefferson Barracks was the scene of the first parachute jump from an airplane.** Albert Berry made the jump from a Benoist "pusher" biplane (the propellers faced the rear) piloted by Tony Jannus. The son of a balloonist and a professional parachute jumper, Berry admitted that he felt uneasy before the drop but said the greatest danger was probably to the pilot of the plane.

*Courtesy Wikipedia*

### March 1, 1851

**Carondelet was incorporated as a city with a population of about 1,200.** It was named after Baron Francisco Luis Héctor de Carondelet, the Spanish governor of Upper Louisiana. The original village was located just south of the hill where Bellerive Park is today. It was also referred to as "Vide Poche," meaning "Empty Pockets," which was either a comment on the poor people of the village or their gambling ability. St. Louis annexed Carondelet in 1870.

*Courtesy Missouri Historical Society, St. Louis*

### March 1, 1914

**Harry Christopher Carabina was born in St. Louis.** He grew up at 1909 LaSalle Street and attended Dewey School and Webster Groves High School. As Harry Caray, he began broadcasting Cardinals and Browns away games in 1945 and became the Cards' broadcaster in 1947. He was the lead voice of the Cardinals before being fired in 1969. Caray then called games for the Oakland A's for one season, the Chicago White Sox for 11 seasons, and the Chicago Cubs from 1982 until 1997. *(facing page)*

### March 2, 1821

**President James Monroe approved the Second Missouri Compromise, clearing the way for Missouri to be admitted to the Union.** The first Missouri Compromise allowed the territory to draft a constitution. But some northern lawmakers objected to a passage preventing free Negroes from settling in Missouri. The second compromise removed the offending language.

*Courtesy Smithsonian Libraries*

## March 2, 1803

**President Jefferson authorized Robert Livingston and James Monroe to negotiate with France to purchase New Orleans and western Florida.** They were authorized to pay $10 million. Livingston and Monroe were stunned when the French offered to sell the entire Louisiana Territory. The negotiators agreed to a $15 million deal for 828,000 square miles. That came out to about four cents per acre.

## March 3, 1875

**The St. Louis area was hit with a 15-inch snowstorm, the biggest since 1860.** Transportation was at a standstill, since the horses couldn't find the streetcar tracks. The *St. Louis Globe-Democrat* reported that "thousands of children" were unable to make it to their places of labor.

## March 3, 1962

**Jackie Joyner-Kersee was born in East St. Louis.** Considered one of the best all-around female athletes ever, she won three Olympic gold medals, along with silver and a bronze. She once held the American record for the long jump. Her score of 7,161 in the heptathlon in 1986 still stands as the world record.

*Courtesy Wikipedia*

## March 4, 2010

**Pinnacle Entertainment opened the $392 million River City Casino in Lemay.** Part of the 80-acre site was formerly occupied by the National Imagery and Mapping Agency and National Lead Industries, which required extensive environmental cleanup. Pinnacle also built a road connecting the casino complex with Interstate 55.

*Courtesy Wikipedia, credit RamblingGambler*

## March 4, 2007

**Statesman Thomas Eagleton died at the age of 77.** He served 18 years in the US Senate and was chosen as George McGovern's vice presidential candidate in 1972. Just 18 days later, Eagleton was dropped following reports of his treatment for depression. In 1995, he was a major factor in bringing the Rams to St. Louis. The federal courthouse downtown is named in his honor.

*Courtesy Wikipedia*

## March 4, 2021

**The Clayco Construction firm announced that the 100 Above the Park Building on Kingshighway across from Forest Park was complete.** The 385-foot tiered tower houses residential apartments, retail, amenities, and parking. Each tier includes four angled stories. The top of each tier gives an outdoor space to a quarter of the apartments.

*Courtesy St. Louis Media History Foundation*

## March 5, 1790

**Daniel Page was born in York County, Maine.** A great philanthropist and the second mayor of St. Louis, he served four consecutive one-year terms from 1829 to 1833. Under his administration, a night watch was set up and the first business regulations were passed. Street cleaning and garbage collection services were also started. Page Avenue/Page Boulevard is named for him.

## March 5, 1950

**The children's show *The Wrangler's Club* premiered on KSD-TV.** Harry Gibbs starred as the beloved "Texas Bruce." He would entertain kids and show cartoons until 1963. When Gibbs retired, *Corky the Clown* took over the slot. Weatherman Clif St. James played Corky until 1979.

## March 6, 1857

**The US Supreme Court made a landmark decision that polarized the nation.** Dred Scott's owner had taken him from the slave state of Missouri to the free state of Illinois and later to the Wisconsin Territory. Scott sued upon being returned to St. Louis, claiming he had resided in a free state. The Supreme Court ruled that slaves

*Courtesy Missouri Historical Society, St. Louis*

were not citizens, and thus could not sue. Scott's ownership was transferred to abolitionist Henry Taylor Blow, who freed him. He lived out his days as a porter at Barnum's Hotel.

## March 7, 1988

**The Blues made one of the better deals in their history.** They swapped Rob Ramage and Rick Wamsley to Calgary for Steve Bozek and a young winger named Brett Hull. Hull would spend the next 10 seasons in St. Louis, notching 100 points four consecutive times from 1989 to 1993. His greatest season in St. Louis came in 1990–91, when Hull racked up 86 goals and 45 assists.

**One of the best trades in Blues history**

*Courtesy Getty Images*

## March 8, 1887

**James Buchanan Eads died in Nassau in the Bahama islands at age 66.** Eads was not content to rest on his laurels after the great bridge at St. Louis was completed in 1874. He developed a system of jetties where the Mississippi empties into the Gulf of Mexico. The jetties cause the natural flow of the river to keep the channel clear of silt. He also promoted a railway across the Isthmus of Tehuantepec, in Mexico, as an alternative to the proposed Panama Canal.

*Courtesy Library of Congress*

## March 5, 1996

**Wayne Gretzky played his first game at Kiel Center in a Blues uniform.** The largest home crowd in Blues history, 20,725, saw the Blues beat the Florida Panthers, 2–0. Unfortunately, "The Great One" didn't spend much time here. He signed a free-agent contract with the New York Rangers at the end of the season.

## March 6, 1907

**The Western Brewery in Belleville announced the winner of a contest to find a name for its newest brew.** Seventeen-year-old George Wuller won $25 for suggesting the name "Stag." The named lived on even after the brewery closed for the last time in 1988. Stag is now brewed by Pabst.

## March 7, 1849

**Mayor John Darby and a group of prominent citizens established Rural Cemetery on a 138-acre site at the Hempstead farm.** It wasn't long before the name was changed to Bellefontaine Cemetery. During the cholera epidemic of 1849, 30 burials a day were taking place there. Famous names buried at Bellefontaine include William Clark, Thomas Hart Benton, James Eads, Adolphus Busch, and the Lemp family.

## March 7, 1974

**Regina Marie "Jenna" Fischer was born in Ft. Wayne, Indiana.** Raised in St. Louis, she attended Nerinx Hall High School before leaving for Los Angeles. Best known for playing Pam Beesly on NBC's *The Office*, she has appeared in movies like *Blades of Glory*, *Walk Hard: The Dewey Cox Story*, and *Hall Pass*. She also appeared in *You, Me and the Apocalypse* on NBC and in Clint Eastwood's *The 15:17 to Paris*.

## March 8, 1804

**It was the last day that the Spanish flag flew over St. Louis.** Almost the entire village of 925 turned out to watch as the flag was lowered. The French flag, symbolizing the return of the territory to France, replaced it. But the French flag came down just 24 hours later and the American flag was raised.

# MARCH

### March 9, 1896

**Granite City, Illinois, was incorporated.** Industrialists F. G. and William Niedringhaus laid out the town. Its name came from their principal product, "Graniteware" kitchen products. By 1899, the Niedringhaus plant was called NESCO, for National Enameling and Stamping Company and the immigrants it drew attracted other heavy industrial firms, including Granite City Steel.

### March 10, 1804

**Captain Amos Stoddard, the first American commandant of Upper Louisiana, raised the American flag over St. Louis.** The previous day, Stoddard had represented France in the ceremony transferring the territory to the French from Spain. To the delight of most village residents, he allowed the French flag to fly for 24 hours.

### March 10, 1849

**St. Charles was incorporated as a city, and the first city charter was adopted.** Louis Blanchette established a post at the site in April 1769. The village was originally known as *Les Petites Cotes* or "Little Hills." It was named San Carlos after the first church was established and was later anglicized to "St. Charles" when the Americans took over.

### March 10, 1971

**Jonathan Daniel "Jon" Hamm was born in St. Louis.** He attended John Burroughs School and post-college, briefly returned to teach acting. The Emmy-winning actor is best known for his role as ad executive Don Draper in the AMC series *Mad Men*.

*Courtesy Missouri Historical Society, St. Louis*

### March 9, 1914

**The deadliest fire in St. Louis history killed 33 people staying in the Missouri Athletic Club Building at 4th and Washington.** The director of Boatmen's Bank removed $100,000 from vaults on the main floor of the seven-story building the following morning. The building commissioner declared that the walls were safe, but six days later a wall fell onto an adjacent building, killing six more people.

### March 10, 1956

**The new, ultramodern terminal building at Lambert Field was dedicated by Mayor Raymond Tucker.** The St. Louis architectural firm of Hellmuth, Yamasaki and Leinweber designed the terminal. It replaced a terminal built in 1933, which stood on the north end of the airport at Lindbergh Boulevard and Bridgeton Station Road. The old terminal was eventually torn down in 1978.

### March 11, 1942

**Blues great Bob Plager was born.** Bob and his brother Barclay were two of the most popular players ever to wear the blue note, with Bob being especially feared

*Courtesy Getty Images*

for his checking. On February 2, 2017, his number was retired. As the banner rose, Barclay's number 8 came down to meet it and both ascended to the rafters together. Bob Plager died on March 24, 2021.

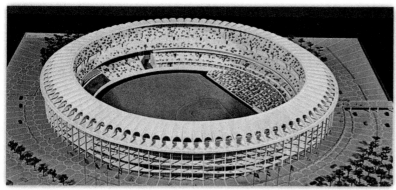

*Courtesy author*

## March 12, 1963

**Architect Edward Durell Stone unveiled a $12,000 plastic model showing his design for a new downtown stadium.** He called the design "a 20th century version of the Roman Coliseum." The design featured 96 arches along the top, each repeating the catenary curve of the Gateway Arch. Other works by Stone include the General Motors Building in New York, the National Geographic Building, and the Kennedy Center for the Performing Arts in Washington.

*Courtesy Wikipedia*

## March 13, 1960

**The NFL announced that the Chicago Cardinals were moving to St. Louis.** The legendary George Halas of the Chicago Bears played a key role in the move. The Bears could not televise road games because the Cardinals would be at home. It also didn't hurt that the upstart AFC was interested in placing a franchise in St. Louis.

## March 14, 1899

**The bankrupt Browns of the National League were sold for $33,000 and taken over by Mathew Stanley Robison and Frank de Haas Robison, owners of the Cleveland Spiders.** The Robisons sent the best Cleveland players to St. Louis and shipped the hapless Browns players to Cleveland. The Browns became the Perfectos and the players donned red hats and stockings. Will Hale of the *St. Louis Republic* newspaper overheard a fan commenting that the socks were "a lovely shade of cardinal," and a new nickname was coined.

*Courtesy Library of Congress*

### March 11, 1980

**The landmark riverfront McDonald's opened.** The restaurant was built on a 702-ton, 185-foot-long riverboat on top of a barge moored on the levee. The restaurant could seat 350 people. It closed in November 2000 due to financial reasons.

### March 12, 1989

**The curtain came down on the Ambassador Theatre.** The chandeliers, staircases, and even sections of plasterwork were auctioned off. The Ambassador was once the home of the "Skouras Brothers Missouri Rocket Girls," which evolved into the world-famous Radio City Music Hall "Rockettes." It was torn down in 1997 to make room for a plaza in front of the Mercantile Bank (now US Bank) headquarters.

### March 13, 1914

**Edward "Butch" O'Hare was born in St. Louis.** During World War II, he was awarded the Medal of Honor for shooting down five Japanese bombers attacking the USS *Lexington*. O'Hare was shot down over Tarawa in 1943. Chicago's airport was named in his honor in 1946.

### March 14, 1859

**The Missouri State Legislature approved the establishment of the Missouri Botanical Garden.** Henry Shaw established the garden at his country estate, Tower Grove. He enlisted the help of leading botanists, including Dr. George Engelmann of St. Louis, and also donated 276 acres around the garden for Tower Grove Park.

## March 15, 1962

**The population of St. Louis County was reported to have exceeded that of the city for the first time.** The Metropolitan Census Committee of the St. Louis Chapter, American Statistical Association, put the county population at 762,000. The city population was put at 740,000.

## March 16, 1972

**The first building was blown up at the notorious Pruitt-Igoe housing project.** The demolition of the 11-story building at 2207 O'Fallon Street was a test to see if the entire 35-building complex could be demolished using dynamite. Pruitt-Igoe stood as a monument to the well-intentioned but failed social programs of the 1950s and '60s.

*Courtesy Missouri Historical Society, St. Louis*

## March 16, 2020

**A Saint Louis University student who had traveled abroad was the first COVID-19 case reported in the City of St. Louis.** Area officials banned gatherings of 50 or more people, and schools would be closed two days later. In Illinois, schools were already closed and bars were ordered closed to dine-in customers by that evening. Missouri officials were considering the same action.

*Courtesy Pixabay*

*Courtesy Missouri Historical Society, St. Louis*

## March 15, 1884

**The "New" Post Office and Customs House on Olive was dedicated.** General William T. Sherman presided over the ceremonies dedicating the building designed by Alfred Mullett in the French Second Empire style. In 1959, the federal government moved to sell the building to a developer, who planned to tear it down. Public outcry saved the building, and it was redeveloped in 2006.

*Courtesy Wikipedia*

## March 16, 1964

**Walt Disney unveiled plans for a proposed entertainment complex on the St. Louis riverfront.** At the Bel Air East Hotel, Disney emphasized that his proposed "Riverfront Square" was not an amusement park. A popular story says that the plans fell through because Gussie Busch wanted to allow beer sales and Disney refused. Actually, Civic Center Redevelopment and other St. Louis interests balked at the cost—and Disney had already bought up 25,000 acres in Central Florida.

## March 17, 1820

**The first recorded St. Patrick's Day parade in St. Louis was held.** At that time, there were about 100 Irish out of a total population of 7,000. A wave of immigrants arrived after the potato famine of 1845–47. By 1851, there were about 8,000, or one-seventh of the population. The Irish first settled in the notorious Kerry Patch neighborhood roughly centered around 16th and 18th Streets between Cass and O'Fallon.

Many Irish moved to the area we now know as Dogtown to work the clay mines in the early 1900s. Contrary to myth, the neighborhood did not receive its nickname because the Igorot tribesmen at the 1904 World's Fair ate dogs from the neighborhood. They ate dog on special occasions and were encouraged by fair officials to do it more often to boost attendance. But the area was known as Dogtown by 1876. "Dogtown" is a miners' term for the shacks and huts around the operations, and "doghole" is a term for a small mine. Prominent Irish in St. Louis history include John Mullanphy, Missouri's first millionaire and a generous philanthropist who funded the first hospital in St. Louis, established by the Sisters of Charity. Jeremiah Connor was the first St. Louis sheriff and donated the land for Washington Avenue. O'Fallon, Missouri, and O'Fallon, Illinois, are named after railroad promoter Colonel John O'Fallon. His estate is now O'Fallon Park. Firefighter Phelim O'Toole became a folk hero for saving at least a dozen lives during the Southern Hotel Fire in 1877.

*Courtesy Wikipedia*

## March 18, 1955

**Francis G. Slay was born in St. Louis.** As a boy, he worked in his family's restaurant. He attended Epiphany and St. Mary's High School as well as the Saint Louis University School of Law, and he worked for a law firm. He served as an alderman and became the 45th mayor of St. Louis in 2001. The first mayor of the city of St. Louis to be elected to the office four consecutive times, Slay was the longest-serving mayor in St. Louis history.

Saint Patrick's Day Procession in Saint Louis 1874

*Courtesy Missouri Historical Society, St. Louis*

## March 18, 1999

**A St. Louis landmark came back to life as 90 display apartments were unveiled and the famous Zodiac and Starlight Rooms were reopened at the renovated Chase Park Plaza.** The Chase Hotel opened in 1922 and hosted nearly every president along with celebrities such as Frank Sinatra, Dean Martin, Nat King Cole, Liberace, and even the Rolling Stones. It was combined with the Park Plaza Hotel in 1961.

## March 19, 1944

**George "Buzz" Westfall was born.** He was elected as the St. Louis County executive in 1990 and reelected three times. On October 5, 2003, he checked into the hospital suffering from back pain. He died of a staph infection on October 27. Route 364 from I-270 to the Veterans Memorial Bridge is named in honor of Westfall, who pushed for its completion.

## March 19, 1982

**Workers put the finishing touches on Richard Serra's $250,000 sculpture on the Gateway Mall downtown.** The sculpture consists of eight 10-by-40-foot structural steel panels. They were designed to rust with age. Serra said he expected initial public reaction to his work to be negative. But he predicted people would soon be entranced.

## March 20, 1805

**Thomas K. Skinker was born in Virginia.** He came to St. Louis in the 1830s to practice law and owned a large estate he called Ellenwood, along the River des Peres. Much of his land became Forest Park, and Skinker Road was the road to his home. In 1902, there was a failed effort to rename it Rochambeau, which proponents thought was a more dignified name for the road running through the World's Fair. Skinker carried an alignment of US 66 from 1926 to 1933.

## March 18, 2017

**Chuck Berry died at age 90.** Charles Edward Anderson Berry, "the Father of Rock 'n' Roll," was born on October 18, 1926, in St. Louis. According to the Rock & Roll Hall of Fame, "While no individual can be said to have invented rock and roll, Chuck Berry comes the closest of any single figure to being the one who put all the essential pieces together. It was his particular genius to graft country & western guitar licks onto a rhythm & blues chassis in his very first single, 'Maybellene.'"

*Courtesy author*

## March 19, 1994

**About 100 people watched as the screen at the 66 Park-In Theater on Watson Road in Crestwood came down in a cloud of dust.** The drive-in was being demolished by the Spirtas Wrecking Company to make way for a National Supermarket. The drive-in opened in 1947 and closed on October 17, 1993.

*Courtesy author*

*Courtesy Missouri Historical Society, St. Louis*

## March 20, 1878

**Businessmen Charles and Alonzo Slayback proposed a yearly pageant, similar to the Mardi Gras in their native New Orleans.** They created the Mystic Order of the Veiled Prophet. The organization staged a parade for the masses and a ball for the elite. Civil rights protests, including the prophet's "unmasking" by activists at the 1972 ball, forced the group to diversify. In 1981, its leaders put on the first VP Fair on the riverfront. In 1995, the celebration became known as Fair St. Louis.

*Courtesy Missouri State Archives*

## March 21, 1972

**A city ordinance changed Easton Avenue and part of Franklin to Doctor Martin Luther King Boulevard.** Easton was named for Rufus Easton, the city's first postmaster, who also founded the city of Alton and named it after his son. His daughter, Mary Sibley, cofounded Lindenwood University. More than 40,000 people each day once passed through the bus and streetcar loop on Easton Avenue in Wellston.

## March 22, 1952

**Bob Costas was born in New York.** At age 22, he came to KMOX to broadcast games of the St. Louis Spirits of the ABA. He also was the voice of Mizzou basketball from 1976 to 1981. He started his career at NBC in 1980 and anchored the network's prime-time Olympic coverage 11 times before stepping down in 2017. From 1988 until 1994, he hosted his own late-night talk show, *Later with Bob Costas*.

*Courtesy Getty Images*

## March 23, 1994

**After forecasting sunny weather for the next day, the top-rated meteorologist in St. Louis climbed into his Piper Cherokee and took off from Spirit of St. Louis Airport.** A few days earlier, the media had reported that Bob Richards had an affair with a Farmington, Missouri, woman and she had petitioned a judge for a restraining order. Morning radio personalities had a field day. The devastated Richards nosed his plane 440 feet to the runway below at over 80 miles per hour.

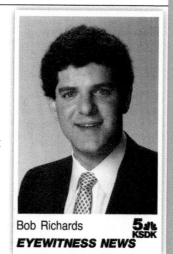

Bob Richards
**5 KSDK**
**EYEWITNESS NEWS**

*Courtesy author*

## March 21, 1975

**Redbird great Joe Medwick died of a heart attack at age 63.** Medwick won the Triple Crown in 1937. He led the league in average and runs batted in and tied for the lead in home runs. But he is best remembered for being taken out of the last game of the 1934 World Series for his own safety. When he returned to his position after sliding hard into third, Detroit fans pelted him with debris.

## March 21, 2006

**Jack Dorsey, who grew up in St. Louis, sent out the first public tweet: "just setting up my twttr."** Around 12 minutes later, he added, "inviting coworkers." Twttr launched to the public on July 15, 2006, and was renamed later that year to Twitter. As a teenager, Dorsey started out listening to police scanners and wrote a graphics program illustrating vehicles as they moved about St. Louis.

## March 22, 1928

**Ed Macauley was born in St. Louis.** He acquired the nickname "Easy" while helping lead the Billikens to the 1948 NIT championship. In the NBA, he played for the St. Louis Bombers, the Boston Celtics, and the St. Louis Hawks. The seven-time All-Star was elected to the Basketball Hall of Fame in 1960. He went on to become a sportscaster for KTVI. "Easy Ed" died in November 2011.

*Courtesy Wikipedia*

Courtesy author

## March 23, 1904

**St. Louisans were hailing the work of chemical engineer John Wixford.** He had found a way to clean up the city's notoriously muddy water supply in time for the fair. Wixford developed settling basins at Chain of Rocks and used chemicals to clear out the mud and bacteria. The plant had been working for two days, and every tap in the city was dispensing an unfamiliar clear liquid.

## March 24, 1961

**The St. Louis Board of Alderman changed the name of Olive between Whittier and Pendleton to Gaslight Square.** The area had risen from the rubble of the 1959 tornado to become a trendy district of nightclubs, coffee shops, restaurants, and stores along a street lined with old-fashioned gaslights. Stars such as Barbra Streisand, the Smothers Brothers, Woody Allen, Lenny Bruce, and Miles Davis performed there early in their careers. But it was mostly over by the late 1960s due to publicity over crime. The area is now a residential community.

## March 25, 1904

**A trainload of Filipino "wild people" and "half-savage tribes" arrived to be put on exhibit at the World's Fair.** Nearly all of the Igorots and savage headhunters were ill because of the change in climate. The Igorots became a major attraction due to their diet of dog meat on special occasions. Fair officials encouraged them to do it more often to boost attendance, and legend says the Rover roundups gave the Dogtown area its name. But the area had been known as Dogtown since before the Civil War.

*Courtesy Missouri Historical Society, St. Louis*

## March 24, 1826

**The commander of the Western Department, General Edmond, and his field commander, Colonel Henry Atkinson, were ordered to select a position within 20 miles of the mouth of the Missouri for a new fort.** The post would become Jefferson Barracks. Robert E. Lee, Jefferson Davis, Ulysses Grant, William T. Sherman, George Custer, John J. Pershing, and Dwight Eisenhower are among those who served there.

## March 25, 1979

**General Motors announced it was relocating the Corvette Assembly Plant.** 'Vettes had been built on Natural Bridge since 1954. GM officials said they would meet with Mayor Conway and state officials and try to find a site in St. Louis or at least in Missouri. But rumors said a decision had already been made to move production to Bowling Green, Kentucky.

*Courtesy Pixabay*

## March 26, 1941

**Blues great Barclay Plager was born in Ontario.** The Rangers traded him to the Blues in 1967 along with Red Berenson. Number Eight was a crucial part of the Blues teams that reached the Stanley Cup Finals in the franchise's first three seasons. He coached the team in 1978–79 and 1982–83, and his number was retired on March 24, 1981. Barclay died of brain cancer in 1988.

*Courtesy Getty Images*

*Courtesy Library of Congress*

## March 27, 1819

**The town of Belleville was incorporated.** In 1814, St. Clair County commissioners were seeking to move the county seat from Cahokia and they chose a site on a farm owned by George Blair. He donated 25 acres, including one acre to be set aside as a public square. At that time, the area was known as Compton Hill. Blair said the town should be called "Belleville," which means "beautiful city" in French. Belleville was incorporated as a city in 1850.

## March 28, 1899

**August Busch Jr. was born.** As chairman from 1946 to 1975, he built Anheuser-Busch into the largest brewery in the world. The firm built nine regional breweries and increased its annual sales from three million barrels in 1946 to more than 34 million in 1974. "Gussie" was the first brewer to advertise on a national television show and guided introduction of the Budweiser "bow tie." He was most beloved for his work as president of the Cardinals from 1953 until he died in 1990.

*Courtesy Wikipedia*

## March 29, 1969

**The ill-fated replica of the *Santa Maria* arrived at the St. Louis riverfront.** The ship was part of the Spanish exhibit at the World's Fair in New York. Mayor A. J. Cervantes acquired it as a tourist attraction, but it sank in a storm in June 1969. Raised and repaired, it was sold to a promoter for $1 and returned to the riverfront. In March 1973 it was sold and moved to Florida. On June 24, 1974, it was destroyed by fire.

*Courtesy Missouri Historical Society, St. Louis*

### March 26, 1776

**Peter Lindell was born.** He made a fortune as a merchant and bought up land that now makes up the Central West End, where Lindell Boulevard runs today. Spring Avenue was named for a spring on his land. His eastern land was the site of the 1861 encampment of the state militia known as "Camp Jackson." At least 28 people died in the violence after federal troops seized the camp in May 1861.

### March 27, 2002

**After 96 years, the D'Arcy Masius Benton and Bowles advertising agency announced it would close its doors by June.** The firm created such advertising icons as the Coca-Cola Santa Claus, the Budweiser frogs and lizards, and the Ralston Purina dog food chuck wagon. The firm suffered a major blow when it lost the Budweiser account in 1994. That was followed by the loss of TWA and Southwestern Bell.

### March 27, 2014

**After years of planning and construction, the $100 million first phase of Ballpark Village opened.** The 120,000-square-foot facility, located just north of Busch Stadium, started out with the Cardinals Nation restaurant, the new Cardinals Hall of Fame Museum, the Budweiser Brew House, and Fox Sports Midwest Live!

### March 28, 1902

**Marlin Perkins was born in Carthage, Missouri.** He began his career at the Saint Louis Zoo cutting grass and cleaning cages. Two months later, he took over the reptile collection. Perkins nearly died in 1928, when a Gaboon viper bit him. He left to direct the Buffalo Zoo in 1938. In 1962, he returned to become director of the Saint Louis Zoo and began hosting television's *Mutual of Omaha's Wild Kingdom*. The show ran for 23 years.

## March 29, 1957

**A sellout crowd of 10,819 along with 90 law enforcement personnel standing by saw Elvis Presley perform at Kiel Auditorium.** A writer for the *St. Louis Globe-Democrat* described Elvis as a "side-burned virus who infected 10,000 teenagers." The writer said Elvis "sang, groaned, shimmied and shook his way through 16 offerings," wearing a gold suit. It marked the first sellout at Kiel since a show by Liberace.

*Courtesy Getty Images*

## March 30, 1890

**The Great Blizzard of 1890 began.** Officially, 20.4 inches of snow fell here on the 30th and 31st. That's still the all-time record for the worst snowstorm in St. Louis history. Despite that, the storm was covered on page six of the *St. Louis Globe-Democrat*. The *Post-Dispatch* gave the "Queer Local Storm" a few paragraphs on page two.

## March 31, 1964

**Seven months of protests at Jefferson Bank and Trust came to an end as the bank hired four Black clerical workers.** The St. Louis Chapter of the Congress of Racial Equality, or CORE, organized the protest over the bank's hiring practices. Many demonstrators were arrested. Some of those who took part included 2nd Ward Alderman and future US Representative William L. Clay, Louis Ford, J. B. (Jet) Banks, Charles and Marian Oldham, and Norman Seay.

*Courtesy Wikipedia*

## March 30, 1931

**The *St. Louis Globe-Democrat* reported that Betty Grable of St. Louis had signed a contract with Fox Studios that assured her of "talkie stardom."** She had made her first appearance in 1930, dancing in *Let's Go Places*. She would go on to appear in 42 films and become the most famous pin-up girl of World War II. Grable felt she was not a great actress. She once said, "My legs saved me."

**Betty Grable of St. Louis signed a contract with Fox Studios that assured her of "talkie stardom."**

## March 31, 1984

**The HBE Corporation's Adam's Mark Hotel at Fourth and Chestnut downtown opened.** The Adam's Mark was constructed around the Pierce Building, built in 1907. A pair of nine-foot-tall bronze horses, created by Venetian artist Ludovico De Luigi, dominated the lobby of the 910-room hotel, which became the Hyatt Regency St. Louis at the Arch.

*Courtesy Missouri Historical Society, St. Louis*

# APRIL

## April 1, 1904

**The Union Electric powerhouse at the foot of Ashley Street on the Mississippi River was completed.** The impressive industrial building with classical details was designed by engineer-architect Charles Ledlic. The Trigen Energy Corporation bought the plant in the 1980s, and it now powers the downtown steam loop.

*Courtesy Wikipedia, credit Marcus Qwertyus*

## April 2, 1908

**Christian Ludolf Ebsen Jr. was born in Belleville.** He rose to fame as "Buddy Ebsen." Ebsen was originally cast as the Tin Man in the film *The Wizard of Oz*, but an allergic reaction to the silver paint dust in the makeup nearly killed him. His most famous role is that of Jed Clampett in *The Beverly Hillbillies*. He also starred as Georgie Russell in *Davy Crockett* and as Barnaby Jones.

*Courtesy Wikipedia*

## April 3, 1950

**The St. Louis Board of Aldermen moved to stop that great scourge of the 1950s, the comic book menace.** A measure was passed making it a misdemeanor to sell lurid comic books or crime comics to kids under 18. The bill, introduced by Alderman Alfred F. Harris and endorsed by several civic organizations, provided for fines from $50 to $500 per violation and exempted comics published in the newspapers.

*Courtesy Wikipedia*

### April 1, 1841

**The first luxury hotel in St. Louis opened.** The Planter's House hosted the great names of the day, including Henry Clay, Daniel Webster, and Charles Dickens. It was the birthplace of the famous "Planter's Punch."

### April 2, 1896

**The city of Webster Groves was incorporated.** Webster Groves was originally five separate communities along the Missouri Pacific and Frisco lines: Webster, Old Orchard, Webster Park, Tuxedo Park, and Selma. The developers of Webster Park had promoted it as "The Queen of the Suburbs," and that nickname endures.

### April 2, 2001

**A 21-year-old hitter by the name of Albert Pujols made his Major League debut with the Cardinals.** Pujols had torn apart spring training and locked himself into a roster spot following an injury to veteran Bobby Bonilla. Pujols started in left field as the Cardinals fell 8–0 to the Colorado Rockies at Coors Field.

*Courtesy Wikipedia, credit Dave Herholz*

### April 3, 1977

**Barclay Plager played his final game for the Blues.** Two of Barc's brothers, Bob and Bill, also played in the NHL. All three were teammates on the Blues from 1968–69 through 1971–72. Barclay coached the Blues for parts of four seasons. "The Spirit of the Blues" died of cancer on February 6, 1988.

## April 4, 1928

**Maya Angelou was born Marguerite Johnson.** Her childhood home still stands at 3130 Hickory Street in St. Louis. She was raised in rural Arkansas and recounted her upbringing there in *I Know Why the Caged Bird Sings*. She was nominated for an Emmy Award for her role in *Roots*. Her screenplay *Georgia, Georgia* was the first by an African American woman to become a motion picture. Maya Angelou died on May 28, 2014.

## April 4, 1933

**Bernard F. Dickmann was elected mayor of St. Louis, the first Democratic mayor here in 24 years.** He would call together a group of businessmen to set in motion Luther Ely Smith's plans for a riverfront memorial. The Poplar Street Bridge was officially the Bernard F. Dickmann Bridge until 2013.

## April 5, 1976

**Sterling Kelby Brown was born in St. Louis.** He grew up in Olivette and attended Mary Institute and Saint Louis Country Day School. He originally planned to become a businessman before starting to pursue acting at Stanford. Brown won critical acclaim and a Primetime Emmy for starring in *The People v. O. J. Simpson: American Crime Story* in 2016 and starred as Randall Pearson in the NBC series *This Is Us*.

## April 5, 1991

**Sisters Robin and Julia Kerry were raped and pushed off the old Chain of Rocks Bridge to their deaths.** Marlin Gray was executed for the crime in 2005. Antonio Richardson's sentence was commuted to life with no parole in 2003. Suspect Daniel Winfrey was sentenced to 30 years. The Missouri Supreme Court threw out the conviction of Reginald Clemons on a technicality in 2015 and he pleaded guilty in exchange for a life sentence in December 2017.

## April 4, 1968

**Martin Luther King Jr. was assassinated.** That night, Mayor Alfonso Cervantes went from TV station to TV station to appeal for calm. The streets mostly stayed quiet. In the 1970s, a House committee found that James Earl Ray of Alton had killed King as part of a plot involving his brothers, Jerry and John, and two St. Louis businessmen, John H. Sutherland and John Kauffmann. Kauffmann and Sutherland, who were dead by the time the probe began, allegedly put up a $50,000 bounty.

*Courtesy Wikipedia*

*Courtesy Pixabay*

## April 5, 1885

**Flamboyant Englishman Hugh M. Brooks, alias Walter Lennox Maxwell, murdered his friend Charles Arthur Preller at the old Southern Hotel and stuffed the nude body in a trunk.** A message left behind read "Thus perish all traitors to the great cause." St. Louis Police spent the unheard sum of $400 for a telegram to New Zealand, where Brooks had fled. The press across the nation eagerly followed his 69-day journey back to St. Louis. Some historians compare it to the O. J. Simpson chase. Brooks was hanged on August 10, 1888.

## April 6, 2021

**St. Louis Treasurer Tishaura Jones became the first Black woman elected as mayor of St. Louis.** She defeated Alderwoman Cara Spencer with 51.68 percent of the vote.

*Courtesy Wikipedia, credit New America*

Courtesy Missouri Historical Society, St. Louis

# April 7, 1933

**A crowd of 25,000 gathered at the Anheuser-Busch Brewery and cheered as the clock struck midnight and Prohibition ended.** Speaking on a CBS Radio Network broadcast from the brewery, Gussie Busch said, "There is a song in our hearts: it's 'Happy Days Are Here Again.'" The Clydesdales made their debut the next morning, bringing one of the first cases of legal Budweiser down Pennsylvania Avenue to present to President Roosevelt. Today, there are six Clydesdale hitches.

Courtesy Wikipedia

# April 8, 1964

**Ed and Margie Imo opened their pizza parlor at Thurman and Shaw.** Imo's was the first pizza place west of the Mississippi to deliver to the customer's home. Loved or hated for its provel cheese and thin, crispy crust cut into squares, Imo's now has over 90 stores across Missouri, with 80 in the St. Louis area.

# April 9, 1859

**After serving two apprenticeships, Samuel Clemens was licensed as a Mississippi River pilot at St. Louis.** In *Life on the Mississippi*, Clemens said, "The first time I ever saw St. Louis, I could have bought it for $6 million, and it was the mistake of my life that I did not do it." It was while working on the river that he picked up a term used to measure the water's depth, which he later took as his pen name: Mark Twain.

Courtesy Library of Congress

**April 6, 1917**

**Congress declared war on Germany.** The names of 1,075 St. Louisans who gave their lives in World War I are listed in the Court of Honor at the Soldiers Memorial. Three St. Louisans were awarded the Medal of Honor. Captain Alexander Skinker died attacking iron pillboxes on the Hindenburg Line. Sergeant Arthur Forrest took six German machine gun nests, and Sergeant Michael Ellis single-handedly captured 44 Germans and 10 machine guns in one day.

**April 7, 1823**

**William Carr Lane was elected the first mayor of St. Louis.** The former post surgeon at Fort Belle Fontaine was so popular that he would be reelected to five more one-year terms. He returned to office seven years later and was reelected two more times.

**April 7, 1981**

**U2 played St. Louis for the first time.** They were paid $750 for a show at Washington University's Graham Chapel and performed before a crowd of about 600. The band played "I Will Follow" twice because they didn't have enough material.

**April 8, 1904**

**The newspapers reported that the latest figures from the US Census Bureau showed that St. Louis was the fourth-largest city in the country.** The population of the city was put at 612,279. That ranked behind only New York, Chicago, and Philadelphia.

**April 9, 1865**

**Ulysses S. Grant and Robert E. Lee, two men who had lived in St. Louis, met at Appomattox and signed the documents ending the Civil War.** There were more than 1,100 battles or skirmishes in Missouri during the war, behind only Tennessee and Virginia. More than 14,000 Missourians died fighting for the Union. About 4,000 died fighting for the Confederacy.

## April 10, 1987

**The body of Walter Scott, lead singer for Bob Kuban and the In-Men, was found in a cistern in rural St. Charles County.** It marked the beginning of one of the most bizarre murder cases in St. Louis area history. James Howard Williams, who was having an affair with Scott's wife, was convicted of killing Scott and his own wife, Sharon. Scott's wife, JoAnn, would plead guilty to hindering the prosecution.

## April 10, 2006

**At 3:14 p.m., Mark Mulder threw a called strike past Brady Clark of the Milwaukee Brewers, the first regular-season pitch at the new Busch Stadium.** The Cardinals won the game 6–4. The first hit was a single by Carlos Lee of the Brewers. Bill Hall of Milwaukee hit the first home run. Albert Pujols hit the first Cardinals home run in the third inning.

## April 11, 1842

**Charles Dickens arrived in St. Louis.** He later wrote that St. Louis must be an unhealthy place: "it is very hot, lies among great rivers, and has vast tracts of undrained swampy land around it, I leave the reader to form his own opinion." He described Belleville as "a small collection of wooden houses, huddled together in the very heart of the bush and swamp." He felt St. Louis "is not likely ever to vie, in point of elegance or beauty, with Cincinnati."

## April 11, 1877

**A fire at the Southern Hotel killed 21 people and made a folk hero out of firefighter Phelim O'Toole.** He saved a dozen people trapped beyond the reach of his primitive hook-and-ladder apparatus. O'Toole instructed victims to lower bedsheets after tying them around the bedposts. He then swung out on a rope, climbed up the sheet, and brought them to safety. The citizens of St. Louis awarded him a check for $500, which he promptly donated to orphans.

*Courtesy Wikipedia*

## April 10, 1847

**Joseph Pulitzer was born in Mako, Hungary.** He was penniless when he came to St. Louis. He rose to the state legislature and later became a partner in the *Westliche Post*, an influential German-language newspaper here. In December of 1878, he purchased the bankrupt *St. Louis Dispatch* and merged it with the *Evening Post*. His will established the Pulitzer Prizes for journalism, letters, drama, and education.

## April 11, 1898

**The new St. Louis City Hall opened.** Mayor Henry Ziegenheim led a parade of city employees from the old offices at 11th and Chestnut. The new building had been under construction for years. The building was not completely finished until 1904.

*Courtesy Missouri Historical Society, St. Louis*

## April 12, 1892

1899 St. Louis Perfectos
*Courtesy Library of Congress*

**The current St. Louis National League franchise played its first game.** The Browns lost to Chicago 14–10 before 8,160 fans at old Sportsman's Park. St. Louis had a franchise when the NL was founded in 1876, but the team folded. In 1882 the Browns joined the American Association. The AA folded after the 1891 season, and the Browns rejoined the newly reformed National League.

New owners Stanley and Frank Robison named the team the Perfectos in 1899 and the team became the Cardinals in 1900.

## April 13, 1954

**Tom Alston started at first base on opening day.** He was the first Black player in Cardinals history. Alston appeared in 91 big-league games for the Cardinals over four seasons, but his career was hampered by mental issues that eventually led to his hospitalization. He died at age 67 on December 30, 1993.

*Courtesy Missouri Historical Society, St. Louis*

*Courtesy Missouri Historical Society, St. Louis*

## April 14, 1893

**The first "horseless carriage" ever seen in St. Louis appeared on Garrison Avenue.** Twenty-year-old Perry Lewis converted an old wagon into an electric car that could reach a speed of 10 miles per hour. George Dorris would build the first internal combustion automobile made in St. Louis in 1898. Lewis would receive License Number One when St. Louis began regulating automobiles in 1902.

## April 15, 1912

**The newspapers were reporting that the passengers aboard the *Titanic* had been saved and the richest heiress in St. Louis was among those rescued.** Georgette Madill and her mother, Elisabeth Robert, had gone on a European trip to recover from the death of Elisabeth's second husband. A court order had given 15-year-old Georgette an allowance of $7,500 per year for clothing and her education until she turned 18.

### April 12, 1976

**The *St. Louis Post-Dispatch* reported on the demise of the Holiday Hill Amusement Park at Brown Road and Natural Bridge in Berkeley.** The rides had been relocated to Chain of Rocks Fun Fair. At its height in the 1950s, Holiday Hill covered 45 acres that had once been the Champ Dairy Farm. The land was eventually lost to airport expansion.

### April 13, 1743

**Thomas Jefferson was born in what is now Albemarle County, Virginia.** There are more than 40 streets, parks, and institutions in the St. Louis area named for Jefferson. On this date in 1913, the Jefferson Memorial in Forest Park was dedicated. The World's Fair Company had it constructed using funds left over from the fair, and it is located on the former site of the fair's main entrance. It was the first national monument to Jefferson, as the Jefferson Memorial in Washington was not completed until 1943.

### April 13, 1948

**The St. Louis County Court approved the incorporation of St. Ann with a population of 2,249.** Charles F. Vatterott began developing the community as a defense housing project. The first 100 homes in Mary Ridge opened in 1940 and were only sold to families with four or more children. Vatterott built 638 more homes on the site of the Stein farm.

### April 14, 1913

**Voters approved incorporation of Clayton and chose William Broadhead as the first mayor.** Clayton was established as the county seat in 1877. E. G. Lewis wanted to make the area part of his planned University City, but word leaked out and a group of Clayton residents stayed up all night to prepare the paperwork for incorporation. Lewis's people arrived at the courthouse to find the papers were already filed.

## April 15, 1916

**"Miss Jim" the elephant arrived, and Mayor Henry Kiel formally dedicated the Saint Louis Zoo.** Children in the public schools raised $2,385 to purchase an elephant that was to be named in honor of Board of Education President James Harper. But the animal turned out to be a "she," so they settled on "Miss Jim."

## April 16, 1963

**The new planetarium in Forest Park formally opened.** The first show was called "New Skies for St. Louis." The decision to build the planetarium on the site of the old mounted police academy caused a controversy over the use of the park for new buildings.

## April 16, 1978

**Bob Forsch pitched the first no-hitter in St. Louis in 54 years, blanking the Phillies 5–0.** It was the first no-hitter ever in Busch Stadium II but was not without controversy. The official scorer charged Ken Reitz with an error on a hard liner by Gary Maddox in the eighth inning that went off Reitz's glove. Forsch would throw another no-hitter at Busch on September 26, 1983.

## April 17, 1918

**William Beedle was born in O'Fallon, Illinois.** He changed his name to William Holden when he signed a movie contract. His first major role came in *Golden Boy* with Barbara Stanwyck in 1939. He also played Joe Gillis, the writer who romanced Norma Desmond in *Sunset Boulevard*. Holden won an Academy Award for his role in *Stalag 17* and also made a memorable appearance in *Network*.

*Courtesy Missouri Historical Society, St. Louis*

## April 16, 1917

**Construction began on a permanent outdoor theater in Forest Park.** The site had been chosen earlier in the year for a presentation of *As You Like It*, marking the 300th anniversary of the death of William Shakespeare. The St. Louis Advertising Club put up half the money for the permanent theater in order to host a presentation of *Aida* for a major advertising convention. The future "Muny" was completed in just 49 days, and the curtain went up on *Aida* on June 5, 1917.

## April 17, 1945

**The Browns' legendary one-armed outfielder, Pete Gray, made his major-league debut.** Gray singled once off Les Mueller of the Detroit Tigers in four at bats. He did not handle any chances in the outfield. Gray was called up as many of the players were serving in the war. He finished the season with a .218 average and was sent to the minors when players began returning from overseas.

*Courtesy Getty Images*

*Courtesy Missouri Historical Society, St. Louis*

## April 18, 1949

**The incident that inspired the book and movie *The Exorcist* ended in St. Louis.** The Reverend William Bowdern of St. Francis Xavier performed the exorcism on a 13-year-old Maryland boy over several weeks at the old church rectory and old Alexian Brothers Hospital. An account of the horrifying and violent afflictions suffered by the boy and the ordeal of the priests was reportedly recovered from a sealed room just before Alexian Brothers was demolished in 1978. The child recovered.

*Courtesy Wikipedia, credit Limulus*

## April 19, 1983

**It appeared as if only a miracle would keep the Blues in St. Louis.** The vice president of Ralston Purina signed papers selling the team to a group from Saskatoon, Saskatchewan. The president of another team said, "Hockey obviously isn't as important anymore in St. Louis. They have baseball and football and I guess that's what the fans want to see."

*It appeared as if only a miracle would keep the Blues in St. Louis.*

## April 20, 1970

**The Spanish Pavilion closed its doors.** Brought here from the 1965 New York World's Fair, it was open for less than a year before the foundation formed to bring it here went bankrupt. Developer Donald Breckenridge bought the building, which became the lobby of the Marriott, which became the Hilton at the Ballpark.

*Courtesy Missouri Historical Society, St. Louis*

## April 21, 1972

**Demolition work began on the main portion of the Pruitt-Igoe housing project.** When the two complexes were built in the 1950s, Pruitt-Igoe was hailed as a milestone. But the vacant and vandalized buildings became a national symbol of the failure of large-scale high-rise public housing. The photo was made when the complex first opened.

*Courtesy Missouri State Archives*

### April 18, 1942

**Colonel James Doolittle and a squadron of B-25s took off from the carrier *Hornet* and made the first bombing raid on Tokyo.** Doolittle headed the aviation department of the Shell Oil Corporation in St. Louis in the 1930s. He flew for the Missouri Air National Guard before joining the Air Corps in 1940. Lieutenant Charles Lee McClure of University City also took part in the raid. The town of Centerville, Missouri, on Route 66 changed its name to Doolittle in honor of the raiders in 1946.

### April 19, 1912

**The *St. Louis Post-Dispatch* scooped the world with the first eyewitness accounts of the *Titanic* disaster.** Reporter Carlos Hurd was returning from a vacation aboard the *Carpathia* when it steamed to the aid of survivors. The captain of the *Carpathia* ordered all passengers to remain in their rooms, but Hurd managed to shoot pictures and gather accounts from survivors. The wireless operator refused to send the story. Joseph Pulitzer sent a tug to meet the *Carpathia* at New York, and Hurd tossed a buoy with the story attached to the crew of the tug.

### April 20, 1769

**The great Ottawa Chief Pontiac was assassinated by a Peoria warrior near Cahokia, Illinois.** Governor Saint-Ange de Bellerive sent for his body to be brought across the river.

*Courtesy Wikipedia*

Pontiac, who united several of the Great Lakes tribes in a revolt against the British, was buried at present-day Broadway and Walnut, where the Southern Hotel was later constructed and the Stadium East Garage is located today.

Courtesy Missouri Historical Society, St. Louis

## April 22, 1856

**The first railroad bridge over the Mississippi River opened at Rock Island, Illinois.** It was an important date for St. Louis because it would be almost 20 years before a bridge was built here, and the Rock Island bridge made Chicago a greater railroad hub. Steamboat interests here had fought to prevent railroads from being allowed to bridge the river. Abraham Lincoln defended the railroad in one such court case.

## April 22, 1857

**Washington University (founded as Eliot Seminary in 1853) was formally inaugurated with ceremonies in the Mercantile Library Hall.** The speaker at the ceremony was Edward Everett. In 1863, Everett would speak for two hours at a cemetery dedication in Gettysburg, Pennsylvania, but his 14,000-word oration was overshadowed by a 272-word, two-minute speech Abraham Lincoln made that day.

## April 22, 1952

**A grand jury indicted Cardinals owner Fred Saigh on income tax evasion charges.** He was eventually sentenced to 15 months and was forced to sell the team. He turned down an offer of substantially more money from Milwaukee interests and sold to Anheuser-Busch. The brewery's purchase of the Redbirds doomed the Browns.

## April 23, 1869

**The St. Louis County Lunatic Asylum opened atop the hill at Arsenal and Sublette.** One hundred twenty-nine

Courtesy Wikipedia

patients were admitted on opening day. William Rumbold designed the dome for the Old Courthouse and the asylum. When the city and county separated in 1876, it became the St. Louis City Insane Asylum. Renamed City Sanitarium in 1911, it was sold to the state in 1948 and renamed St. Louis State Hospital. The facility is now the St. Louis Psychiatric Rehabilitation Center.

## April 23, 1967

Courtesy Missouri Historical Society, St. Louis

**The first fully professional St. Louis soccer team played its first game at Busch Stadium.** A crowd of 18,000 saw the St. Louis Stars' 2–1 win over the Oakland Clippers. The Stars played in the National Professional Soccer League and then moved to the North American Soccer League in 1968. The team moved to California in 1977.

## April 23, 1999

**Fernando Tatis of the Cardinals belted two grand slams in the third inning of a game against the Dodgers in Los Angeles.** Dodgers pitcher Chan Ho Park became the first hurler since Bill Phillips of the Pirates in 1890 to give up two grand slams in an inning.

## April 24, 1953

**About 100 policemen shot it out with bandits from Chicago at the Southwest Bank on Kingshighway.** Robber Frank Vito shot himself to death. Police wounded John Frederick and William Scholl. Officer Robert Heitz was wounded. In 1958, directors Charles Guggenheim and John Stix restaged the holdup for the movie *The Great St. Louis Bank Robbery*. Steve McQueen played the getaway driver. Many of the customers and officers involved were featured in the film.

Courtesy Missouri Historical Society, St. Louis

About 100 policemen shot it out with bandits from Chicago at the Southwest Bank on Kingshighway.

## April 25, 1969

**Joe Buck was born.** The youngest of Jack Buck's eight children, Joe did play-by-play for the Cardinals from 1991 to 2007, although he first called an inning on his 17th birthday. Joe started on NFL broadcasts for FOX when he was 25 and is one of only three broadcasters ever to serve as a network's lead announcer for MLB and the NFL.

*Courtesy Wikipedia, credit FOX Sports*

## April 26, 1921

*Courtesy Pixabay*

**Saint Louis University president Reverend William Robison became the first voice on the St. Louis airwaves, broadcasting over Station 9YK.** The station, operated by SLU and overseen by Brother George Rueppel of the meteorological department, was the second in the United States. On July 16, 1921, Rueppel held a microphone up to a gramophone, becoming the first St. Louis disc jockey. The station became WEW in 1922.

## April 27, 1896

**Rogers Hornsby was born in Winters, Texas.** "The Rajah" played for the Cardinals from 1915 to 1926 and returned in 1933. He played for the Browns from 1933 to 1937 and managed the Browns in 1952. His lifetime batting average of .358 is the highest in National League history and the third highest in major-league history. He was named to the Baseball Hall of Fame in 1942.

**"The Rajah" played for the Cardinals from 1915 to 1926 and returned in 1933.**

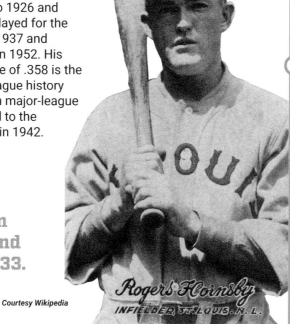

*Courtesy Wikipedia*

### April 24, 1902

**The St. Louis Browns of the American League played their first game and beat Cleveland, 5–2.** Businessman Robert Hedges had moved the cellar-dwelling Milwaukee Brewers to St. Louis and took the name abandoned by the Cardinals a couple of seasons earlier. The Cardinals sued but lost when seven players, including Bobby Wallace, jumped to the Browns. Wallace became the highest-paid player in baseball at $6,500 per season.

### April 25, 1214

**Our city's namesake was born near Poissy, France.** Louis IX became king of France in 1226 at the age of 11. He took up the sword in 1244, vowing to recapture Jerusalem from the Muslims, but he was captured and held for ransom. Louis embarked on another crusade in 1270. He got as far as Tunis, where he fell ill and died in August. Louis IX was canonized by Pope Boniface VIII in 1297.

### April 26, 1974

**The St. Louis Regional Commerce and Growth Association kicked off a massive promotion campaign with the theme "St. Louis Has It All from A to Z."** Remember the jingles? "Gimme an A . . . We've got the Gateway Arch, antiques, amusement parks . . . B . . . boat rides and boulevards, baseball and beer."

### April 27, 1916

**Enos "Country" Slaughter was born in Roxboro, North Carolina.** Slaughter was beloved for his hustle and determination and for dashing from first to home on a hit by Harry Walker in game seven of the 1946 World Series. Slaughter spent three years in the service at the height of his career, but he still played in five World Series.

## April 28, 1959

**St. Louis's first independent television station signed on.** KPLR Channel 11 was to air its first program that night, a telecast of the game between the Cardinals and the Reds, but the game was rained out. The next night, Jack Buck, Harry Caray, and Joe Garagiola called the action as the Cards played the Milwaukee Braves.

## April 29, 1825

**St. Louis welcomed General Marie Joseph Paul Roche Yves Gilbert du Motier, the Marquis de Lafayette.** Officials weren't sure if they could use city money to entertain their important guest. They invited the governor, reasoning that the state might then pick up the bill. But Governor Frederick Bates said no state money would be used, and he would not meet Lafayette. Aldermen voted to go ahead and use city money to pay the expenses, which amounted to $37.

## April 30, 1803

**The US and France signed the Louisiana Purchase.** Napoleon planned to use Louisiana to supply an empire on Hispaniola. But Toussaint L'Ouverture led a slave revolt that forced the French from Hispaniola, making Louisiana useless to France. President Thomas Jefferson sent James Monroe and Robert R. Livingston to purchase the Port of New Orleans and western Florida to guarantee free navigation of the Mississippi. They were stunned when the French offered to sell the entire territory. *(facing page)*

1803 Louisiana Purchase Lithograph
*Courtesy Missouri Historical Society, St. Louis*

F/A-18E Super Hornet
*Courtesy Wikipedia*

## April 28, 1967

**McDonnell Aircraft and Douglas Aircraft merged.** The deal with essentially a takeover by McDonnell of the financially ailing Douglas. James McDonnell would be chairman, and the St. Louis headquarters would be retained. McDonnell Douglas went on to build several notable aircraft here, including the F-15 Eagle fighter (1972) and F/A-18 Hornet fighter (1978). The firm merged with Boeing in 1997.

## April 29, 1944

**Jim Hart was born in Evanston, Illinois.** Hart starred at SIU–Carbondale but was ignored by NFL teams because he played for a small school. In 1966, the Big Red signed him as a free agent. Hart became the starting quarterback when the Army drafted Charley Johnson, and he would start for the Cardinals until 1981. He was released in 1983.

*Courtesy State Historical Society of Missouri*

## April 30, 1904

**A crowd of 200,000 people watched the World's Fair opening ceremonies.** John Philip Sousa's band played, and Exposition Company President David R. Francis and Secretary of War William Howard Taft spoke. At 1:06 p.m., Francis raised his hands and said, "Swing wide ye portals. Enter herein ye sons of men and behold the achievement of your race." Water gushed from the Cascades as the machinery roared to life. The 1904 World's Fair was open.

*Courtesy Missouri Historical Society, St. Louis*

THE INSTRVMENT
VE
HAVE SIGNED
VILL PREPARE
CENTVRIES OF
HAPPINESS
FOR
INNVMERABLE
GENERATIONS
OF THE HVMAN
RACE
THE MISSISSIPPI
AND
THE MISSOVRI VILL
SEE THEM PROSPER
AND INCREASE IN
THE MIDST
OF
EQVALITY VNDER
JVST LAWS

MONROE·LIVINGSTON
MARBOIS·
·1803·

Stan Musial
*Missouri Historical Society, St. Louis*

# MAY

## May 1, 1995

**Conrad Properties bought Coral Court Motel.** The site of this iconic motel would be used for a new subdivision, Oak Knoll Manor. The Coral Court was constructed in 1941 along Route 66. It became notorious for its attached garages but was treasured for its beautiful Deco Moderne design.

*Courtesy Wikipedia*

## May 1, 1955

**Chuck Berry signed a contract with Chess Records of Chicago.** Owner Leonard Chess was impressed with Berry's performance of an old country song called "Ida Red." Berry reworked the lyrics and changed it to "Maybellene." Recorded on May 21, 1955, and released in July 1955, "Maybellene" became Berry's first hit.

## May 2, 1968

**The St. Louis Hawks were sold to Atlanta interests led by the governor of Georgia.** Owner Ben Kerner said efforts to find a St. Louis buyer failed because "They just don't want our product here." Fewer than 9,000 fans had turned out for three playoff games here the previous season when the Hawks were fighting San Francisco for the division title.

*Courtesy Missouri Historical Society, St. Louis*

## May 2, 1954

**Stan Musial slammed five home runs and drove in nine in a doubleheader against the Giants in St. Louis.** The Cardinals won the first game 10–6 but lost the nightcap, 9–7. Musial also set a record with 21 total bases in the two games. He went 4-for-4 with a walk in game one and 2-for-4 with a walk in game two. Eight-year-old Nate Colbert was in attendance that day. In 1972, Colbert would become the only other player to hit five homers in a doubleheader. *(facing page)*

## May 3, 1918

**An ordinance was introduced in the Board of Aldermen to change the name of Berlin Street to Pershing.** It was the first of several ordinances purging the city of German street names. Von Versing was changed to Enright to honor one of the area's first war dead. Kaiser was changed to Gresham, Brunswick to January, Wiesenhan to Bonita, Helvetia to Stole, and Hasburger to Cecil Place.

Berlin Hotel, at the corner of Taylor and Berlin Avenue
*Courtesy Missouri Historical Society, St. Louis*

## May 3, 1948

**The US Supreme Court ruled in the landmark case of *Shelley v. Kraemer*.** Many St. Louis neighborhoods had remained segregated, and African Americans faced a critical housing shortage because property owners would enter into agreements forbidding the sale of homes to non-Whites. Neighbors sued when the Shelleys bought a home at 4600 Labadie, but the high court ruled that racial covenants were not enforceable.

## May 4, 1876

**The first National League game in St. Louis took place.** A crowd of 4,000 was on hand at the Grand Avenue Ball Grounds to see the Brown Stockings face the Chicago White Stockings. The game was rained out in the third inning, but management refused to make refunds or allow fans to use their tickets for the makeup game the next day. The Browns disbanded after a game-fixing scandal in 1877. The team was resurrected when the American Association was founded in 1881, and those Browns evolved into the Cardinals.

## May 5, 1834

**Francois Lemais was granted permission to operate a ferry on the Meramec River.** The road leading to the ferry was the Road to Carondelet, also known as Middle Road or Meramec Road. Sometime after the Civil War it became the Lemay Rock Road and later Lemay Ferry.

*Courtesy Flikr, credit Wampa-One*

## May 5, 1904

**The Palace of Fine Arts at the World's Fair was opened to the public.** Most of the great palaces at the fair were built of plaster of paris, but architect Cass Gilbert's $1 million Art Palace was designed as a permanent museum. It became the first major US art museum to be municipally funded when residents passed the Art Museum Tax in 1907.

## May 6, 1971

**Ike & Tina Turner were awarded their only gold record, for "Proud Mary."** Tina met Ike at the Club Manhattan in East St. Louis. They began performing together regularly at spots such as the Club Imperial at Goodfellow and West Florissant and then broke big nationally with "A Fool in Love" in 1960.

*Courtesy Missouri State Archives*

## May 4, 1819

**Nineteen-year-old Henry Shaw arrived in St. Louis aboard the Mississippi steamboat *Maid of Orleans*.** The immigrant from England brought with him a small stock of cutlery to make his fortune. Shaw became such a successful importer-exporter and real estate investor that he was able to retire at age 40. In 1851, he visited the Royal Gardens and the gardens at the Duke of Devonshire's estate in England. The visits inspired Shaw to construct his own garden at his estate, Tower Grove.

## May 5, 1961

**Alan Shepard became the first American in space.** His space capsule was built here at McDonnell Aircraft. The photo shows the "Clean Room" at McDonnell where the Project Mercury space capsules were assembled.

*Courtesy Arthur Witman Collection, State Historical Society of Missouri*

## May 6, 1942

**Mayor Becker signed an ordinance changing the name of the Municipal Bridge to the MacArthur Bridge.** The long-awaited "Free" bridge opened in January 1917. The span carried Route 66 traffic

*Courtesy Wikipedia, credit Paul Sableman*

from 1929 to 1935 and "City Route 66" from 1936 to 1955. It closed to vehicle traffic in 1981 but still carries trains.

## May 7, 1947

The *Sporting News* listed some of Dizzy Dean's contributions to the English language during his broadcasts on WIL. The article mentioned gems such as "Slaughter slud safe into second," "Marion threw Rieser out at first" and "the runners held their respectable bases." Diz got around the wartime ban on mentioning weather conditions by telling his audience, "If you folks don't know what's holdin' up the game, just stick your heads outta the window."

*Courtesy Missouri Historical Society, St. Louis*

## May 8, 1966

The Cardinals played their last game at old Busch Stadium, losing to the Giants, 10–5. Willie Mays hit the final home run in the old ballpark. Alex Johnson hit into a double play to end it. August Busch Jr. presented the deed to Richard Amberg, president of the Herbert Hoover Boys Club. Retired groundskeeper Bill Stocksick, who had installed the original home plate in 1906, struggled to dig up the current one. The plate was put aboard a helicopter and flown to new Busch Stadium.

*Courtesy author*

## May 7, 1945

At 8:36 a.m., KSD radio flashed word of the German surrender. The city waited to celebrate until the following morning, when VE Day would be officially declared. The *Post* reported that 1,246 St. Louisans had lost their lives in the European theatre and 621 were listed as missing. The following day, vital war industries continued business as usual. The main gathering was an interfaith service at Memorial Plaza.

## May 7, 1974

Nine-year-old Vonda Clark of Shipman, Illinois, became the five millionth visitor to the Arch. Among her prizes: a case of wine and tickets to the Playboy Club.

## May 8, 1900

Streetcar workers walked off the job, beginning the most violent strike in St. Louis history. At least 14 people were killed and 200 injured in the 55-day walkout. The elite of the city formed an armed posse of 1,600 citizens to keep order. Most of the strikers were replaced, but the episode is a major turning point in St. Louis labor history.

## May 9, 1953

The $40 million Chain of Rocks Canal was dedicated. A flower-bedecked barge carrying Veiled Prophet Queen Sally Baker Shepley led a parade of 150 vessels. The canal bypassed the treacherous "Chain of Rocks" stretching across the river below the bridge that also bears that name.

## May 9, 1929

A crowd of 20,000 celebrated the dedication at the grand opening of the new Soulard Market and Civic Center. The building is modeled after the Ospedale degli Innocenti (Hospital of the Innocents) constructed in 1419 in Florence, Italy. It currently houses the Grand Hall Shops on the first floor and a gymnasium/theater on the second floor.

*Courtesy Wikipedia, credit Paul Sableman*

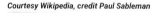

# MAY

## May 10, 1861

**Federal volunteers under Nathaniel Lyon surrounded the pro-Southern militia at Camp Jackson on the western edge of the city.** A huge crowd assembled on Olive Street and hurled insults at the "damned Dutch" as the mostly German Union volunteers marched the prisoners toward the arsenal. No one knows where the first shot came from, but the untrained Home Guard turned and fired into the crowd. At least 27 civilians and eight soldiers died. The president of a St. Louis streetcar company barely escaped injury by diving into a ditch. His name was William T. Sherman.

## May 10, 1957

**Annie Turnbo Pope Malone died.** Her line of Poro Beauty Care products made her one of the first female African American millionaires. She opened Poro College here in 1917. Malone pioneered the practice of hiring women to sell the products. She founded a finance company to help Blacks buy homes and donated the money to the St. Louis Colored Orphans Home, now the Annie Malone Children and Family Service Center. She moved her business to Chicago in 1930.

## May 11, 1906

**A huge crowd watched as the great Ferris wheel from the World's Fair was blown up.** It took two explosions of 50 sticks of dynamite to do the job. Pittsburgh bridge builder George Washington Gale Ferris originally constructed the wheel for the Columbian Exposition of 1893 in Chicago, inspired by the design of the merry-go-round. The wheel was 264 feet tall and could hold 2,100 people. Its 45-foot axle was the largest single piece of forged steel in the world at the time.

*Courtesy Missouri Historical Society, St. Louis*

## May 10, 1970

**Bobby Orr's overtime goal gave the Boston Bruins the Stanley Cup and gave Blues fans another heartbreak.** Noel Picard flattened Orr right after the goal, a moment captured in one of the most famous hockey photos of all time. It was the third year the Blues had reached the finals, only to be swept in four straight.

*Courtesy Getty Images*

*Courtesy Don Korte*

## May 11, 1940

**The *Meeting of the Waters* fountain in front of Union Station was dedicated.** Swedish sculptor Carl Milles designed the fountain depicting the "marriage" between the Missouri and the Mississippi. Its nude figures caused a bit of a controversy when the plans were announced. The fountain and Aloe Plaza replaced the flophouses, saloons, and brothels that once awaited travelers as they left the station.

## May 12, 1966

**A crowd of 46,048 was on hand as the new Busch Stadium II opened.** First pitch by Ray Washburn of the Cardinals to Felipe Alou of the Braves

*Courtesy Missouri Historical Society, St. Louis*

(a ball) came at 8:04 p.m. Hometown hero Mike Shannon got the first Cardinals hit at Busch II. Second baseman Jerry Buchek, who also grew up in St. Louis, scored the first Cardinals run in the new ballpark as the Cards beat the Braves 4–3 in 12 innings. The fan who caught the first home run ball off the bat of Felipe Alou told a reporter he planned to sell it for $50. Don Dennis became the first pitcher to win a game at Busch II.

## May 13, 1958

**In the sixth inning of a game against the Cubs at Wrigley Field, Stan Musial lined a double to left field for the 3,000th hit of his career.** The Cardinals originally planned to keep Stan on the bench for the final game of the Cubs series so the hometown crowd could see the historic moment. But with the Cards trailing in the game, skipper Fred Hutchinson called on Musial to hit for pitcher Sam Jones. The Cardinals went on to win the game and Musial became the only player whose 3,000th was a pinch hit.

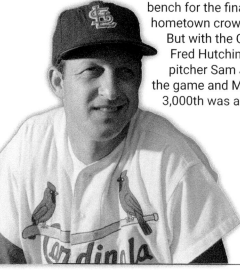

*Courtesy Missouri Historical Society, St. Louis*

## May 14, 1904

**Ceremonies marked the start of the 1904 Olympic Games in St. Louis.** The first event was actually an interscholastic track meet, but all sporting events under the auspices of the fair were billed as "Olympic." The international competitions began in July. The track-and-field event, considered the true Olympics, began on August 29. The games were actually a success, but the oft-quoted memoirs of Olympic founder Pierre de Coubertin insisted they were a failure and that the Olympic organization was forced to hold interim games at Athens in 1906 to restore credibility.

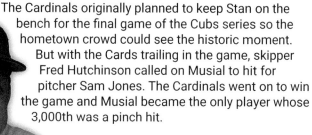

*Courtesy Missouri Historical Society, St. Louis*

*Courtesy Missouri Historical Society, St. Louis*

## May 15, 1850

**Bellefontaine Cemetery was dedicated.** Among the more than 82,000 people buried there are fur trader Manuel Lisa, kindergarten creator Susan Blow, poet Sara Teasdale, James Eads, Senator Thomas Hart Benton, and Adolphus Busch. Flamboyant Browns owner Chris Von der Ahe rests beneath a life-size statue he built before going bankrupt. The grave of explorer William Clark faces the confluence of the Missouri and Mississippi.

## May 12, 1925

**Lawrence Peter "Yogi" Berra was born in St. Louis.** He grew up at 5447 Elizabeth Street on "the Hill," across the street from his best friend, Joe Garagiola. Berra would go on to play on 10 world championship clubs. He was elected to the Baseball Hall of Fame in 1973. Berra died on September 22, 2015, at the age of 90.

*Courtesy Wikipedia*

## May 13, 1961

**The last public city bathhouse was closed.** City Bathhouse #6 was located at 1128 St. Louis Avenue, and the building still stands. The *Post-Dispatch* reported that fewer than 60 people were using it each day.

## May 14, 1804

**The Lewis and Clark Expedition departed Camp DuBois, near present-day Wood River, Illinois.** Clark noted in his journal that the journey began at 4 p.m. under "a gentle brease." On the first day, the 41 men, a 55-foot keelboat, and two smaller boats known as "pirogues" made about six miles and camped across from the mouth of Coldwater Creek. The crews spent the two-day journey to St. Charles becoming accustomed to their boats and the Missouri currents. Lewis would remain in St. Louis until May 20.

*Courtesy Wikipedia*

# MAY

## May 16, 1970

**The gates were closed on the dam as Lake St. Louis was dedicated.** Developer R. T. Crowe intended the 600-acre lake to be the centerpiece of a 2,700-acre residential development modeled after planned "New Towns" such as Reston, Virginia, and Columbia, Maryland. Part of the area was incorporated as Harbor Town in 1975 and the name was changed to Lake St. Louis in 1977.

## May 16, 1979

**The Streckfuss Lines announced that the *Admiral*'s summer cruise season would be cancelled for the first time since World War II.** The Coast Guard had discovered that the hull of the ship had been weakened, and the *Admiral* would leave for a New Orleans drydock in December 1979. By 1981, the ship appeared to be destined for the scrap heap.

*Courtesy Missouri Historical Society, St. Louis*

## May 17, 1849

**Fire broke out aboard the steamboat *White Cloud*, moored at the foot of Franklin Avenue.** Within a half hour, the blaze spread to 23 boats. The worst fire in St. Louis history had begun. The flames jumped to the buildings crowded along the levee. Four hundred thirty buildings, 11 city blocks, and 23 riverboats were reduced to ashes by morning.

## May 16, 1804

**The Lewis and Clark expedition arrived at St. Charles.** Clark described it in his journal as "one mile in length, situated on the North Side of the Missourie at the foot of a hill from which it takes its name, Peetiete Coete or the Little hill." He described the 450 inhabitants as "pore, polite and harmonious." While in St. Charles, two members of the expedition were court-martialed for being absent without leave. One of them received 50 lashes for behaving in an "unbecoming manner" at a ball.

*Courtesy Wikipedia*

## May 17, 1673

**Cartographer Louis Joliet and Jesuit missionary Father Jacques Marquette began their expedition down the Mississippi River.** Marquette wrote of a scene near present-day Alton: "While Skirting some rocks, which by Their height and length inspired awe, We saw upon one of them two painted monsters which at first made Us afraid, and upon Which the boldest savages dare not Long rest their eyes." The Indigenous Peoples called it "Piasa."

*Courtesy Wikipedia, credit Burfalcy*

*Courtesy Missouri Historical Society, St. Louis*

## May 18, 1849

**By 8:00 am, the Great Fire of 1849 was under control.** The blaze destroyed 15 city blocks, 430 buildings, 23 steamboats, nine flatboats and barges, the post office, three banks, and $2,750,000 in property. Volunteer Fire Captain Thomas Targee, who died in an explosion while throwing a keg of powder into Nathaniel Phillips's music store, was the hero of the Great Fire. His heroism created a gap that kept the flames from wiping out the cathedral and the entire business district. Targee Street was named in his honor. It ran south of Market between 14th and 15th, where the Enterprise Center now stands.

## May 19, 1926

**Ground was broken for the new $4.5 million civil courthouse downtown.** The courthouse was to occupy the block bounded by Market, Chestnut, 11th, and 12th Streets. As he turned the first spadeful of earth, Mayor Victor Miller uncovered a rusty old horseshoe and exclaimed, "Oh! Good luck!"

### Ground was broken for the new $4.5 million civil courthouse downtown.

THE CIVIL COURT HOUSE

STONE SET TO 2/2/2
7560-4'
STONE SET FROM 2/2
THRU 6/7/28-192,604-2
STONE SET SINCE
CORNER SETTING
192,604 Cu.Ft.
This Photo taken - 6-7-1928

*Courtesy Missouri Historical Society, St. Louis*

### May 18, 1875

**An army of police officers were guarding city hall after supporters of Henry Overstolz threatened to take over city government by force.** Overstolz had been narrowly defeated in a special mayoral election by James Britton, who was sworn in, even though widespread fraud was alleged. The resulting dispute made St. Louis a national laughingstock until Overstolz was declared the winner in February 1876.

### May 19, 1957

**The *St. Louis Post-Dispatch* reported that contracts for the largest bowling alley between Chicago and California had been signed.** Construction of the 48-lane center at the Arena was set to begin on June 15. After the 1959 tornado destroyed the adjacent roller-skating rink, another 24 lanes were added.

### May 19, 1962

**Stan Musial set a new National League record with his 3,431st hit.** The hit that broke Honus Wagner's old record came in the ninth inning off Ron Perranoski of the Dodgers. By the time he retired in 1963, Musial had set or tied 29 National League records, 17 Major League records, and nine All-Star records, including most home runs in All-Star Games.

*Courtesy Wikipedia*

# MAY

## May 20, 1855

**Mary Meachum tried to help several slaves escape across the Mississippi.** They were caught, and Mary was indicted on charges of "enticing people held in slavery to escape to another state." She was acquitted on one charge and another was dropped. The site of their attempt is now the Mary Meachum Freedom Crossing on the North Riverfront Bike Trail.

## May 20, 1931

**Cardinals great Ken Boyer was born in Liberty, Missouri.** A Cardinal from 1955 to 1965, he was a four-time Gold Glove winner. He won the National League MVP award in 1964 and managed the Cardinals from 1978 to 1980. He died of cancer in 1982.

## May 21, 1927

**The *Spirit of St. Louis* landed at Le Bourget in Paris, two and a half hours ahead of schedule.** Charles Lindbergh had made the trip in 33 hours, 30 minutes, and 29.8 seconds. He had not slept in 55 hours. The Browns were playing the Red Sox at Sportsman's Park when the news was announced to the cheering crowd. Major Albert Bond Lambert, one of the flight's backers, said the *Spirit of St. Louis* would be returned here for exhibition at the airport.

## May 22, 1937

**Construction began on the landmark fountain in the Belleville public square.** It was dedicated in honor of war veterans on October 10, 1937. The fountain stands on land donated by George Blair for the county seat in 1814. It has hosted a pen for stray cattle, two trees that once stood there were used for whipping posts, and it was the site of a lynching in 1903.

*Courtesy Getty Images*

## May 20, 1927

**St. Louisans sat by their radios eager for news of Charles Lindbergh's flight.** The headline in the *Globe* screamed, "Lindbergh off to Paris in daring non-stop dash." The *Spirit of St. Louis* had taken off from Roosevelt Field, Long Island. The plane staggered under its heavy load of fuel and barely made it aloft. 33½ hours later, Lindbergh brought the plane down safely at Le Bourget.

## May 21, 1966

**Car 1628 of the Hodiamont line made its final run, and the streetcar disappeared from the streets of St. Louis.** In 1902, when the system was at its peak, St. Louis City and environs had 560 miles of streetcar lines. On the opening day of the 1904 World's Fair, 927,000 people rode the streetcars. The last day of the line drew about 2,500 riders.

## May 22, 1958

**What to name the new four-lane highway bridge at St. Charles was a hot topic.** There was considerable support for naming it after Harry Truman, though the County Court had approved naming it after the first governor of Missouri, Alexander McNair. The St. Charles Historical Society wanted it named after Benjamin Emmons, who helped write the first state constitution and was a member of the first state legislature. The highway department didn't want the bridge named after anyone.

*Courtesy Wikipedia, credit Americasroof*

## May 23, 1896

The *St. Louis Republic* carried a small notice that Forest Park Highlands, "the finest and largest open-air enterprise in the West," was open for business. The paper said the Highlands offered "ten

new and novel features including a scenic railway." Admission to the grounds was free. Comedienne Marie Dressler was appearing at Col. John D. Hopkins' vaudeville theater.

*Courtesy Missouri*
*Historical Society, St. Louis*

*Courtesy Missouri Historical Society, St. Louis*

## May 24, 1940

The first drive-in theater in the St. Louis area opened on Manchester Road west of Ballas with a showing of *Raffles* starring David Niven and Olivia de Havilland. At first, it was simply called the Drive-In. But as the ozoners became more popular, the name was changed to the Manchester Drive-In. The Manchester could accommodate 500 cars and even offered Easter sunrise church services. It closed in 1967, and West County Center now stands on the site.

*Courtesy State Historical Society of Missouri*

## May 25, 1968

*Courtesy Missouri Historical Society, St. Louis*

Vice President Hubert Humphrey and US Secretary of the Interior Morris Udall presided over a rain-soaked ceremony marking the formal dedication of the Gateway Arch. Officials moved the ceremony indoors under the Arch as water poured down the entryways and across the floor. The public was not admitted. Phillip Russell of ACTION, a civil rights group, briefly interrupted Udall's remarks to loudly accuse Mayor Cervantes of racism.

## May 23, 1820

**James B. Eads was born in Lawrenceburg, Indiana.** At age 22, Eads developed the first diving bell for use in salvage operations, and during the Civil War he built some of the first "ironclad" ships. Eads had little formal education and was a self-taught engineer. After the great bridge at St. Louis was completed, Eads went on to devise a system of jetties south of New Orleans that to this day keep the mouth of the Mississippi from filling with silt.

## May 23, 1959

*Wrestling at the Chase* premiered on KPLR-TV, Channel 11, with Joe Garagiola as the first commentator. Over the next 24 years, over 1,100 episodes would run. The show featured the biggest names from the National Wrestling Foundation, mostly run by promoter Sam Muchnick. St. Louisans still fondly remember watching Rick Flair, Harley Race, "Dick the Bruiser" Afflis, Ted DiBiase, and many others.

## May 24, 1964

**General Manager Bing Devine, manager Johnny Keane, and several other Cardinals players watched as ground was broken for the new Busch Stadium.** Home plate for the new ballpark would be located on the site occupied by the Comfort Printing and Stationery Company, 200 South Seventh Street. Charles Farris, director of the Land Clearance Authority, first proposed a downtown stadium in December 1958 as a way to bring people downtown.

## May 25, 1793

**Johann Adam Lemp was born in Gruningen, Germany.** He came to St. Louis in 1838 and began brewing the first lager beer in St. Louis in about 1840. Lager comes from the German term "lagern," meaning to stock or to store, and Lemp aged his beer in caves below the city. Lager beers also use yeast that ferments on the bottom. Adam's son William built the brewery into the largest in St. Louis by the 1870s.

*Courtesy Wikipedia*

## May 26, 1857

**Dred Scott and his family were freed.** After the infamous Supreme Court ruling in 1857, ownership of Scott; his wife, Harriet; and their daughters, Eliza and Lillie, was transferred to Taylor Blow, and antislavery civic leader who supported the Scotts during their 11-year legal battle. Blow quickly freed them. Scott worked as a porter at Barnum's Hotel before dying of tuberculosis on September 17, 1858.

**In 1873, Blow's daughter, Susan, founded the first kindergarten.**

## May 26, 1926

**Miles Davis was born in Alton.** He moved to East St. Louis and took up the trumpet at age 13. He played in the jazz band while attending Lincoln High School and moved to New York in 1944 to play with his idol, Charlie Parker. He later formed his own bop group and invented a style known as "cool jazz." In 1970, his *Bitches Brew* album combined rock with jazz and became one of the best-selling jazz albums of all time.

## May 27, 1911

**Actor Vincent Price was born in St. Louis at 3748 Washington Avenue.** A graduate of Country Day, he made his first film appearance in 1938 in *Service de Luxe*. It was his role in the 1953 3D movie *House of Wax* and several 1960s Roger Corman adaptations of Edgar Allan Poe tales that made him the "king of the horror movie." He also played in some lighter films, such as the unforgettable *Doctor Goldfoot and the Bikini Machine* (1965) and the Elvis film *The Trouble with Girls*. His last film appearance was in *Edward Scissorhands* in 1990.

*Courtesy Wikipedia*

## May 26, 1780

**Residents of St. Louis and 150 Spanish militia defeated a force of about 1,000 Indigenous Peoples led by the British in the only American Revolution battle fought west of the Mississippi.** The Native Americans were turned back by fire from a hastily constructed tower dubbed Fort San Carlos, at what is now Fourth and Walnut. At least 21 settlers were killed, most caught outside the village when the attack began. At the same time, an attack on Cahokia was thwarted by the timely arrival of forces commanded by George Rogers Clark.

## May 27, 1896

**Shortly after 5 p.m. a tornado touched down near the present site of the State Hospital on Arsenal Street.** The twister then roughly

*Courtesy Missouri Historical Society, St. Louis*

paralleled the path of today's I-44 before slamming into East St. Louis. At least 306 people died. Seventh and Rutger was the deadliest spot, where 14 died in the destruction of the Mauchenheimer family tenement, which today is the site of a parking lot under I-55. A year earlier, the Reverend Irl Hicks had forecast a tornado would hit St. Louis in May 1896, basing his forecast on the moon and the planets. No one paid much attention.

*Courtesy Missouri Historical Society, St. Louis*

## May 28, 1904

**At 2:02 p.m. the Great Ferris Wheel opened to the public.** Dr. L. C. Shutt of 2323 Eugenia purchased the first ticket. The first wedding on the wheel also took place that day. Eddy Rogers and Miss Florence Benton of Wamego, Kansas, were married in Car 21, to be known as "the Marriage Car." The wheel was dynamited in May 1906 and an urban myth persists that the axle was buried nearby. However, witnesses said it was cut up into pieces, placed on flatcars, and shipped to Chicago, and that only a few steel rods stuck in the ground were cut off and left. The axle sat in the wrecking company warehouse before being cut up for scrap in 1918.

## May 29, 1977

**Bob Gassoff was killed in a motorcycle accident on Route M near Garry Unger's farm, where the team had gathered for a postseason party.** Number three may have been the roughest player in St. Louis Blues history. He only played four seasons but still ranks high on the Blues all-time penalty minutes list. His number was retired on October 1, 1977.

*Courtesy Getty Images*

*Courtesy Missouri State Archives*

## May 30, 1947

**Art Wild opened the Palace of Poison.** Probably the most unique drive-in and cruising spot ever in the St. Louis area, its sign at 1500 Lemay Ferry Road read, "Eat Here if it Kills You." Customers who polished off treats such as the Doomsday Delight could get a "death certificate" declaring they were "null, void, and all shook up." The teenagers and the hot-rodders loved it. The Palace of Poison closed in 1964, shortly after a Steak 'n Shake opened a block away.

## May 31, 1948

**The World War II Court of Honor in Memorial Plaza, was dedicated by General Jonathan Wainwright, the hero of Corregidor.** The names of 2,500 St. Louisans who lost their lives in World War II were inscribed on 16 granite tablets.

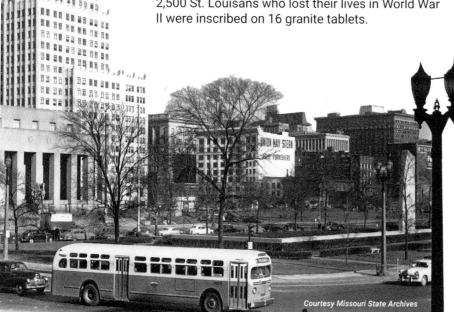

*Courtesy Missouri State Archives*

### May 28, 1890

**Plans were unveiled for a building at Seventh and Chestnut to house the brewery syndicate of Ellis Wainwright.** Designer Louis Sullivan would create the first artistic design for the modern skyscraper. In 2013, PBS named the Wainwright Building one of the "Ten Buildings That Changed America." It was nearly torn down for a parking lot in the 1970s before the state stepped in and converted it to offices.

### May 29, 1964

**Ground was broken for the largest residential and commercial development in the nation at that time.** Mayor Raymond Tucker said the $45 million Mansion House development signaled the return of residents to the riverfront for the first time in a century.

### May 30, 1954

**The only drive-in theater within the St. Louis city limits opened.** The Broadway Drive-In was located on South Broadway across from the old City Workhouse. It was closed in October 1964, in part to make room for Interstate 55, and a strip mall occupies the site today.

### May 31, 1925

**The *St. Louis Star-Times* was launching a unique subscription promotion.** With a new subscription, readers would receive a 20-by-100-foot lot near the Meramec River. The promotion marked the birth of the ill-fated community of Times Beach. The government bought out and razed the town after dioxin contamination was discovered and a disastrous flood struck in December 1982.

# JUNE

## June 1, 2003

**The 5400 block of Elizabeth Avenue was renamed "Hall of Fame Place" in honor of former residents Yogi Berra, Jack Buck, and Joe Garagiola.** Berra and Garagiola grew up across the street from each other on Elizabeth. Jack Buck lived there in the late 1950s.

## June 1, 2005

**The *St. Louis Post-Dispatch* reported that Falstaff Beer was history.** The Pabst Brewing Company, which acquired the Falstaff brand after production in St. Louis ceased in 1977, cited lack of sales. The Lemp Brewing Company created Falstaff in 1903, and in the late 1950s it was the third most popular brand in the nation.

## June 2, 1959

**The Missouri Highway Department announced an agreement had been reached to preserve the historic Bissell Mansion.** The 129-year-old home was in the path of the Mark Twain Expressway. Captain Lewis Bissell was a veteran of the War of 1812. He was a member of the 1818 Yellowstone Expedition, which founded the City of Omaha, and his father was the first commandant of Fort Belle Fontaine. The oldest remaining home in St. Louis, the mansion was a murder mystery dinner theater for 40 years.

## June 3, 1906

**Josephine Baker was born Freda Josephine McDonald in St. Louis.** The daughter of a washerwoman and a vaudeville drummer, she would become the highest-paid entertainer in Europe, beginning with her exotic performances in La Revue Negre in 1925. During World War II she served the French Resistance, smuggling secret messages written on her music sheets. Baker returned to the US in the 1950s and '60s to fight racism, but she seldom came back to St. Louis.

*Chesterfield - 1934*
*Courtesy Missouri State Archives*

## June 1, 1988

**The city of Chesterfield was incorporated.** There actually were three Chesterfields over the years. Justus Post laid out the first in 1816 near what are now Wild Horse Creek and Wilson Roads. The second sprang up in the early 1900s next to the railroad tracks that ran beside Olive. The third community developed around the Chesterfield Mercantile on Highway 40.

## June 2, 1942

*Courtesy Wikipedia*

**The US War Department ordered the Village of Madison, Illinois, to do something to make the Chain of Rocks Bridge less visible from the air.** At the time, the bridge carrying US 66 was silver and parts of it had been painted red. The bridge was repainted in olive drab, which must have worked because it was never bombed. The olive paint is still visible on the bridge.

*Courtesy St. Louis Public Library*

## June 3, 1904

**On a hot day at the World's Fair Ceylon Pavilion, Englishman Richard Blechynden was having a hard time getting people to drink his tea.** Blechynden poured the tea over ice, and folks were soon lining up. Blechynden is often credited with inventing iced tea, but he merely helped popularize the beverage. Iced tea had appeared on menus as early as the 1860s.

## June 4, 1916

**The *St. Louis Post-Dispatch* reported on plans for the new Bevo Mill Restaurant on Gravois.** August A. Busch chose a site exactly halfway between the brewery and the Busch Estate. He wanted to show that drinks could be served at a "high class" restaurant. Busch named it after Bevo, the brewery's nonalcoholic beer. Prohibition made Bevo a huge success for a time. But the public decided they liked illegal booze better, and Bevo flopped.

*Courtesy Missouri Historical Society, St. Louis*

## June 5, 1971

**The Six Flags over Mid-America amusement park opened in Eureka.** The 220-acre park was expected to draw nearly two million visitors per year and provide a financial windfall for the town. There were 16 rides and attractions at the time, including the Super Sports car ride, the Hannibarrels, the Skyway, the Hoo Hoo (log flume), and the River King Mine Train. Admission for the day was $6.50 for adults and $5.50 for children 3 to 11 years old.

*Courtesy Wikipedia/Flikr, Chris Hagerman*

### June 4, 1931

**A fire destroyed part of the landmark Beers Hotel at Grand and Olive.** The 136-room hotel was famous for its Victorian architecture and fancy tower at one corner. It was torn down the following year, and the Woolworth's Building, originally planned to be 15 stories tall, was built on the site. Woolworth's closed in 1993, and the building became the Big Brothers Big Sisters and the Kranzberg Arts Center.

### June 5, 1937

**The Cardinals signed a young pitcher from Donora, Pennsylvania, to his first contract.** An injury to his arm would necessitate a move to the outfield for Stanley Frank Musial.

### June 5, 1957

**The City of Sunset Hills was chartered.** The name dates back to 1911, when August Busch Sr. and Eberhard Anheuser built the Sunset Inn. The inn featured a rooftop restaurant, a pool, and hunting facilities. It eventually grew into the Sunset Hills Country Club.

### June 6, 1967

**The Blues made their picks in the NHL expansion draft.** They chose Glenn Hall from the Blackhawks, Jimmy Roberts and Noel Picard from the Canadiens, Al Arbour from the Maple Leafs, and Rod Seiling from the Rangers. The Blues then made their first trade. They sent Seiling back to the Rangers for Gary Sabourin, Bob Plager, and Tim Ecclestone.

*Courtesy Freepik*

# JUNE

## June 6, 2018

**Albert Fred "Red" Schoendienst died at age 95.** The native of Germantown, Illinois, was a 10-time All-Star, three-time World Series champion, and the oldest living member of the National Baseball Hall of Fame at the time of his death. Schoendienst spent 67 years with the Cardinals and 76 in professional baseball. He managed the Cardinals from 1965 to 1976 and on an interim basis in 1980 and 1990, spent 17 seasons as a coach, and had worked as a senior special assistant to the general manager since 1996.

## June 7, 1970

**Over 20,000 hardhats, union members, and others marched down Lindell in support of the war in Vietnam.** Marchers beat up several antiwar protestors.

## June 7, 1983

**California business consultant and investor Harry Ornest offered Ralston Purina $8 million for the Blues.** Ralston had turned the team over to the league after the NHL refused to approve the sale of the club to a group from Saskatoon. Ornest said he would keep the Blues here.

## June 8, 1966

**Organist, gadget guru, and local TV regular Stan Kann made his first appearance on *The Tonight Show*, demonstrating his collection of antique vacuums.** He was such a hit that Johnny Carson extended the scheduled eight-minute segment to 14 minutes. Kann would appear on the show a total of 77 times. He appeared on *The Mike Douglas Show* show 89 times.

## June 6, 1904

**The Apache Chief Geronimo arrived at the St. Louis World's Fair to be part of the Indigenous Peoples anthropological exhibit.** Visitors could pay a dime for his autograph and up to $2 for a photo. The 75-year-old warrior was scared when his guards took him aboard "curious little houses" that took him to a great height. He was on the Ferris wheel. Geronimo also appeared in the Wild West shows on "the Pike." He lived in the Apache Village until October 2.

*Courtesy Missouri Historical Society, St. Louis*

## June 7, 1843

**Susan Elizabeth Blow was born in St. Louis.** She studied the work of Friedrich Froebel, a German educator who developed the concept of teaching children ages 3 to 6 through play. Susan persuaded St. Louis Superintendent of Schools William Torrey Harris to set up the first public "kindergarten" in the US at Des Peres School in 1873. By 1880, she had designed more than 50 kindergarten rooms in St. Louis and was helping develop them around the nation.

*Courtesy Missouri Historical Society, St. Louis*

*Courtesy Missouri Historical Society, St. Louis*

## June 8, 1904

**About 75,000 children welcomed the Liberty Bell.** A petition by public school children resulted in the bell coming to St. Louis. Two troops of cavalry, along with Mayor Rolla Wells, accompanied the bell from the Jefferson Hotel to the grounds of the World's Fair. The symbol of liberty was placed in the Pennsylvania Building, where it could be visited free of charge under the watchful eyes of Philadelphia Police.

## June 9, 1980

**Whitey Herzog was named manager of the Cardinals, replacing Kenny Boyer.** Under the "White Rat," the Kansas City Royals had won three consecutive AL West titles from 1976 to 1978. Herzog would also take over the general manager position in August 1980 and manage the Cardinals to three pennants and one World Championship during his 10 years behind the bench. He resigned in disgust in 1990, with the Birds mired in last place.

*Courtesy Wikipedia, credit John Mena*

## June 10, 1999

**Missouri Governor Mel Carnahan signed a bill naming part of the Mark Twain Expressway/Interstate 70 in St. Louis in honor of Mark McGwire.** A five-mile stretch in the city limits was designated as the "Mark McGwire Highway," but in 2010, the Missouri Legislature voted to strip McGwire of the honor and restore Twain's name.

*Courtesy Wikipedia, credit formulanone*

**A five-mile stretch in the city limits was designated as the "Mark McGwire Highway."**

*Courtesy Library of Congress*

## June 11, 1861

**Pro-Southern Governor Claiborne Jackson and Missouri State Guard commander Sterling Price met with Union General Nathaniel Lyon and Congressman Frank Blair at the Planter's Hotel.** Lyon said he would see "every man, woman and child in the state dead and buried" before conceding that the state had the right to dictate orders to "my government." He turned to the governor and said, "This means war." Price and Jackson fled to Jefferson City, burning the bridges behind them.

## June 9, 1939

**The city of Overland, named for the Overland Trail, was incorporated.** Originally, the town was to have been named Ritenour City, after the school district that was named for a local landowner.

## June 9, 1955

**Groundbreaking ceremonies took place for Crestwood Plaza, at Highway 66 and Sappington Road.** Louis and Milton Zorensky were developing the 31-acre shopping center. Speakers included Crestwood Mayor Oliver Wilkins and County Supervisor Luman Mathews. The site of Crestwood Plaza is now a mixed-use retail and housing development.

## June 10, 1702

**Jesuit missionary Father Jacques Gravier landed at the mouth of a river emptying into the Mississippi, south of what is now St. Louis.** He established a mission, the first European settlement in what is now Missouri. The mission only lasted about a year, but the stream became known as "River des Peres," or "River of the Fathers."

## June 10, 1950

**President Harry Truman dedicated the site of the Jefferson National Expansion Memorial on the riverfront.** The ceremony followed a parade of Truman's old World War I outfit through downtown. The Korean War and a controversy over who would pay to remove the elevated railroad tracks on the riverfront delayed any actual construction for another nine years, during which time the riverfront remained a giant parking lot.

# JUNE

**June 11, 1875**

**George Herbert Walker was born in St. Louis.** He was son of Eli Walker, who founded the largest dry-goods firm west of the Mississippi. George founded an investment firm and once controlled 17 companies. His daughter Dorothy married Captain Prescott Bush, who worked for Simmons Hardware. Their first son was George Herbert Walker Bush, and his son is George Walker Bush.

**June 12, 1940**

**The new, streamlined SS *Admiral* made its first cruise.** The 375-foot-long, five-decked *Admiral* was originally built in 1907 as the steamer *Albatross*. Cruising and dancing on the *Admiral* would be a favorite activity of St. Louisans until hull deterioration was discovered in 1979. It was converted into an entertainment complex, which flopped, and it became a casino in 1994. The *Admiral* went to the scrapyard in July 2011.

*Courtesy Wikipedia*

**June 13, 1997**

**The Vatican designated the Cathedral of St. Louis a basilica.** The church at Lindell and Newstead was renamed the Cathedral Basilica of St. Louis. St. Louis became one of the few cities in the world with two basilicas recognized by the Vatican, as the "old" cathedral downtown is also a basilica.

**June 14, 1862**

**John Cardinal Glennon was born in Kinnegad, Ireland.** In October 1903, he became the third archbishop of St. Louis and Glennon is best remembered for spearheading construction of the "New" Cathedral on Lindell. Glennon died in his native Ireland while returning to St. Louis following his installation as cardinal in 1946.

*Courtesy author*

**June 12, 2019**

**For the first time in their 52-year history, the Blues were the Stanley Cup champions, as they beat Boston 4–1 in Game Seven at TD Garden.** Goalie Jordan Binnington kept the Blues in it, and Ryan O'Reilly scored the critical first goal. Boston was stunned when Jaden Schwartz fed Alex Pietrangelo for the second goal with just 7.9 seconds left in the first period. Ryan O'Reilly took home the Conn Smythe Trophy as the playoff MVP.

*Courtesy Missouri Historical Society, St. Louis*

**June 13, 1921**

**The first of the famous bear pits at the Saint Louis Zoo was dedicated.** The zoo was one of the first in the world to replace cages with open enclosures surrounded by moats. The rocks and walls were cast from plaster molds made of actual cliffs near Herculaneum. Three black bears, six-year-old Joe, Frank, and Bessie, took up residence in the first pit. The pits were torn out in 2013 for construction of the new Polar Bear Point.

**June 14, 1991**

**The Riverport Amphitheater opened.** The first concert featured Steve Winwood and Robert Cray. Now known as the Hollywood Casino Amphitheatre, it remains one of the premier outdoor concert venues in the country and entertains more than 500,000 people each year. It can accommodate about 20,000 per show.

*Courtesy Wikipedia, credit LittleT889*

*Courtesy Wikipedia*

## June 15, 1964

**The Cardinals made the best trade in their history.** The Birds sent pitchers Ernie Broglio and Bobby Shantz and outfielder Doug Clemens to the Cubs. In return, the Cardinals picked up pitchers Jack Spring and Paul Toth, along with an outfielder named Louis Clark Brock. Brock would lead the Cardinals to the pennant and star in the World Series. Broglio would win just seven more games in his career. Shantz only played 20 more games.

*Courtesy Missouri Historical Society, St. Louis*

## June 16, 1919

**The Muny Opera opened its first season with a production of *Robin Hood*.** The Muny dates its origins to the lavish "Pageant and Masque" staged in Forest Park in 1914 to

*Courtesy Missouri Historical Society, St. Louis*

commemorate the 150th anniversary of the founding of St. Louis. The success of the pageant inspired the building of the Muny. To commemorate opening night, St. Louis Mayor Henry Kiel made a cameo appearance riding a mule on stage.

## June 17, 1904

**The great floral clock on the slope of a terrace north of the World's Fair Palace of Agriculture began operating at noon.** Over 13,000 plants covered the 112-foot-diameter face of the world's largest clock. The tip of the 2,500-pound minute hand traveled 352 feet each hour. Over 1,000 lights illuminated the clock at night.

*Courtesy Missouri Historical Society, St. Louis*

### June 15, 1859

**Henry Shaw opened his botanical garden to the public.** Shaw had transformed his Tower Grove estate into a scientific complex that would become internationally famous. Original buildings still on the grounds include the Linnean House, Tower Grove House, and the Museum Building, which reopened as the Stephen and Peter Sachs Museum in 2018. Founder Henry Shaw, by will upon his death, left the garden in trust to a group of St. Louis citizens and their successors, to be maintained "for all time" for the public benefit.

### June 16, 1896

**The Republican National Convention opened at an auditorium erected just for the occasion on Washington near City Hall.** "The Wigwam" had a seating capacity of 40,000. The convention nominated William McKinley for president and Garret A. Hobart as his running mate.

### June 17, 1845

**A group from Frankfort, Kentucky, came to St. Charles County to exhume the bodies of Daniel Boone and his wife.** Boone had left specific instructions that he was to be buried at Defiance in St. Charles County. Legend says that Boone's angry relatives directed those officials to the wrong grave. In 1983, a forensic anthropologist said the remains in the Frankfort grave are not those of Daniel Boone.

### June 17, 1927

**Factory, steamboat, and railroad whistles shrieked a welcome as 20 planes escorted the *Spirit of St. Louis* over the city.** Thousands gathered on rooftops as Charles Lindbergh performed stunts then turned toward Lambert Field. He touched down at 3:37 p.m. Bad weather kept the crowd at the airport down to about 12,000, plus 2,000 soldiers to hold them back. Lindbergh spent the night at the home of Harry Hall Knight and told reporters he considered only St. Louis to be his home.

## June 18, 1939

**Louis Clark Brock was born in El Dorado, Arkansas.** As a youth, Brock learned about hitting by listening to KMOX as Harry Caray described each player's stance. Brock stole over 50 bases per season 12 times. In 1974, he swiped 118, a record at the time. He banged out 3,023 hits in his career. Brock also set the World Series record with a .391 batting average. Lou was elected to the Baseball Hall of Fame in 1985, and he died on September 6, 2020.

## June 18, 2002

**Cardinals broadcaster Jack Buck died at the age of 77.** He had been hospitalized for five and a half months due to complications following surgery for lung cancer. In 1954, Buck beat out Chick Hearn, who went on to become the Los Angeles Lakers announcer, for the Cardinals broadcasting job. He teamed with Harry Caray for 14 years and with Mike Shannon for almost three decades. Buck was inducted into the broadcasting wing of the Baseball Hall of Fame in 1987.

## June 19, 1950

**The city of Bellefontaine Neighbors was incorporated with a population of 766.** Within 18 months, the population had risen to over 5,000 as the rolling woods and farmland along Route 66 were being transformed into subdivisions. The French called the area "Bellefontaine," or "beautiful fountain," named for a nearby spring.

## June 20, 1952

**Actor John Goodman was born.** The Affton High School graduate made his film debut in 1983's *Eddie Macon's Run*. He starred as Dan on the television show *Roseanne* from 1988 until 1997, during the 2018 revival, and on the spinoff *The Connors*. He played leading roles in *The Babe* and *The Flintstones*, made a memorable appearance as Walt in *The Big Lebowski*, and voiced the character Sully in *Monsters, Inc.* He also starred in the HBO comedy *The Righteous Gemstones*.

## June 18, 1927

**More than 500,000 people packed the streets and ticker tape rained down on Charles Lindbergh.** A crowd at Sportsman's Park cheered as Lindbergh led a procession with Mayor Victor Miller, Secretary of War Dwight Davis, Baseball Commissioner Kenesaw

*Courtesy State Historical Society of Missouri*

Mountain Landis, and NL President John Heydler. Lindbergh raised the 1926 championship banner and then presented World Series rings to the team. That night at the Chase Hotel, Lindbergh said he expected St. Louis to be the aviation hub of the United States.

*Courtesy Missouri Historical Society, St. Louis*

## June 19, 1917

**The Bevo Mill at Gravois and Morganford opened.** Anheuser-Busch donated the landmark to the city after the InBev takeover in January 2009, and the restaurant closed three months later. Pat and Carol Schuchard took over in 2016 and reopened as "Das Bevo" in May 2017. The restaurant closed in 2019, and the Bevo Mill now hosts special events.

*Courtesy Flikr, credit inkknife_2000*

## June 20, 1965

**Frank Sinatra, Dean Martin, and Sammy Davis Jr. performed at a "Rat Pack" summit to benefit Dismas House, a halfway house for convicts.** The Kiel Auditorium show was broadcast via closed-circuit TV to movie theaters around the country. Johnny Carson was pressed into service as an emcee when Joey Bishop hurt his back. A tape of the show turned up in a closet at Dismas House in 1997.

## June 21, 1949

*Courtesy Missouri Historical Society, St. Louis*

**The city opened the swimming pool in Fairgrounds Park to African Americans.** About 40 Black youths were swimming without incident, but a hostile crowd gathered outside. Police escorted the children out when the swimming period ended and violence erupted. It took 150 police officers to bring it under control. Twelve people were hospitalized and seven were arrested. Mayor Joseph Darst immediately segregated the pools again, an order lifted without incident in 1950. The incident was an important turning point in St. Louis civil rights history.

## June 22, 2002

*Courtesy Don Korte*

**Just 24 hours after the funeral for Jack Buck, Cardinals fans were dealt another stunning blow.** Pitcher Darryl Kile was found dead of heart disease in his Chicago hotel room. He was 33. A sellout crowd had already assembled at Wrigley Field when Cubs catcher Joe Girardi made the announcement that the game was called off. Kile had pitched the Cardinals into first place on the same night Jack Buck died.

## June 23, 1972

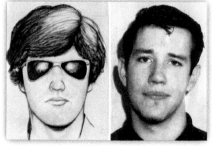

*Courtesy Wikipedia*

**Martin McNally hijacked American Airlines Flight 119 and made the pilot return to St. Louis, where most of the 92 passengers were released.** Authorities delivered a $500,000 ransom and the plane rolled toward takeoff with McNally, three crewmen, a stewardess, and a young hostage on board. David Hanley of Florissant became angry as he watched the drama unfold on TV in the bar at the Marriott. The drunken man got in his Cadillac, crashed through a fence, and slammed into the plane's landing gear at 80 mph, seriously injuring himself. McNally got a new plane and a parachute, bailed out over Peru, Indiana, and was later captured.

McNally and another convicted hijacker, Thomas Trapnell, attempted to escape from the federal prison at Marion, Illinois, on May 24, 1978. Trapnell's girlfriend, Barbara Ann Oswald, hijacked a helicopter in St. Louis and ordered pilot Allen Barklage to land inside the prison. Barklage grabbed the woman's gun in midair and killed her.

## June 21, 1923

**President Warren G. Harding, while visiting St. Louis, became the first president to give a speech over the radio.** The speech to the Rotarian Convention at the old Coliseum was broadcast over KSD. It was also one of the earliest network programs, picked up by WEAF in New York and WCAP in Washington.

## June 21, 1930

**The $4.5 million Civil Courts Building downtown was dedicated.** The courthouse is a traditional office building to the 12th floor. Then there's an Ionic Greek temple, topped with an Egyptian pyramid roof. Two aluminum griffins top it all off. The courthouse was one of the projects paid for by a 1923 bond issue.

## June 22, 1933

**Jimmie Wilson, Bill Hallahan, Frankie Frisch, and Pepper Martin of the Cardinals were named to the first National League All-Star Team.** The first All-Star game would take place on July 6 in Chicago as a part of the World's Fair.

## June 22, 1971

**Kurtis Eugene Warner was born in Burlington, Iowa.** Warner was making $5.50 an hour at the Hy-Vee in Cedar Rapids when he met his future wife, US Marine intelligence officer Brenda Meoni, at a country music bar in 1993. In 1995 he signed with the Iowa Barnstormers of the Arena Football League and then was signed by the Rams in 1998 as a third-string quarterback. He got the top job when starter Trent Green suffered a

season-ending injury before the 1999 season, and he led the Rams to the Super Bowl.

*Courtesy Wikipedia, credit Sean Daly*

# JUNE

**June 24, 1770**

**The first church in St. Louis was dedicated by Father Pierre Gibault of Kaskaskia.** That first one-room log church stood on the same block at Second and Market where the Old Cathedral stands today. It was replaced by a church of white oak timbers in 1776, and work began on a brick church in 1818. That structure was never finished and was supplanted by the Basilica of St. Louis, King of France, or Old Cathedral, consecrated on October 26, 1834.

**June 24, 1876**

**More than 50,000 people were on hand as Forest Park was officially opened to the public.** A speaker at the ceremony said, "I present to you, the people of St. Louis, your own, this large and beautiful Forest Park for enjoyment of yourselves, your children and your children's children forever. . . . The rich and poor, the merchant and mechanic, the professional man and day laborer, each with his family and lunch basket, can come here and enjoy his own . . . all without stint or hindrance . . . and there will be no notice put up, Keep Off the Grass."

**June 25, 1965**

**The National Park Service announced that the Gateway Arch was now the tallest man-made national monument.** The addition of another 12-foot section on the North Leg brought the Arch up to 562 feet, two inches. That was six feet taller than the Washington Monument.

**June 26, 1950**

**The last streetcar run was made over the 05 Line to Creve Coeur Lake.** The line was completed in 1899 and ran west from University City over Midland to the Crow's Nest Loop. Then it ran over light-rail-grade tracks through rural Maryland Heights to the lake, where there was once an amusement park. When the tracks were torn out, Midland was paved over the old right of way west from Ashby.

*Courtesy Wikipedia, credit Richie Diesterheft*

**June 24, 2010**

**The President Casino on the *Admiral* closed for good.** Due to poor performance, the Missouri Gaming Commission had wanted to revoke its license, and eventually Pinnacle Entertainment decided to move on. It actually closed earlier than expected due to flooding on the Mississippi River at the time. The *Admiral* was scrapped after no buyer came forward.

**June 25, 1989**

**The St. Louis Walk of Fame on Delmar was dedicated.** The first 10 inductees were Chuck Berry, Katherine Dunham, James B. Eads, T. S. Eliot, Scott Joplin, Charles Lindbergh, Stan Musial, Vincent Price, Joseph Pulitzer, and Tennessee Williams. Blueberry Hill owner Joe Edwards founded the organization to advance awareness of great St. Louisans and their accomplishments.

*Courtesy Don Korte*

*Courtesy Unsplash, credit Jack FitzWilliam*

**June 26, 1981**

**The John Carpenter film *Escape from New York* opened.** The movie was largely filmed in St. Louis. The Chain of Rocks Bridge, Union Station, and other sites filled in for 1997 New York City, which in the film had been turned into an armed maximum-security prison camp. On opening day, costar Isaac Hayes appeared at several St. Louis area theaters.

*Courtesy Don Korte*

## June 27, 2000

**Nelly's first full-length album was released.** *Country Grammar* would knock Eminem from the top of the album chart on August 26. It would garner three Grammy nominations and go on to sell over nine million copies, putting St. Louis on the hip-hop map.

*Courtesy Getty Images*

### June 27, 1970

**Jim Edmonds was born in Fullerton, California.** Edmonds came to the Cardinals in a trade that sent Adam Kennedy and Kent Bottenfield to the Angels on March 23, 2000. Edmonds won eight Gold Glove Awards for his spectacular play in center field. He also hit the home run in extra innings that gave the Cardinals the win in Game Six of the 2004 NLCS.

### June 28, 1930

**Curtiss-Steinberg Airport at Cahokia was dedicated.** Financier Mark Steinberg (as in Steinberg Rink) and the aircraft firm of Curtiss-Wright developed the field. In 1940, Oliver Parks moved his air college there from Lambert Field, and the name changed to Curtiss-Parks Airport. The field was renamed St. Louis Downtown-Parks Airport in 1984 and St. Louis Downtown Airport in 1999.

### June 29, 1949

**Dan Dierdorf was born in Canton, Ohio.** He played for the football Cardinals from 1971 to 1983. Dierdorf anchored an offensive line that permitted the fewest sacks in the NFC for five years in a row in the 1970s. He went on to become one of the *Monday Night Football* announcers and was elected to the Football Hall of Fame in 1986.

### June 29, 1950

**The US Men's National Soccer team shocked England 1–0 in what many regard as the greatest upset in World Cup history.** The team had played just one tryout game in St. Louis and three practice matches. Five of the starters were from St. Louis, and four of those were from "the Hill." The five St. Louis–based players were Frank Wallace, Gino Pariani, Charles Columbo, Frank Borghi, and Harry Keough. In 2003, the story became the basis for the motion picture, *The Game of Their Lives*.

## June 28, 1969

**During a violent thunderstorm, the riverboat restaurant *Becky Thatcher* was torn from her moorings and drifted down the river with 100 terrified people on board.** The replica of the *Santa Maria*, brought here from the 1964 World's Fair by Mayor Cervantes, also broke free. The *Becky Thatcher* snagged a Monsanto dock, and the passengers were rescued. The badly damaged *Santa Maria* ran aground in Illinois.

## June 30, 1904

**A group of African "pygmies" arrived for display at the World's Fair.** Anthropology department director W. M. McGee said, "I know nothing about them other than they offer an interesting subject for scientific study." Ota Benga was in the group, and after the fair, he was displayed in the monkey house at the Bronx Zoo. Resentful of being a curiosity, Benga shot himself in 1916.

*Courtesy Missouri Historical Society, St. Louis*

## June 30, 1916

**The most famous restaurant in St. Louis closed forever.** Anthony Faust, a plasterer from Russia, opened his first restaurant in 1862. In 1871, Tony Faust's Oyster House and Restaurant moved to Broadway and Elm and became the center of the city's downtown activity. It was the first building in St. Louis to be equipped with electric lights. The building was demolished in 1933.

*Tony Faust's Oyster House and Restaurant.*
*Courtesy Missouri Historical Society, St. Louis*

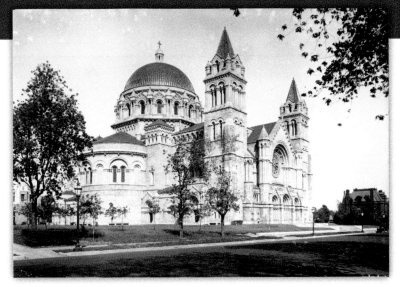

*Courtesy Missouri Historical Society, St. Louis*

## June 29, 1926

**The magnificent "new" cathedral on Lindell was consecrated.** Cardinal John Glennon, "the Eloquent Builder," began construction in 1906. Between 1912 and 1988, 20 artists worked on the 83,000 square feet of mosaics. The Cathedral of St. Louis was designated a basilica by Pope John Paul II on April 4, 1997.

## June 30, 1847

**A St. Louis Circuit Court began hearing the case of slaves Dred and Harriet Scott.** The two sued for freedom after their owner took them into free territory. The court ruled against them on a technicality, but the Scotts temporarily won their freedom in a retrial. That decision was reversed by the Missouri Supreme Court in 1852. Dred Scott appealed to the US Supreme Court, which ruled on March 6, 1857, that slaves were not citizens and thus could not sue. The family was sold to abolitionist Taylor Blow, the son of the Scotts' original owner, and they were freed on May 26, 1857. Dred Scott died of tuberculosis in September 1858, and he is buried at Calvary Cemetery.

A St. Louis Circuit Court began hearing the case of slaves Dred and Harriet Scott.

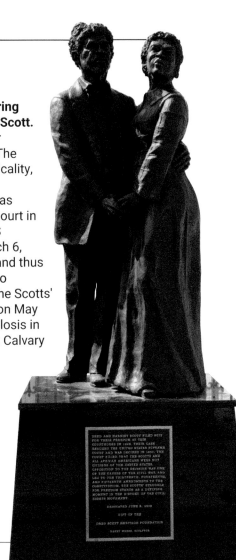

*Courtesy Don Korte*

## July 1, 2009

**Citygarden opened downtown and quickly became a top attraction.**
The spectacular 2.9-acre urban sculpture park on the Gateway Mall
was created by the Gateway Foundation and is divided into themes
representing river bluffs, floodplains, and an urban garden.

*Courtesy Don Korte*

## July 2, 1991

**Axl Rose yelled, "Because of the lame-ass
security, I'm out of here," and halted the
Guns N' Roses concert at the Riverport
Amphitheatre.** Fans went wild, causing
$200,000 in damage as they ripped up seats
and trashed equipment. At least 60 people
were injured and 16 arrested. After being
charged with assault and destruction of
property, Rose was ordered to pay $50,000 to
local charities.

*Courtesy Wikipedia*

## July 3, 2018

**A ribbon-cutting ceremony marked
the opening of the new $176 million
Museum of Westward Expansion
under the Gateway Arch.** It was the
culmination of a $380 million project
to reunite the city with the Arch
grounds by constructing a block-wide
park over Interstate 70 as well as
pedestrian and bicycle paths.

*Courtesy Wikipedia, credit Lewis Hulbert*

## July 1, 1826

**St. Louis adopted the Philadelphia
street-naming system.** East–west
streets were named for trees, except
for Market. North–south streets
were numbered. The Colonial streets
of Grand Rue (Main), Rue d'Eglise
(Church), and Rue des Granges
(Barn) became First, Second, and
Third Streets. Seventh Street was
the western city limit.

The tree streets were Sycamore
(became LaSalle), Hazel (Papin),
Lombard, Mulberry (Gratiot), Cedar,
Plum (Cerre), Poplar, Almond
(Valentine), Spruce, Myrtle (Clark),
Elm (gone), Walnut, Chestnut, Pine,
Olive, Locust, Vine (St. Charles),
Laurel (Washington), Prune (Lucas),
Oak (Delmar), Cherry (Franklin/MLK),
Hickory (Cole), Pear (Carr), and
Willow (Biddle).

## July 2, 1917

**A deadly race riot was sweeping East
St. Louis. Tensions had risen when
an aluminum plant hired Blacks to
replace strikers.** On July 1, Whites in
a car fired into a Black neighborhood.
Two White officers were killed when
they responded. Blacks were pulled
from streetcars and beaten. Some
were lynched or shot down as they
tried to escape their burning homes.
At least 39 Blacks and nine Whites
died, but unofficial counts put the
toll much higher.

## July 2, 1951

**The flamboyant Bill Veeck bought
the St. Louis Browns from Bill and
Charlie DeWitt.** Veeck would go
down in history for his stunts,
including sending three-foot,
seven-inch Eddie Gaedel to the plate
and letting fans vote on the plays.
He bought the Browns with the
intention of forcing the Cardinals
out of St. Louis. But Anheuser-Busch
bought the Cardinals, and the
Browns moved to Baltimore to
start the 1954 season.

### July 3, 1940

**Fontella Bass was born in St. Louis.** Her mother was a gospel singer in a group that toured with the Reverend C. L. Franklin, Aretha Franklin's father. Fontella started out singing gospel and began performing with Oliver Sain. Little Milton persuaded her to join his band in the early 1960s. In 1965 she reached the top five with "Rescue Me." The record label controlled most of the royalties until 1990, when Bass sued over the use of the song in an American Express commercial.

### July 4, 1870

**At 11:24 a.m., the *Robert E. Lee* steamboat arrived in St. Louis a little more than six hours ahead of the *Natchez*.** The *Lee* made the run from New Orleans in three days, 18 hours, and 14 minutes. Captain John Cannon of the *Lee* stripped his boat for the race and refueled from barges while underway. The *Natchez* might have won if Captain T. P. Leathers had refused to carry cargo or passengers as Cannon did.

### July 5, 1879

**Dwight F. Davis was born in St. Louis.** An excellent tennis player, he served as the city parks commissioner and installed tennis courts in Forest Park. They were the first public courts in the nation. In 1900, he donated the "Davis Cup" for the international lawn tennis competitions. He played for the winning US team in the first two cup finals and won US and Wimbledon doubles titles in 1901. He also served as secretary of war under President Coolidge.

*Courtesy Freepik*

*Courtesy Missouri Historical Society, St. Louis*

### July 4, 1862

**Ceremonies were held marking the completion of the building we now know as the "old" courthouse.** The first courthouse on the site was built in 1828. Expansion was begun in 1839, but the dome was not finished until 1862.

*Courtesy Missouri Historical Society, St. Louis*

### July 5, 1871

**The City Council passed the "Social Evil" ordinance.** The measure authorized the Board of Health to issue licenses and regulate prostitutes. Doctors were told to attempt to lead the wayward to a life of virtue, and the ordinance set up the "Social Evil Hospital and House of Industry" at Arsenal and Sublette. The measure was repealed in March 1874.

An FH-1 Phantom, 1948
*Courtesy Wikipedia*

### July 6, 1939

**James S. McDonnell opened the McDonnell Aircraft Company with $165,000 of his own money.** He had one employee, a tiny building at Lambert Field rented from American Airways, and no orders. McDonnell was very interested in the spirit world, so he named the firm's second plane the "Phantom" and continued the trend with the "Banshee," the "Demon," and the "Voodoo."

*Courtesy Wikipedia*

## July 7, 1906

**This is the date generally listed as the birthday of Satchel Paige.** In the Negro Leagues, Paige once won 21 games in a row and won 31 games in a season. MLB.com says he may have won roughly 2,000 games before making his major-league debut at age 42 with Cleveland in 1948. Bill Veeck brought him to the St. Louis Browns in 1951, and Paige pitched here for two more seasons. Paige tossed three innings for the Kansas City Athletics in 1965 at the age of 59.

## July 8, 1954

**The second television station in St. Louis signed on the air with a half-hour broadcast featuring Mayor Raymond Tucker.** KWK-TV broadcast on Channel Four from the KWK radio studios on Cole Street. CBS bought the station in August 1957 and it became KMOX-TV in March 1958. The studios moved to One Memorial Drive in June 1968, and the call letters changed to KMOV when Viacom took over in 1986.

**The second television station in St. Louis signed on the air with a half-hour broadcast featuring Mayor Raymond Tucker.**

*Courtesy St. Louis Media History Foundation Archive*

*Courtesy Missouri Historical Society, St. Louis*

## July 9, 1841

**Four Black men—Charles Brown, James Seward, Alfred Warrick, and Madison Henderson—were hanged on Duncan's Island for the murder of two White bank tellers during a burglary in May 1841.** As many as 20,000 people, 75 percent of the city's population, watched, some arriving by special excursion boats. After the executions, their heads were displayed in a drugstore window for several days.

**Whitey Herzog announced he was stepping down as manager of the Cardinals.** He had piloted the Redbirds since 1980, leading them to the World Series three times. Joe Torre was named as his replacement on August 2.

## July 7, 1964

**The Cardinals called up a St. Louis native who had made All-American as a football player at CBC High School.** He was also named as the top high school basketball player in the state. Mike Shannon had spent some time with the Cards in 1962 and 1963, but this time, he was in the big leagues to stay. Shannon provided valuable offense down the stretch as the Cardinals won the 1964 pennant and World Series.

## July 8, 1924

**Legendary piano player Johnnie Johnson was born in Fairmont, West Virginia.** He came to St. Louis in 1952 and joined Chuck Berry in the Sir John Trio on New Year's Eve 1953. Johnson's piano playing is featured on all of Chuck Berry's 1950s rock-and-roll classics, and Berry is said to have written "Johnny B. Goode" partly in his honor. Johnson's playing in the film *Hail! Hail! Rock 'n' Roll* revived his career.

## July 9, 1878

**Henry Tibbe of Washington, Missouri, patented the improved corncob pipe.** Tibbe and the local druggist came up with a plaster of paris mixture that kept the pipes from becoming too porous. He had created the Missouri Meerschaum Pipe, still made today in Franklin County.

## July 10, 1994

**The final hockey game was played at the Arena.** It was a match between the North and the South in the gold-medal game at the US Olympic Festival. South defenseman Ashlin Halfnight scored the last goal in the Arena, an overtime goal at 5:52 p.m.

## July 11, 1739

**Louis-Pierre Blanchette was born in Canada.** A trapper and trader known as "Le Chasseur," he was chosen by the Spanish to open a trading post on the Missouri River. He chose a site that would become the city of St. Charles.

## July 12, 1966

**The Rolling Stones played St. Louis for the first time.** Only about 3,000 fans paid to see the concert at Kiel Auditorium. The Stones had toured the United States four times before they made a stop in St. Louis. The Trade Winds, the Standells, and the McCoys were on the bill for the show before the half-full hall. The Stones played for about 30 minutes, closed with "Satisfaction," and left without an encore.

*Courtesy Wikipedia*

## July 12, 1973

**A general-alarm fire swept the Military Records Center on Page in Overland.** Irreplaceable records were lost covering servicemen discharged between 1912 and the early 1960s. The fire haunts the military establishment to this day.

*Courtesy Missouri Historical Society, St. Louis*

## July 10, 1904

**Police in St. Louis responded to citizen complaints about the "automobile menace."** The St. Louis Police Department became one of the first in the nation to use its own automobiles to go after the "scorchers." The police car was a high-speed "St. Louis" model made by George Preston Dorris and John French's St. Louis Motor Car Company on Laclede.

## July 11, 1863

**Joseph Griesedieck was born in Stromberg, Germany.** He operated the National Brewery, and was one of the founders of Griesedieck Brothers in 1917. In 1921, he bought the Falstaff trademark from the Lemp Brewery and became president of Falstaff. Griesedieck Brothers shut down during Prohibition but came back strong during the 1940s and 1950s. Falstaff acquired the brand in 1957, and Ray Griesedieck revived it in 2002.

*Courtesy Missouri Historical Society, St. Louis*

## July 12, 1966

**The brand-new Busch Stadium hosted the All-Star Game.** The National League won 2–1 in 10 innings, as Tim McCarver scored the winning run, and Brooks Robinson was named MVP. But the weather was the big story. The high that day hit 105 degrees, and as Casey Stengel noted, the new park "holds the heat well." One hundred twenty-five people in the crowd of 49,936 were treated for heat-related problems.

*Courtesy Missouri Historical Society, St. Louis*

## July 13, 1982

**Yadier Benjamin Molina was born in Bayamón, Puerto Rico.** He made his debut as the Cardinals catcher on June 3, 2004, after Mike Matheny was injured. Molina would go on to win nine Gold Gloves. On April 14, 2021, Molina caught his 2,000th game with the Cardinals, the most by a catcher for one team. When he retired after the 2022 season, Molina ranked first all-time among catchers in putouts and second all-time among catchers with 130 Defensive Runs Saved.

*Courtesy Wikipedia, credit Sector001*

*Courtesy Wikipedia*

## July 14, 2009

**President Barack Obama threw out the first pitch after a tribute to Stan Musial as the 80th Major League Baseball All-Star Game took place at Busch Stadium.** Sheryl Crow sang the US national anthem before the game, and the American League won 4–3. It was the first time the All-Star Game had been played here since 1966.

## July 15, 1939

**Mike Shannon was born in St. Louis.** Shannon starred in three sports at Christian Brothers College High School (CBC) and was named Missouri's number one basketball and football player. He was awarded a football scholarship to Mizzou but signed with the Cardinals in 1958, playing for them from 1962 until 1970, when a kidney ailment cut his career short. He moved to the KMOX broadcast booth in 1972 and stayed for 50 years.

*Courtesy Wikipedia*

## July 13, 1948

**The American League beat the National 5–2 in the All-Star Game at Sportsman's Park in St. Louis.** Stan Musial of the Cardinals hit a home run, as did St. Louis native Hoot Evers of Detroit.

## July 13, 2008

**The Anheuser-Busch board of directors announced they had agreed to a $52 billion takeover bid from the Belgian firm InBev.** The deal created a single company controlling one-fourth of the beer market worldwide with St. Louis as its North American Regional Headquarters. After 156 years, the brewery was no longer under control of the Busch family.

## July 14, 1936

**It hit 108 degrees, the hottest day of the worst heat wave in St. Louis history.** It was the sixth straight day in which the temperature rose to over 100 degrees, and the 10th day out of 11 with temperatures over 100 degrees. Seven more such days would follow. The death toll from the heat had already reached 139 and would eventually climb to at least 421.

## July 15, 1931

**Louie McGinley, inventor of the curb service car tray, opened a drive-in restaurant to show that in-car dining would work in St. Louis.** The Parkmoor at Clayton Road and Big Bend became a St. Louis icon. There eventually were six locations in the St. Louis area and one in Indianapolis. The original building was replaced, but the Clayton Road and Big Bend location was the last survivor, closing its doors in 1999.

*Courtesy Missouri Historical Society, St. Louis*

## July 16, 1921

**Brother George Rueppel, S.J., brought a gramophone into the Saint Louis University campus studio of WEW.** He put on a record and held the station's microphone up to the horn of the gramophone, becoming the first radio disc jockey in St. Louis.

## July 16, 1935

**Route 66 was rerouted over MO Route 77 (Lindbergh Boulevard) and across the Mississippi River on the Chain of Rocks Bridge to avoid congestion in St. Louis.** S. F. Wilson, divisional engineer for the Illinois State Highway Department, said the move would also relieve congestion on the Municipal Bridge. Lindbergh and present-day Dunn Road carried mainline 66 until 1955, when it was designated as By-Pass 66 until 1965.

## July 17, 1903

**Construction began on "the Pike," the area of the World's Fair set aside for amusements.** Visitors could see a re-creation of the Boer War, watch a naval battle fought with real shells and miniature ships, meet the people in the "Eskimo Village" or "Mysterious Asia," and see infants in incubators. It gave us the expression "What's coming down the Pike" to refer to something new or unusual. After the fair there were plans to make the Pike a permanent amusement area, but opposition from Washington University officials killed the plan.

## July 17, 1974

**Bob Gibson recorded his 3,000th career strikeout.** César Gerónimo of the Reds was the player who fanned to give Gibson 3,000.

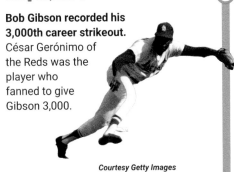

*Courtesy Getty Images*

*Courtesy Missouri State Archives*

## July 16, 1925

**This is truly a landmark day in culinary history.** The first White Castle restaurant in St. Louis opened, at 18th and Olive. The first White Castle in the nation opened in Wichita, Kansas, in 1921.

## July 17, 1917

**Phyllis Diller was born as Phyliss Ada Driver.** She became a regular at the Crystal Palace in Gaslight Square and moved to Mason Avenue in Webster Groves while beginning her rise to national fame. She costarred with her friend Bob Hope in three films. She also accompanied him to Vietnam and appeared in 22 of his specials. In 1992, Diller played the Wicked Witch in the Muny's production of *The Wizard of Oz*. She died on August 20, 2012.

*Courtesy Wikipedia*

## July 18, 1940

**Joe Torre was born in Brooklyn, New York.** He played for the Cardinals from 1969 to 1974. Torre hit .363 in 1971, capturing the Most Valuable Player award in the National League. He managed the Cardinals from 1990 to 1995. Torre then led the Yankees to World Championships in 1996, 1998, 1999, and 2000 and managed the Dodgers from 2008 to 2010. In 2011, he became Major League Baseball's executive vice president for baseball operations.

*Courtesy Missouri Historical Society, St. Louis*

## July 19, 1963

**Charlotte Peters was filming her TV show at the Forest Park Highlands when a fire broke out at the restaurant.** Peters ended up reporting on a disaster that wiped out the

*Courtesy Missouri Historical Society, St. Louis*

beloved amusement park next to the Arena. The carousel survived and was sold to businessman Howard C. Ohlendorf, who spent $250,000 to restore the carousel, which now resides at Faust Park. The ruins of the park were cleared, and St. Louis Community College at Forest Park stands on the site today.

## July 20, 1969

**St. Louisans were glued to their TV sets as Neil Armstrong became the first man to walk on the moon.** St. Louis police reported an increase in burglaries that night. The moon walk kept the crowd at the Mississippi River Festival in Edwardsville down to just 700, the smallest crowd of the season, but a big crowd saw the final night of *Mame* at the Muny. It was announced that 30,000 employees at McDonnell Aircraft would be given the next day (Monday) off.

## July 21, 1930

**The Continental Building on Grand opened.** It was constructed by Edward Mays as the headquarters for his Continental Insurance Company and Grand National Bank. In May 1930, before a permanent vault door could be installed, thieves made off with almost a million dollars in cash, jewelry, and securities from the bank, and the crime was never solved. The building declined during the 1960s and closed in 1973. The interior was ruined but developer Stephen Trampe transformed the 24-story Art Deco masterpiece into luxury apartments in 2002.

*Courtesy Missouri Historical Society, St. Louis*

## July 18, 1877

**The separation of St. Louis City and County was completed.** Mayor Henry Overstolz and the city comptroller presented their report settling the debts between the city and county to the judges of the former county court. The population of the county was about 30,000 at the time, and the separation seemed like a good idea. Unfortunately it is now to blame for many of the region's most pressing problems.

## July 19, 2011

**The SS *Admiral* was towed from her berth one last time, headed for the scrap heap.** The 375-foot-long Art Deco masterpiece, which had been a major destination since 1940, could accommodate 4,000 people. The *Admiral* made her last cruise in 1979 and became a casino in 1994, closing in 2010.

## July 20, 1917

**The US War Department changed the name of its new training base for aviation cadets in St. Clair County.** Known originally as the Belleville Aviation Camp, it was renamed after Corporal Frank Scott, a pioneer airplane mechanic who is believed to be the first enlisted man to die in a plane crash. Scott is the only base named for an enlisted man, and training there began on September 11, 1917.

## July 21, 1901

**A sportswriter for the *St. Louis Globe-Democrat* commented on what he called "an unpleasant innovation permitted at league park."** During a Cards game, they were selling beer to fans! The writer said, "It was doubtless the bilious practice was indulged in without the consent of Mssrs. Robison (the owners of the club) but it was indulged in, and caused considerable adverse comment."

# JULY

## July 22, 1877

**The great railroad strike spread to East St. Louis, and workers seized the rail yards.** The next day, a general strike was declared in St. Louis, led by a small socialist organization. Strikers pushing for an eight-hour workday and an end to child labor ruled the streets until July 27, when police and militia organized by business leaders marched on strike headquarters. No one was killed, but dozens were arrested and the workers gained nothing. In reaction to the strike, business leaders would organize the Mysterious Order of the Veiled Prophet to reestablish the social order with a parade for the masses and a formal ball for the elite.

## July 23, 1885

*Courtesy Missouri Historical Society, St. Louis*

**Ulysses S. Grant died of throat cancer at Mount McGregor, New York.** Grant only returned to St. Louis briefly after the Civil War. He had planned to retire here before the Whiskey Ring scandal engulfed his presidency. Grant was outraged to learn many of his St. Louis friends had used their ties to him to defraud the government of liquor taxes.

## July 24, 1800

**Henry Shaw was born in Sheffield, England.** He came to St. Louis at the age of 18 and turned a few pieces of his father's Sheffield cutlery into a hardware business that amassed him a fortune by age 40. On a trip to Europe in 1851 he visited the gardens at Chatsworth and decided to create a garden on his country estate, soon to be known as "Tower Grove."

*Courtesy Freepik*

*Courtesy Wikipedia*

## July 22, 1893

**Jesse "Pop" Haines was born in Clayton, Ohio.** Haines pitched for the Cardinals from 1920 to 1937, winning 218 games. On July 17, 1924, he threw the first no-hitter in Cardinals history. Pop won two games in the 1926 World Series, and he still ranks number two on the all-time Cardinals win list, behind only Bob Gibson. He was inducted into the Hall of Fame in 1970.

*Courtesy Wikipedia, credit RuthAS*

## July 23, 1973

**The worst air disaster in St. Louis history took place.** An Ozark Airlines Fairchild-Hiller FH-227 turboprop slammed into a hillside near the University of Missouri–St. Louis during a violent thunderstorm, killing 38 out of 44 people on board. Flight 809 from Nashville went down near Florissant Road and Interstate 70 on the campus of Mount Providence School.

The National Transportation Safety Board concluded that the crash was caused by the aircraft encountering severe downdrafts on approach—what we now know as wind shear.

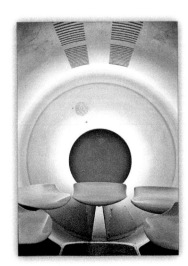

## July 24, 1967

**The unique trams that take visitors to the top of the Gateway Arch were dedicated, nearly two years after the arch was finished.** The trams are operated by Bi-State. Financial difficulty and administrative bickering within the agency delayed completion of the system. Al Carter of Chicago, Illinois, was first in line to buy a ticket to the top.

*Courtesy Wikipedia, credit Nan Palmero, MBA*

## July 25, 1972

**Democratic vice-presidential nominee Thomas Eagleton revealed that he had received psychiatric help and shock treatments while a Missouri state official.** He said the treatments were for nervous exhaustion and fatigue. Presidential nominee George McGovern expressed full confidence in Eagleton, but less than a week later, Eagleton was out.

*Courtesy Missouri Historical Society, St. Louis*

# Gondola Plunge Kills 3 in Family

ST. LOUIS (UPI) — Safety experts have been called in to examine a tower of the Skyway ride at the Six Flags Over Mid-America amusement...

**N.J. Ride Closed**

JACKSON, N.J. (UPI) — In the...

*Courtesy Newspapers.com*

## July 26, 1978

**A support beam broke and a gondola from the "Skyway" ride at Six Flags over Mid-America plunged to earth.** Ten-year-old Trisha Weeks, 15-year-old Kristen Johnson, and 25-year-old Clark Johnson died. Another girl was seriously injured. Nearly 100 people were stranded in the cars up to 200 feet in the air, and firefighters used ladders to rescue them as severe weather moved in. A park spokesman said the ride had been inspected the day before. The Skyway ride was closed in 1981.

## July 27, 2014

**Tony La Russa was inducted into the National Baseball Hall of Fame.** As a player, La Russa ended his career with a .199 average. He became manager of the Cardinals on October 23, 1995, and led the team to three National League championships and the 2006 and 2011 World Series titles. On October 31, 2011, he announced his retirement after 33 seasons as a major-league manager. He came out of retirement in 2020 to manage the Chicago White Sox.

*Courtesy Wikipedia, credit Monowi*

## July 25, 2020

**Regis Philbin died at age 88.** Philbin was recognized by the *Guinness Book of World Records* for having logged the most broadcast hours on air by a TV personality, including as the host of a syndicated morning show and the game show *Who Wants to Be a Millionaire*. From 1971 to 1975, Philbin flew to St. Louis once per month to film episodes of *Saturday Night in St. Louis*, which ran on KMOX-TV, Channel 4. In 1975, it regularly beat NBC-TV's upstart *Saturday Night Live* in the local ratings.

## July 26, 1901

**St. Louisans learned that "Uhrig's Cave" at Jefferson and Washington was to be demolished.** Uhrig's Cave was originally used by a brewery to keep beer cool and then became a beer garden. Uhrig's was the first entertainment spot in St. Louis to use electric lights. At its peak, it could accommodate 3,000 people for concerts and even opera. In 1908, the St. Louis Coliseum was built on the site. It was demolished in 1953 and the site became Jefferson Bank and Trust.

## July 27, 1977

**Ralston Purina purchased the Blues and announced that the Arena would now be known as the Checkerdome.** The franchise was near financial ruin, with just three people left on staff. Fortunately, one of them was General Manager Emile "The Cat" Francis, who made the Blues competitive. But the team fell on hard times again, and Ralston abandoned the club when the league refused to approve a move to Saskatoon. Harry Ornest bought the team in 1983.

*Courtesy Missouri Historical Society, St. Louis*

## July 28, 1943

**William Warren Bradley was born in Crystal City.** The only former pro basketball player to serve in the US Senate, he was considered the best high school player in Missouri. He went on to star with Princeton and the New York Knicks and was named to the Basketball Hall of Fame in 1983. Bradley served three terms as a Senator from New Jersey.

## July 28, 2002

**Ozzie Smith was inducted into the Baseball Hall of Fame.** In his induction speech, "The Wizard" used a baseball and imagery from *The Wizard of Oz* to symbolize his career. Smith led NL shortstops in fielding percentage eight times, assists eight times, and double plays five times. He played 2,511 games at shortstop, won 13 Gold Gloves, and was named to 15 All-Star teams.

*Courtesy Getty Images*

## July 29, 1983

**The movie *National Lampoon's Vacation*, starring Chevy Chase, Beverly D'Angelo, and Anthony Michael Hall, premiered.** A scene shows the Griswold Family Truckster exiting off the westbound Poplar Street Bridge into downtown. But a brief shot in the original cut also shows a sign reading "East St. Louis" before the family stops for directions and their car is stripped.

## July 29, 1985

**Cardinal greats Lou Brock and Enos Slaughter were inducted into the Baseball Hall of Fame.** Brock was baseball's all-time leading base burglar before Rickey Henderson came along. Brock set the NL record with 118 steals in 1974. Slaughter is best remembered for his mad dash from first to home in the eighth inning of Game Seven of the 1946 World Series.

## July 28, 1969

**Commissioner Ford Frick repeated his quote "Here stands baseball's perfect warrior, here stands baseball's perfect knight" as Stan Musial was inducted into the Hall of Fame.** Musial established National League records for games played, at bats, hits, runs in a season, RBIs in a season, and lifetime total bases. A seven-time NL batting champion, he was named MVP three times and appeared in 24 All-Star Games.

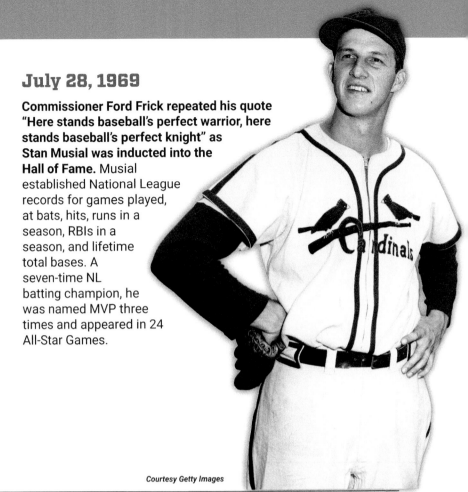

*Courtesy Getty Images*

## July 29, 1904

**The International Association of Ice Cream Makers says Syrian immigrant Ernest Hamwi invented the ice-cream cone at the World's Fair on this date.** Hamwi sold zalabia, a crisp, wafer-like pastry from Syria. When ice-cream vendor Charles Menches ran out of dishes, Hamwi supposedly plunked a scoop of ice cream atop a zalabia.

*Courtesy Missouri Historical Society, St. Louis*

Several sources list other inventors, including Italo Marchiony of New York City. On September 22, 1903, he filed a patent for a device that was "split in two like a waffle iron and producing small pastry cups with sloping sides." They were cups, not cones. After cones became popular, Marchiony sued but failed to protect his patent.

*Courtesy National Weather Service*

## July 30, 1993

**The Monarch Levee gave way, inundating the Chesterfield Valley.** Spirit Airport and 500 businesses were swamped. Highway 40 was underwater, cutting off the Boone Bridge as a route into St. Charles County. Thousands were evacuated in South St. Louis as 51 propane tanks were floating in the floodwaters and officials feared an explosion. Today, a $26 million levee is designed to protect the Chesterfield Valley from a 500-year flood.

*Courtesy Don Korte*

## July 31, 1993

**It was a surreal day in St. Louis.** Dramatic live television footage showed helicopter rescues from the flooded Chesterfield Valley. A tornado swept across the flooded areas near St. Peters, Portage des Sioux, and West Alton. A planned benefit concert by John Cougar Mellencamp, Bob Dylan, and Blind Melon at Riverport was cancelled because officials feared tying up traffic on the only bridge for miles.

Lost amid all the bad news from the river was some good news for commuters. The MetroLink light-rail system was opened from East St. Louis to the Hanley Road station. It was extended to Lambert Field in 1994. Within a year, the number of riders had exceeded the wildest projections.

### July 30, 1998

**After 27 years, the family of Michael Blassie of Florissant learned he had rested in the Tomb of the Unknowns in Washington, DC.** DNA tests had identified the remains. The family planned to bury him at Jefferson Barracks.

*Courtesy Don Korte*

### July 30, 2001

**St. Louis Mayor Francis Slay and other area leaders took part in a ceremony near Natural Bridge and Fee Fee marking the first phase of work on the controversial W-1-W project at Lambert Field.** The $1.1 billion first phase of the project included construction of a 9,000-foot-long runway, the removal of 1,937 homes and 70 commercial properties, and relocation of seven major roads. The runway was expected to be ready by 2006.

*Courtesy Freepik*

### July 31, 1981

**The last Corvette rolled off the assembly plant at the General Motors Plant in North St. Louis.** The plant had built about 700,000 'Vettes since 1954. GM moved the Corvette assembly line to Bowling Green, Kentucky.

# AUGUST

## August 1, 1831

**The cornerstone was laid for a "new" cathedral at Third and Walnut in St. Louis.** The building we now know as the Old Cathedral was completed in the fall of 1834. A church has occupied the site of the Old Cathedral since the very beginning of the city.

## August 1, 1943

**A crowd of 5,000 at Lambert Field watched in horror as a Robertson CG-4A glider carrying Mayor William Dee Becker plunged to earth.** The crash also killed Major William B. Robertson, president of Robertson Aircraft; Harold Krueger of Robertson Aircraft; Thomas Dysart, president of the St. Louis Chamber of Commerce; Max Doyne, director of public utilities; Charles Cunningham, deputy comptroller; Henry Mueller, St. Louis County Court presiding judge; Lieutenant Colonel Paul Hazelton; Pilot Milton Klugh; and mechanic J. M. Davis.

## August 2, 1817

**The first steamboat arrived in St. Louis.** The *Zebulon M. Pike* took six weeks to make the trip from Louisville, because it could only run during the day. A big crowd greeted the boat at the riverfront, but the Indigenous Peoples fled at the sight of the fire-breathing monster.

## August 2, 1993

**The Poplar Street Bridge closed because the *Burger King* riverboat was lodged beneath it.** Six miles of Highway 40 were closed in the Chesterfield Valley because of flooding. The Missouri set a new record-high mark at St. Charles, cresting at 39.6 feet. Thousands of people were out of their homes near the River des Peres because officials feared an explosion of propane tanks knocked from their mounts.

## August 1, 1993

**The flood of 1993 hit its peak here, as the Mississippi crested at 49.58 feet, a full 6.58 feet above the record 1973 level.** The raging floodwaters knocked the *Burger King* riverboat and the minesweeper *Inaugural* from their moorings. There was panic along the River des Peres, where water was lapping at the top of sandbags protecting thousands of homes.

*Courtesy National Weather Service*

A levee broke in Monroe County, near Columbia, Illinois, and news helicopters sent dramatic pictures back as the rampaging river washed away the Gummersheimer farm. Those are the most enduring images of the worst flood in US history.

## August 2, 1928

**The Missouri Pacific Building was dedicated.** It was originally planned to be 30 stories tall, but construction halted due to the Depression when only 22 were complete. Union Pacific left for Omaha in 2005. In 2011, the renovated building became Parc Pacific Apartments.

*Courtesy Missouri Historical Society, St. Louis*

## August 3, 1763

**Pierre Laclède left New Orleans to establish a trading post near the confluence of the Missouri and the Mississippi.** He left his family and trading goods at Fort Chartres. Taking a few of his men and his stepson, Auguste Chouteau, he searched the west bank of the Mississippi and picked a spot protected by a low bluff. On February 15, 1764, Auguste and Laclède's men returned to begin construction. The men wanted to call the site Laclede, but Pierre chose to name it after King Louis IX of France.

*Courtesy Missouri Historical Society, St. Louis*

## August 4, 1968

**The 10-foot-tall bronze statue of Stan Musial in front of Busch Stadium was dedicated.** When Stan Musial retired, Commissioner Ford Frick said, "Here stands baseball's perfect warrior. Here stands baseball's perfect knight." The quote is inscribed on the pedestal of the statue. Stan later said the statue by Carl Mose showed him in "too straight a stance" and said he had asked Morse to change the design to no avail.

*Courtesy Missouri Historical Society, St. Louis*

## August 5, 2017

**Former Rams quarterback Kurt Warner was inducted into the Football Hall of Fame.** Warner became the starting quarterback in 1999 after an injury to Trent Green. He went on to become the NFL MVP as the Rams capped the season with a win in Super Bowl XXXIV. He recorded another MVP season two years later as the Rams returned to the Super Bowl. Warner returned to the big game for a third time with the Arizona Cardinals.

*Courtesy Getty Images*

## August 6, 2011

**Marshall Faulk was inducted into the Football Hall of Fame.** Faulk was traded to the Rams from the Indianapolis Colts after the 1998 season and in 1999 helped lead the Rams to the championship. He was named the NFL MVP in 2000. Faulk finished his career with 12,279 career rushing yards (ninth all-time).

*Courtesy Getty Images*

### August 3, 1932

**Work began on the Municipal Auditorium.** The cornerstone was laid on November 11, 1932. The auditorium was dedicated on April 14, 1934, and was later named for Mayor Henry Kiel, whose firm built it. In 1992, the auditorium was torn down to make room for Kiel Center, today's Enterprise Center. The Opera House remains, now the Stifel Theatre.

### August 4, 1968

**Dan Kelly was officially named as broadcaster for all Blues broadcasts on KMOX.** During the Blues' first season, Gus Kyle and famed St. Louis broadcaster Jack Buck called many of their games but Buck decided to leave the booth after one season.

### August 5, 1981

**The MacArthur Bridge was closed to auto traffic.** Originally the Municipal or "Free" Bridge, it opened in 1917 and was renamed for General Douglas MacArthur in 1942. The bridge carried US 66 from 1929 to 1935 and City 66 from 1936 to 1965. The road deck and approaches have been removed, but the old bridge is still used by trains.

### August 6, 1856

**Nicholas Krekel arrived to open a store on land in St. Charles County where he had donated right-of-way for the new railroad.** He named the depot for Colonel John O'Fallon, head of the Northern Missouri Railroad. The Krekel Home on North Main Street was purchased by the city in 2007.

This Day in St. Louis History | 83

## August 6, 2022

**Former Rams coach Dick Vermeil was inducted into the Pro Football Hall of Fame.** Vermeil was the head coach of the Philadelphia Eagles for seven years, the Rams for three seasons, and the Kansas City Chiefs for five. He led the Rams to a win in Super Bowl XXXIV.

## August 7, 1960

**Ike & Tina Turner's first single, "A Fool in Love," debuted on the Billboard charts.** It rose to number two on the R&B chart and number 27 on the pop chart. The first Ike & Tina record came about by accident, as Tina stepped in when the session singer hired to sing with Ike didn't show. Ike & Tina followed "A Fool in Love" with four more top-10 hits over two years. By then, Tina was plainly the star.

## August 7, 2021

**Former Rams wide receiver Isaac Bruce was inducted into the Hall of Fame.** The ceremony at Canton, Ohio, had been delayed for a year because of the COVID-19 pandemic. Bruce played with the Rams for 14 seasons and ranked fifth all time in receiving yards when he retired. He also played for the San Francisco 49ers.

## August 8, 1884

**Poet Sara Teasdale was born in St. Louis.** She is considered one of the foremost lyrical poets of the 20th century. Two of her best-known poetry books are *Love Songs* and *Flame and Shadow*. In 1917, *Love Songs* won the Columbia Poetry Society of America Prize, the forerunner of the Pulitzer Prize.

*Courtesy Wikipedia*

## August 7, 1972

**Yogi Berra was inducted into the Baseball Hall of Fame.** Berra grew up on "the Hill" across the street from Joe Garagiola. The Yankees catcher played on a record 10 World Series championship teams. In 1947, the Cardinals honored him with "Yogi Berra Night." Berra told the crowd, "I want to thank everyone for making this night necessary."

*Courtesy Wikimedia Commons*

## August 8, 1954

**Mayor Raymond Tucker announced a giant slum clearance project for the Mill Creek Valley.** A 330-acre area between 20th Street, Grand Avenue, Olive Street, and Scott Avenue was cleared so completely that the area was

*Courtesy Missouri Historical Society, St. Louis*

known as "Hiroshima Flats" before it was redeveloped. About 20,000 people, mostly African American, were forced to relocate. At least 800 businesses, churches, and institutions were leveled.

## August 9, 2014

**Eighteen-year-old robbery suspect Michael Brown was shot and killed on Canfield Drive during an altercation with Ferguson officer Darren Wilson.** Brown was unarmed but struggled for the officer's weapon. The incident triggered several days of vandalism, looting, and rioting as some accused the police of responding too harshly. Violence broke out again on November 24 when a grand jury refused to indict Wilson. The subsequent US Justice Department investigation cleared Wilson of wrongdoing in the incident.

*Courtesy Wikipedia, credit Jamelle Bouie*

## August 10, 2014

**An evening that began with a candlelight vigil in the wake of the Michael Brown shooting turned into a night of violence, arson, and looting in Ferguson.**
Crowds chanting "No justice, no peace" flooded West Florissant Avenue and were met by

*Courtesy Missouri Historical Society, St. Louis*

300 armed police officers in riot gear. Looters descended on a QuikTrip convenience store and then set it on fire. About two dozen other businesses were also damaged and 32 people were arrested.

*Courtesy Missouri Historical Society, St. Louis*

## August 11, 1904

**The Olympic "Anthropological Field Days" got underway at the World's Fair stadium (Francis Field) featuring competitions between "costumed members of the uncivilized tribes."** Philippine Negritos and Igorrotes, Patagonians, Ainu, Indigenous Peoples, and others took part in two days of competitions in events such as rock throwing, mud fighting, spear throwing, and pole climbing. The events were not part of the official Olympics. They were presented by the Anthropological Department of the Fair and seen as a noble scientific experiment at the time.

*Philippine Negritos and Igorrotes, Patagonians, Ainu, Indigenous Peoples, and others took part in two days of competitions in events such as rock throwing, mud fighting, spear throwing, and pole climbing.*

## August 9, 1949

**Ted Lyle Simmons was born in Highland Park, Michigan.** One of the best offensive catchers of all time came up with the Cardinals in 1968 and played full time from 1970 to 1980. He batted over .300 for six of those seasons. Simmons was elected to the Baseball Hall of Fame in 2020.

## August 10, 1821

**President James Monroe signed the bill admitting Missouri as the 24th state after years of struggle over the balance of free and slave states in the union.** When Missouri first petitioned Congress for admission in 1818, there were 11 free and 11 slave states. It took two Missouri Compromises before Maine was admitted as a free state, and Missouri was admitted with no restriction on slavery.

*Courtesy Wikipedia*

## August 11, 1987

**The Missouri Department of Transportation announced that 41 miles of US 40 between Wentzville and the Illinois line had been designated as part of Interstate 64 by the Federal Highway Administration.** To this day, we still call it Highway Farty.

## August 11, 2021

**The first phase of City Foundry opened in Midtown.** The $300 million mixed-use development, which offers a food hall, shopping, entertainment, and office space, was originally the 15-acre Century Electric Foundry, which closed in 2007.

# AUGUST

Courtesy St. Louis Public Library

## August 12, 1905

A special detachment of police had to be called out as a crowd of 12,000 people gathered at the city's latest purchase, the World's Fair Flight Cage. The city had paid $3,500 for the cage, which had cost the Smithsonian Institution $17,500 to build for the Louisiana Purchase Exposition of 1904. That price didn't include the birds. Parks commissioner Robert Aull called for a zoo "second to none in the country" to be located in Forest Park.

## August 13, 1979

Lou Brock of the Cardinals rapped out his 3,000th career hit. It came off Dennis Lamp of the Cubs in the fourth inning of a game at Busch. Lamp had knocked Brock down on the previous pitch. The Cards won the game 3–2. At age 40, Brock became the 14th player in Major League history to reach 3,000 hits. Brock would bat .304 and steal 21 bases in 1979, his last season.

## August 14, 1861

The Commander of the Army's Western Department at St. Louis, John C. Fremont, put the city under martial law. Fremont seized the property of alleged rebel sympathizers and demanded payments from them. On August 30, he declared martial law in the entire state and freed the slaves of those in rebellion. Fearful of offending border states, President Lincoln demanded that Fremont rescind the order and had him removed from office when he refused.

## August 12, 1904

It was "Automobile Day" at the World's Fair. A parade of 250 machines, 150 of them from St. Louis, paraded from the Jefferson Hotel to the fairgrounds. Police Chief Mathew Kiely led the parade in the department's new "auto catcher."

Courtesy Missouri Historical Society, St. Louis

## August 13, 1956

Construction began on a short stretch of Interstate 70 in St. Charles, near the present-day Fifth Street exit. Those few miles of I-70 were the very first of over 40,000 miles constructed under the Interstate Highway Act. At the time, the population of all of St. Charles County was about 40,000.

Courtesy Missouri State Archives

## August 14, 1971

Bob Gibson threw the only no-hitter of his amazing career. The Cardinals scored five runs in the first and beat the Pirates in Pittsburgh 11–0. Gibson struck out 10 and drove in three runs, and Ted Simmons had four hits and scored three times. José Cruz saved the no-hitter with a spectacular catch off Milt May.

Courtesy State Historical Society of Missouri

AUGUST

Courtesy Missouri Historical Society, St. Louis

## August 15, 1945

**As celebrations of the Japanese surrender continued, the newspapers reported that $250 million in St. Louis area war contracts were cancelled immediately, affecting up to 75,000 workers.** It was also reported that five men from this area were missing and presumed to be among the 880 lost when the heavy cruiser *Indianapolis* was torpedoed on July 30. The news had been kept secret because the ship had just delivered the atomic bomb.

Courtesy Missouri State Archives

## August 16, 1958

**The new 3,900-foot-long highway bridge over the Missouri River at St. Charles was dedicated.** Within two years it was already jammed with traffic, and plans were in motion to build a new one. The second span was completed in 1979 and now carries eastbound traffic. Both bridges are now named for Louis Blanchette, the first settler of St. Charles. The superstructure and deck of the original (now westbound) bridge were rebuilt in 2013.

## August 17, 1889

**The Grand Avenue Viaduct opened.** Before the bridge, the Mill Creek rail yards presented an obstacle to development on the south side. The revolutionary design was a hybrid suspension and truss bridge, with the road deck suspended from a huge eyebar chain supported by two 55-foot-tall steel towers. The span was replaced in 1960. Demolition of the old bridge spelled the end for the Grand Avenue streetcars, which made their final run on January 3, 1960.

Courtesy Missouri State Archives

### August 15, 1797

**Revolutionary War veteran Captain James Piggott received a "perpetual" lease from Spanish Commandant Zenon Trudeau for his ferry between Cahokia and St. Louis.** Back in the winter of 1792–93, Piggott and his sons constructed a few crude buildings on the site that would become the city of East St. Louis. The road from his ferry to Cahokia later became Piggott Avenue.

### August 16, 1971

**The largest crowd in the history of the Mississippi River Festival came out to Southern Illinois University–Edwardsville.** More than 33,000 people saw the Who and Wishbone Ash. President Delyte Morris first organized the summer performing arts festivals in 1969 as a way to publicize SIUE. Performers such as Bob Dylan, the Beach Boys, the Grateful Dead, and Janis Joplin played there. The last one was held in 1980.

### August 16, 1977

**Elvis Presley died in Memphis.** He played St. Louis for the last time on March 22, 1976, at Kiel Auditorium, the last show of his High Standard Tour. He stayed at the Bel Air Hilton. His first appearances here were October 21–23, 1955, at the Missouri Theater. His show on March 29, 1957, at Kiel was the last time Elvis wore his entire gold lamé suit on stage. He also performed at Kiel in September 1970 and June 1973.

Courtesy Wikipedia

## August 17, 1859

**John Queeny was born in Chicago.** In 1891 he took a job as a buyer for a wholesale drug company in St. Louis. In 1901 he established his own company for the production of saccharine and named it Monsanto after his wife, Olga Monsanto Queeny. Queeny Park is named for their son, Edgar, as it was once his estate.

## August 18, 1774

**Meriwether Lewis was born in Virginia.** Thomas Jefferson asked him to lead the expedition to the Louisiana Territory in 1804. Lewis recruited his friend William Clark and insisted that Clark's name be included when the expedition was named. After the journey, Lewis became territorial governor here. He was found shot to death on the Natchez Trace while traveling to Washington in 1809, and the mysterious death was ruled a suicide.

## August 18, 1920

**Shirley Schrift was born in East St. Louis.** She rose to fame as an actress with the name Shelley Winters. Her first major role came in the 1945 film *A Double Life*, for which she received an Oscar nomination. She won Academy Awards for *The Diary of Anne Frank* and *A Patch of Blue*, but her best-known role may have been in *The Poseidon Adventure*. She died on January 14, 2006.

## August 19, 1940

**Bob Kuban was born in St. Louis.** In 1964, he formed the band Bob Kuban and the In-Men, best known for their 1966 hit "The Cheater," which reached number 12 on the Billboard charts. The band had two more records dent the lower reaches of the chart ("The Teaser" number 70 and "Drive My Car" number 93) but never had another big hit. Bob Kuban and the In-Men were on hand to perform at opening ceremonies for Busch Stadium II on May 10, 1966, and before the last game there on October 2, 2005.

*Courtesy Missouri Historical Society, St. Louis*

## August 18, 1960

**Placement of plants began in the ultramodern "Climatron" at the Missouri Botanical Garden.** The geodesic dome was designed to be the new home for the garden's tropical plants. R. Buckminster Fuller developed the geodesic dome, which is a structure shaped like a sphere made of a network of triangles. Fuller was serving as a research professor at SIU-Carbondale when the Climatron was unveiled.

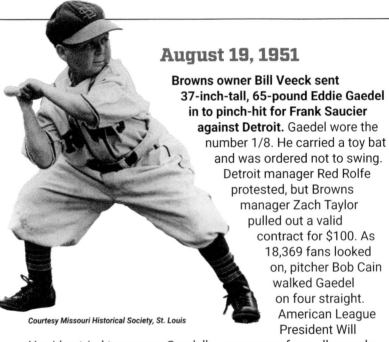

## August 19, 1951

**Browns owner Bill Veeck sent 37-inch-tall, 65-pound Eddie Gaedel in to pinch-hit for Frank Saucier against Detroit.** Gaedel wore the number 1/8. He carried a toy bat and was ordered not to swing. Detroit manager Red Rolfe protested, but Browns manager Zach Taylor pulled out a valid contract for $100. As 18,369 fans looked on, pitcher Bob Cain walked Gaedel on four straight. American League President Will Harridge tried to remove Gaedel's appearance from all records and then promptly set minimum height requirements for players.

*Courtesy Missouri Historical Society, St. Louis*

## August 20, 2019

**Major League Soccer announced that St. Louis would be awarded the league's 28th franchise beginning in 2022.** The date was later pushed back due to COVID. The new team would be the first in the league with female-majority ownership, consisting of Enterprise Holdings Foundation President Carolyn Kindle Betz and female members of the Taylor family.

*Courtesy Wikipedia, credit cornfield948*

Major League Soccer announced that St. Louis would be awarded the league's 28th franchise beginning in 2022.

## August 21, 1966

**A crowd of 23,143 braved the rain to see the Beatles at Busch Stadium.** The band took the stage at 8:30 p.m., having played a show in Cincinnati that afternoon. The Del-Rays from Mascoutah, Illinois; Bobby Hebb; the Ronettes; and the Cyrkle also played. The Beatles appeared third to take advantage of a break in the weather—so the Beatles "opened" for the Ronettes and the Cyrkle that night. They performed 11 songs in 30 minutes. The Beatles would only play four more shows before they stopped touring.

*Courtesy Missouri Historical Society, St. Louis*

## August 22, 1936

**Nellie Muench and three others were found guilty of conspiracy in a sensational case.** Muench was a prominent West End socialite who masterminded a plot by gangsters to kidnap a well-known doctor, Isaac Kelley. Muench was acquitted, but she had stolen a baby from an unwed servant and claimed it as her own to gain sympathy from the jury. She even blackmailed a doctor into giving her money by telling him he was the father! The paternity case involving the child was heard by Judge Rush Limbaugh Sr.

*Courtesy Library of Congress*

## August 23, 1876

**William F. Dierberg was born in Creve Coeur.** He worked as a blacksmith before buying the Creve Coeur House on Olive Street Road in 1914. The general store, stable, and hotel had been established in 1854 as the 14-Mile House. His sons relocated the grocery business to a market next door in 1930, the first Dierberg's Market.

## August 21, 1924

**John Francis Buck was born in Holyoke, Massachusetts.** He began his radio career at Ohio State, where a professor told him he should find another way to make a living. In 1950, he became the announcer for the Cardinals Triple-A team in Columbus. His first TV job was also in Columbus, where Jonathan Winters was a coworker. Promoted to Rochester, he auditioned for the Cardinals in 1953. He initially was number three on the broadcasts, behind Harry Caray and Joe Garagiola, but Buck became number two in 1961 and took the top job when Harry Caray was fired in 1969.

*Courtesy Freepik*

## August 22, 1876

**An election was held on the proposal to separate St. Louis City and County.** It looked like the measure had failed, but allegations of fraud quickly surfaced. A commission found hundreds of fraudulent ballots, and a recount found the plan had passed. The "Great Divorce" was made official on October 22 and is now blamed for many of the region's problems.

*Courtesy Freepik*

## August 23, 1958

**Teddy Nadler, a 47-year-old $70-per-week supply clerk from St. Louis, became the all-time TV quiz show winnings champion.** He raked in $252,000 on the CBS show *The $64,000 Question*. Nadler had an amazing ability to memorize facts that he read, but he repeatedly failed the civil service examination because he lacked reasoning skills.

# AUGUST

*Courtesy Museum of Transportation*

## August 24, 1944

**The Sporting News reported that Commissioner Kenesaw Mountain Landis would not allow Browns broadcaster Dizzy Dean to announce the World Series.** Landis called Dean an embarrassment to baseball and "unfit for a national broadcaster" for his use of the word "ain't." Diz said, "I ain't never met anybody that didn't know what ain't means."

## August 24, 1951

**Browns' owner Bill Veeck pulled another of his crazy PR stunts.** On "Fan Manager's Night," a crowd of 1,115 fans at Sportsman's Park voted "Yes" or "No" on plays held up by the Brownies coaches on placards. "The Clown Prince of Baseball," Max Patkin, served as first-base coach. The Browns beat the A's 5–3. A's GM Art Ehlers condemned the game as "farcical."

## August 25, 1984

**Thousands watched as the Buder and International Buildings downtown were imploded to make room for the Gateway Mall project.** Preservationists had lost a court fight to save the historic buildings that once made up "Realty Row." The city would settle for a half mall, instead of the uninterrupted open space originally proposed between the Old Courthouse and the Civil Courts Building.

## August 25, 2010

**NFL owners unanimously approved Stan Kroenke as the owner of the St. Louis Rams contingent upon his eventual divestment of his Colorado sports interests.** Kroenke complied with the rule when he transferred ownership of the NBA's Nuggets and the NHL's Avalanche to his son Josh Kroenke.

## August 24, 1951

**More than 15,000 people were on hand when St. Louis Mayor Joseph Darst cut the ribbon opening the distinctive Southtown Famous Barr store at City Route 66 (Chippewa) and Kingshighway.** The landmark closed in 1992 and was torn down in 1995 to make room for a Builders Square that was never built. A controversial plan to build a Kmart was scuttled, and it was 2004 before the site was redeveloped as the Southtown Centre.

## August 25, 1270

**Catholic churches celebrate a special Mass and remember our city's patron saint, King Louis the Ninth of France, on this day.** Louis became king at age 12. He was known for his work with the poor, and he led a crusade to the Holy Land from 1248 to 1250. He fell ill during another crusade in Tunisia and died on August 25, 1270. He was canonized in 1297.

*Courtesy Wiiipedia, credit Fredlyfish4*

*Courtesy Missouri Historical Society, St. Louis*

## August 26, 1873

**The school board voted to accept the offer of Susan Blow to establish a kindergarten at Des Peres School in St. Louis.** It was the first public kindergarten in the United States. Mary Timberlake became the first public kindergarten teacher in America.

## August 27, 1895

**The Terminal Hotel at Union Station formally opened.** It was the last part of the station to be completed. The hotel boasted accommodations for 250 guests and was described as one of the finest in the country. It closed in 1970. In 1985, the 550-room Omni Luxury Hotel (now St. Louis Union Station Hotel, Curio Collection by Hilton) opened. It occupies the area of the old Terminal Hotel and part of the train shed to the south.

*Courtesy Missouri Historical Society, St. Louis*

### August 26, 1831

**Major Thomas Biddle and Congressman Spencer Pettis met in a duel on Bloody Island (now part of the East St. Louis riverfront).** The duel stemmed from remarks Pettis made about Biddle's brother during his campaign for reelection to the House. As the word was given, Pettis ducked and fired. But both men fell mortally wounded. A county in Missouri is named in Pettis's honor.

### August 27, 1920

**Alfonso J. Cervantes was born in St. Louis.** He became an alderman from the 15th ward in 1949 and was elected as the 43rd mayor of St. Louis in 1965. The "Salesman Mayor" brought the ill-fated replica of the *Santa Maria* and the Spanish Pavilion to St. Louis. In 1970, *Life* magazine claimed the mayor was linked to the mob and Cervantes filed a $12 million suit against the magazine. The suit was dismissed.

## August 28, 1999

**Rams quarterback Trent Green suffered a season-ending injury when he was tackled by free safety Rodney Harrison of the Chargers in an exhibition game.** His replacement was a little-known former quarterback from the Arena Football League and NFL Europe. Kurt Warner had only taken 14 snaps in the NFL. Warner's first pass was perfect, and was promptly fumbled. Many Rams fans believed the season was over.

**Kurt Warner**
*Courtesy Getty Images*

### August 28, 1963

**Josephine Baker of St. Louis spoke during the March on Washington.** She told the crowd of 250,000 that they looked like "salt and pepper, just as it should be." Wearing her uniform from her days as a French war hero, Baker said, "You are on the eve of a complete victory. You can't go wrong. The world is behind you." Her words would be overshadowed by a speech made by Martin Luther King Jr. that day. About 200 St. Louisans made the trip by bus to take part in the march.

## August 29, 1977

**Lou Brock broke Ty Cobb's career stolen-base mark, swiping his 893rd in a game at San Diego.** The record breaker came off Dave Freisleben. The game was halted while Brock was mobbed by his teammates and Randy Jones of the Padres presented Lou with second base. Brock stole two bases in the game, but the Cardinals lost 4–3. Rickey Henderson broke Brock's record on May 1, 1991.

## August 29, 1985

**Marching bands, speeches, and fanfare marked the reopening of a St. Louis landmark.** After a $150 million renovation, Union Station was reborn as a mixed-use complex. The station had fallen on hard times after the last train left in 1978. Its gloomy interior was featured in the movie *Escape from New York*. The St. Louis Aquarium now occupies the old retail space, a 3D light show dazzles in the Grand Hall, and the 200-foot-high St. Louis Wheel is another attraction.

## August 30, 1958

**The very first McDonald's restaurant in Missouri opened at 9915 Highway 66 (Watson Road).** Bill Wyatt and partner Don Kuehl brought the golden arches to St. Louis. The first store, as was the case with all the early McDonald's stores, was originally a walk-up location only.

## August 31, 1872

**A group of property owners sued real-estate promoter Hiram Leffingwell and the others instrumental in proposing the 3,000-acre Forest Park.** Landowners such as Thomas Skinker, Robert Forsyth, and Charles Cabanne said the park would destroy the value of the little land they would have left. *(facing page)*

*Courtesy Missouri Historical Society, St. Louis*

## August 29, 1963

*Courtesy Wikipedia, credit Robert Lawton*

**The Saint Louis Zoo's Zooline Railroad was completed.** At a ceremony at the original Vierheller Station near the bear pits, Zoo Director Marlin Perkins and Zoo Board Chairman Howard Baer whacked at a "golden spike" to complete the 1.5-mile loop of track. The location where the spike was driven is no longer part of the line. The track was moved in 2003 to create Wild Station.

*Courtesy Missouri Historical Society, St. Louis*

## August 30, 1904

**The temperature soared to over 90 degrees during the Olympic marathon.** Fred Lorz of New York City crossed the finish line first and accepted congratulations from Alice Roosevelt—but he had hitched a ride in a car for 11 miles! Thomas Hicks was carried off the track after winning with a time of 3:28:53. His trainers gave him strychnine mixed with raw eggs during the race.

## August 31, 1972

**Mayor Cervantes unveiled a proposal to use inflatable dams at Lansdowne and at Morganford to turn a**

*Courtesy Wikipedia, credit Millbrooky*

**3.1-mile stretch of the River des Peres into a concrete-lined boating and recreation area.** Cervantes said the $14 million plan was "one of the most unusual and unique plans ever imagined for the city." The public ridiculed the plan as the "River Des Peres Yacht Club."

Forest Park and the Chase Hotel
*Missouri Historical Society, St. Louis*

Mark Twain (Samuel Clemens) and
David R. Francis unveiling tablet at the
dedication of the Eugene Field House
*Missouri Historical Society, St. Louis*

*Courtesy Missouri Historical Society, St. Louis*

## September 1, 1894

**Union Station opened with a gala in the Grand Hall, attended by about 20,000 invited guests.** Architect Theodore C. Link's building was twice as big as any railroad depot in the world. Closed in 1979, it was renovated and turned into a unique shopping area in 1985. It stands on the site of "Chouteau's Pond." An early settler, Joseph Taillon, built a mill and a dam across a stream the French called "La Petite Riviere." Auguste Chouteau acquired the property and built a bigger dam. "Chouteau's Pond" became polluted and was drained in 1849, but the old bed would provide an easy path for the new railroads.

## September 2, 1994

**The Old Barn on Oakland Avenue closed its doors for good.** A concert by Christian recording star Carman Licciardello was the final event at the Arena. The Arena was built in 1929 as the home of the National Dairy Show, and the cavernous old structure hosted the Rolling Stones, Ronald Reagan, Blues hockey, Spirits basketball, and Gypsy Caravans.

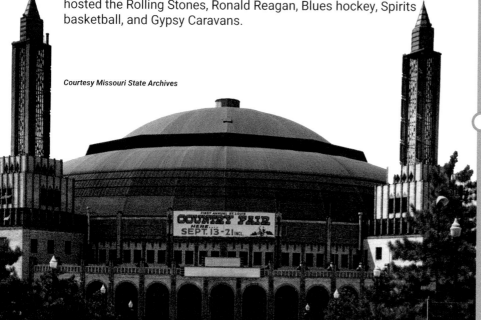

*Courtesy Missouri State Archives*

### September 1, 1940

**The *St. Louis Post-Dispatch* first published a strip featuring local oddities sent in by readers.** Originally called "St. Louis Oddities," it later became "Our Own Oddities" and would be drawn by staff artist Ralph Graczak until February 24, 1991. The strip featured bizarre coincidences, natural oddities, goofy signs, just about anything readers sent in. At first, the paper paid $1 for each item used. That had increased to $10 by the time the last column ran.

### September 2, 1850

**Children's poet Eugene Field was born.** His most famous works are "Wynken, Blynken, and Nod" and "Little Boy Blue." The Field home was originally one of a row of 12, called Walsh's Row, but Field may not have been born at 634 Broadway. When Mark Twain unveiled a plaque there in 1902, Field's brother Roswell told Twain that Eugene was two when the family moved there. Twain remarked, "Officially and for the purpose of the future your brother was born here." *(facing page)*

*Courtesy Missouri Historical Society, St. Louis*

### September 2, 1917

**Major George E. A. Reinburg and civilian flying instructor William H. Couch made the first flight from Scott Field.** The first class of 100 cadets would begin training on September 11, 1917. The base was named after Corporal Frank Scott, the first enlisted man to die in a plane crash. Scott is the only base named for an enlisted man.

*Courtesy State Historical Society of Missouri*

### September 3, 1975

**Bob Gibson made his last career appearance on the mound.** He entered the game in the sixth inning at Busch Stadium, walked three, and gave up five runs, including a grand slam by pinch hitter Pete LaCock of the Cubs. Gibson said, "I knew it was time to go when Pete LaCock hit a grand slam against me."

### September 3, 2021

**Yadier Molina and Adam Wainwright became only the fourth battery in Major League history to start 300 games together.** Molina hit a grand slam as the Cardinals beat Milwaukee at American Family Field 15–4. Wainwright tossed six scoreless innings and even drove in a run.

### September 4, 1987

**One of the worst multiple murders in St. Louis history took place.** Two gunmen entered the National Supermarket at 4331 Natural Bridge after the store closed. The robbers ordered seven workers to lie face down and shot them in the head. Five of them died: Rose Brown, 49, head cashier; Kenneth Bass, 27, a cleaning man; Michael Beam, 34, a stock manager; Michael Marr, 16, a bag boy; and David Spahn, 27, a security guard. Marvin Jennings and Donnie Blankenship were later convicted of the murders.

### September 5, 1936

**John Claggett Danforth was born in St. Louis.** The heir to the Ralston Purina fortune became a lawyer and an Episcopal minister before becoming attorney general of Missouri in 1969. Danforth served 18 years in the US Senate beginning in 1976. He made national headlines in 1999 when he was appointed as an independent investigator into the 1993 siege and fire at the Branch Davidian Compound in Waco, Texas.

## September 3, 1903

**The contract to construct the birdcage at the St. Louis World's Fair was awarded to the St. Paul Foundry Company for $14,634.** Frank Baker of the Smithsonian's National Zoo designed the cage, which measures 228 feet long, 84 feet wide, and 50 feet high. After the fair, the Smithsonian made an effort to send the cage to Washington, DC, but the City of St. Louis purchased it for $3,500. The purchase led to the establishment of the Saint Louis Zoo in 1916.

*Courtesy Missouri State Archives*

## September 4, 1906

**University City was incorporated.** Edward Garner Lewis, the flamboyant publisher of *Women's Magazine*, bought 85 acres for his model city in 1902. The building that now serves as city hall was the magazine's headquarters. Lewis went broke defending himself on fraud charges and left his first planned city to found another in Atascadero, California.

## September 5, 1906

**Bradbury Robinson of Saint Louis University threw the first legal forward pass in football.** The 1906 season was the first in which the forward pass was legal. Because SLU was the first to use the pass effectively, they finished with a perfect record and outscored their opponents 402–11. The first pass thrown—in a practice game against Carroll College—was incomplete, and SLU lost the ball. The next time, Robinson completed a 20-yarder for the first aerial touchdown.

*Courtesy Wikipedia*

# SEPTEMBER

## September 6, 2020

**Hall of Famer Lou Brock died at the age of 81.** Brock began his Major League career with the Cubs in 1961 and was traded to the Cardinals in one of the most lopsided deals in baseball history on June 15, 1964. Brock set the single-season record for stolen bases with 118 in 1974. That record stood until 1982. He finished with 938 career steals, a record that stood until 1991. Brock also had 3,023 hits in his career.

*Celebration of Life*
*St. Louis Cardinal Hall of Famer*
*Louis Clark Brock*
*To God Be The Glory!*
*June 18, 1939 to September 06, 2020*

*Courtesy author*

## September 7, 1982

**The "Fabulous Fox" Theatre reopened with a presentation of the musical *Barnum*.** The theater was restored to its original grandeur under the guidance of Leon and Mary Strauss. The Fox had opened in 1929, and it had been vacant since 1978.

*Courtesy Don Korte*

## September 8, 1998

**At 8:18 p.m., Mark McGwire smashed a line-drive home run on the first pitch he saw from Steve Trachsel of the Cubs.** Number 62 was his shortest home run of the year and broke the previous single-season home run record set by Roger Maris. It cleared the left field wall at Busch Stadium by just two feet. Mark's son met him at home plate again, and Sammy Sosa came in to congratulate him. McGwire embraced the four sons and two daughters of Roger Maris. Groundskeeper Tim Forneris retrieved the ball and presented it to McGwire following the game.

*Courtesy Wikipedia, credit Jon Gudorf Photography*

Mark McGwire
*Courtesy Wikipedia, credit Jon Gudorf Photography*

### September 6, 1808

**Richard J. Lockwood was born in Delaware.** In 1850 he bought 50 acres along the Frisco Railroad that included two orchards, a new one and an old one. The Frisco wanted to name its station after Lockwood but there was already a Lockwood in southwest Missouri. The station house was located in the old orchard and took that name.

### September 6, 1833

**Tragedy struck as James Buchanan Eads and his family arrived in St. Louis.** The 13-year-old Eads and his family lost everything but the clothes they were wearing when fire broke out as their steamboat approached the landing. Eight people aboard were killed. James Eads had to sell apples and newspapers on the streets to help his family survive.

### September 7, 1749

**René-Auguste Chouteau was born in New Orleans.** His father had abandoned the family, and his mother began a relationship with Pierre Laclède. In 1763, Laclède brought 14-year-old Auguste along to choose a spot for a trading post. The following year, Auguste led the men who began construction on the site that his stepfather predicted would become a great city.

### September 8, 1949

**The St. Louis County Court approved incorporation of the Village of Hazelwood.** The court dismissed a petition by Ford and the Wabash Transit Company to incorporate the area as Motorville. All but two of the 55 registered voters in the village, all farmers, signed the petition for incorporation to avoid annexation of the area by Florissant.

# SEPTEMBER

## September 8, 2021

**Ted Simmons was inducted into the Baseball Hall of Fame.** Simmons was a catcher for the Cardinals from 1968 to 1980 and also played for the Brewers and the Braves. At the time of his retirement, Simmons led all catchers in career hits and doubles and ranked second in RBIs behind Yogi Berra and second in total bases behind Carlton Fisk. The Cardinals retired his #23 on July 31, 2021.

## September 9, 1898

**Frank Francis Frisch was born in the Bronx.** He came to the Cardinals in the controversial trade that sent Rogers Hornsby to the Giants after the 1926 season. But the "Fordham Flash" would star for the Redbirds for 11 years. He was named NL MVP in 1931 and managed the team from 1933 to 1938. He was elected to the Hall of Fame in 1947.

## September 10, 1983

**KPLR-TV aired the final episode of _Wrestling at the Chase_.** The show, created by St. Louis Wrestling Club president Sam Muchnick, premiered back in 1959 and featured such wrestlers as "Nature Boy" Ric Flair, "Dick the Bruiser" Afflis, and Ted DiBiase. Wrestling returned to the Chase with the National Wrestling Association in 2021.

## September 11, 1974

**Bake McBride was the hero in the longest game in Cardinals history, which began on the 11th and ended on the 12th.** He opened the 25th inning with a single. McBride then scored on a couple of errors by the Mets, starting with an errant pickoff attempt. Only about 1,000 fans were still on hand at Shea Stadium when the game ended after seven hours and 13 minutes at 3:13 a.m. The teams left a total of 45 men on base. McBride would go on to win NL Rookie of the Year honors in 1974.

*Courtesy Missouri Historical Society, St. Louis*

## September 9, 1977

**After 120 years, Falstaff beer was no longer being brewed in St. Louis.** The Griesedieck Company ended production at its plant at 1920 Shenandoah. Falstaff was originally introduced by the Lemp Brewery, and the beer was named in honor of the Shakespearean character Sir John Falstaff in 1903. When Lemp closed in 1921, the name was sold to Griesedieck. During the 1960s, Falstaff was the third-largest brewer in America.

## September 10, 1941

**Phil the Gorilla arrived at the Ape House.** Phil was named for the man who brought him to St. Louis, animal collector Phil Carroll. the _Guinness Book of World Records_ estimated Phil's weight at 615 pounds, making him one of the largest gorillas on record. Phil was one of the zoo's top attractions, and his death in December 1958 was front-page news. Phil was mounted and displayed publicly for many years. He is now in the zoo's Educational Outpost.

### Phil the Gorilla arrived at the Ape House.

*Courtesy Don Korte*

## September 11, 2001

**That morning, the big news was that Tiger Woods was here to play in the PGA American Express Championship at Bellerive.** The news from New York broke shortly after 7:45 a.m. St. Louis time. Within an hour, air traffic was halted at Lambert Field and armed marshals patrolled the Eagleton Federal Courthouse. The Gateway Arch and the Old Courthouse closed, and the golf tournament was cancelled. By afternoon, most of the shopping malls were closed and blood donation centers were swamped.

*Courtesy Wikipedia*

## September 12, 1962

**John F. Kennedy made his final visit to St. Louis.** At McDonnell Aircraft, he told employees they were engaged in the most important and significant adventure in the history of mankind. Kennedy was scheduled to come to St. Louis again in October 1962, but the trip was cancelled at the last minute and the press was told it was because the president had a cold. The truth was more sinister. Kennedy had just learned of the offensive missile sites in Cuba.

*Courtesy Missouri Historical Society, St. Louis*

## September 13, 1957

**Trading closed for the last time at the Merchant's Exchange downtown.** The building at 111 North Third Street was one of the city's architectural treasures, with a trading room 235 feet long, 98 feet wide, and 65 feet tall. The Democratic National Convention nominated Samuel Tilden for president there in 1876. The building was torn down in 1957 to make way for the Gateway Arch. Construction began on the Adam's Mark Hotel in this location in 1983.

*Courtesy Missouri State Archives*

## September 14, 2022

**Pitcher Adam Wainwright and catcher Yadier Molina of the Cardinals, both age 40, broke a Major League record even older than they were.** With their 325th start together, they topped the 324 games pitcher Mickey Lolich and catcher Bill Freehan had started for the Tigers from 1963 through 1975.

*Courtesy Wikipedia, credit Johnmaxmena*

## September 12, 1930

**The first drive-up banking window in the US went into operation at the new Grand National Bank headquarters in the Continental Building.** It was covered with a steel curtain until the customer pressed a button and was for deposits only. The bank was still reeling from a million-dollar robbery back in May that had occurred while a vault door was being moved to the new building.

## September 12, 1980

**The "South Side Dentist," Doctor Glennon Engelman, was found guilty of the 1976 murder-for-profit slaying of Peter Halm.** Engleman would also be convicted of the 1980 car bombing that killed Sophie Marie Barrera, who had sued him for unpaid lab fees. Engelmann would be linked to murder-for-profit killings of James Bullock in 1958, Eric Frey in 1963, Arthur and Vernita Gusewelle in 1977, and their son Ronald in 1979.

## September 13, 2016

**Monsanto was sold to German pharmaceutical giant Bayer AG in a $66 billion deal.** It was announced that St. Louis would become the commercial headquarters for North America. A spokesperson said the merger would help the city become a "global center" for the seed business, adding, "This is good news for St. Louis" where Monsanto employed more than 4,000 people.

## September 14, 1992

**John C. Vincent, a diver and construction worker from New Orleans, used suction cups to climb to the top of the Arch and parachute to the ground.** He made a getaway in a car as rangers closed in and later told reporters he did it "for the hell of it." Vincent was charged with two misdemeanors, even though the US attorney admitted, "It was clearly a great stunt."

## September 15, 1978

**The seven-month reign of Leon Spinks as heavyweight champion came to an end.** Muhammad Ali regained the title in a 15-round decision at the Superdome in New Orleans. Spinks never trained seriously for the rematch, instead living a flamboyant lifestyle. He blew about $20 million in winnings and was arrested for cocaine possession before declaring bankruptcy in 1986.

## September 15, 1986

**Mike Laga of the Cardinals became the first player to hit a ball out of Busch Stadium II.** Problem was, it was foul by about 150 feet. Nonetheless, it was an impressive feat. It was 130 feet from the roof of Busch Stadium to the field below. The ball was found in a flower bed in the employee parking lot.

## September 16, 1809

**Bryan Mullanphy was born.** His father, John, was the city's first millionaire and a great philanthropist, but Bryan was so generous his father considered him "reckless" and disinherited him. Bryan won a battle over the will and used the money to found the Travelers Aid Society, the St. Vincent DePaul Hospital, and an immigrant home. He also donated land for Mullanphy Park. Bryan Mullanphy served as mayor in 1847–48.

## September 17, 1980

**Mobster James "Jimmy" Michaels was killed when a bomb detonated by remote control ripped his car apart on southbound I-55 near Reavis Barracks Road.** The bombing marked the start of two years of bloody warfare between the rival Michaels and Leisure gangs over control of a St. Louis labor union. David Leisure was convicted of planting the bomb that killed Jimmy Michaels and was executed in 1999.

*Courtesy State Historical Society of Missouri*

## September 15, 1963

**The University of Missouri–St. Louis was dedicated with ceremonies on the present site of Woods Hall.** The campus was once the Bellerive Country Club, and the first classes were held in the old clubhouse shown here. Construction on Benton Hall, the first new building on campus, would begin in 1964. The campus is now St. Louis's largest university by enrollment and the third-largest in the state.

## September 16, 1924

**"Sunny Jim" Bottomley of the Cardinals drove in 12 runs in a single game at Ebbets Field.** Wilbert Robinson, who had set the previous record in 1892, was managing the Brooklyn team at the time and watched from the dugout. Bottomley smacked three singles, a double, and two home runs as the Cardinals romped, 17–3. Mark Whiten of the Cardinals would tie the record in 1993.

*Courtesy Wikipedia*

## September 17, 2001

**On the night that baseball resumed for the first time since September 11, in a trembling voice, Jack Buck read a stirring poem during pregame ceremonies at Busch Stadium.** The poem ended "We've been challenged by a cowardly foe who strikes and then hides from our view. With one voice we say there's no choice today, there is only one thing to do. Everyone is saying the same thing and praying that we end these senseless moments we are living. As our fathers did before, we shall win this unwanted war. As our children will enjoy the future we'll be giving."

*Courtesy Flickr, credit majorvols*

## September 18, 1949

**The new international airport in Chicago was dedicated in honor of Lieutenant Edward "Butch" O'Hare.** O'Hare's father, Edward J. O'Hare, was a St. Louis lawyer who ended up in Chicago running

*Courtesy Wikipedia*

a racetrack for Al Capone. He was instrumental in putting Capone behind bars for tax evasion. E. J. O'Hare was murdered on November 8, 1939. Butch O'Hare was awarded the Medal of Honor for singlehandedly defending the carrier *Lexington* against seven Japanese bombers. He was shot down over Tarawa on November 27, 1943.

## September 19, 1934

**Jay Randolph was born.** The son of US Senator from West Virginia Jennings Randolph, Jay came to St. Louis to work at KMOX in 1966. He served as sports director for KSD-TV Channel 5 from 1967 to 1988 and became a staple on Cardinals broadcasts.

*Courtesy St. Louis Media History Foundation Archive*

*Courtesy Missouri Historical Society, St. Louis*

## September 20, 1954

**Educational television came to St. Louis. KETC signed on at 9 p.m., with a preview of things to come.** The first broadcast was from McMillan Hall at Washington University. Following remarks by Arthur Holly Compton, the station broadcast a play dramatizing the necessity for free speech. Channel Nine was the seventh educational station in the country.

## September 18, 1972

**The city of Arnold was incorporated.** Arnold was created by the incorporation of what had been several small towns: Wickes, Flamm City, Tenbrook, Maxwell, Beck, and Old Town Arnold. Ferd Lang was appointed as the first mayor on November 15, 1972.

## September 18, 2023

**Adam Wainwright joined Jesse Haines and Bob Gibson as the only Cardinals pitchers with 200 wins.** In his last career start, Wainwright pitched seven innings and gave up four hits as the Cardinals beat the Milwaukee Brewers 1–0 at Busch.

## September 19, 1820

**Alexander McNair was inaugurated as the first governor of Missouri at the Missouri Hotel.** William Ashley was named first lieutenant governor, and John Scott became the first representative in Congress. The first state General Assembly was meeting in St. Louis to begin the process of getting the state ready to join the union.

*Courtesy Wikipedia*

## September 20, 1946

**Writing in the *St. Louis Post-Dispatch*, Bob Broeg reported that during a recent series in Brooklyn, Bums fans had begrudgingly bestowed a nickname on Stan Musial.** As he came to the plate, they were heard to murmur, "Here comes the man again." Musial was leading the National League in batting, base hits, runs scored, doubles, and triples.

## September 21, 1948

**The Airway Drive In at St. Charles Rock Road and Ashby in St. Ann opened with a showing of the Disney feature cartoon *Song of the South*.** The Airway could accommodate 1,000 cars and was torn down in 1996. But the sign featuring a baton-twirling majorette was saved to mark the entrance to a shopping center that was located on the site.

## September 21, 1998

**Legendary track star Florence Griffith Joyner died of an apparent seizure at age 38.** "Flo-Jo" was married to East St. Louis Olympian Al Joyner and was the sister-in-law of Jackie Joyner-Kersee. Flo-Jo had suffered a previous seizure while on a flight to St. Louis in 1996.

*Courtesy Wikipedia*

## September 22, 1997

**Demolition was about to begin on a North St. Louis County landmark.** The Central Hardware store at New Halls Ferry and I-270 was torn down to make room for a new Home Depot. When it was built in 1961, the distinctive design reminded people of the Lambert Field Terminal.

## September 23, 1929

**About 3,000 people gathered for a banquet as part of the ceremonies marking the dedication of the Arena.** Secretary of Agriculture Arthur Hyde and Governor Henry Caulfield spoke. According to the *St. Louis Globe-Democrat*, the "almost perfect acoustics of the new structure" were demonstrated by a 50-piece band and the singing of "The Masked Soprano." The Arena was built as the permanent home of the National Dairy Show, but the stock market crash would soon bankrupt the promoters.

## September 21, 1962

**The US 66 National Highway Association petitioned AASHTO (American Society of State Highway and Transportation Officials) to keep 66 as the number for the interstates replacing the old highway.** The request was denied because 66 didn't fit the interstate numbering system. It took five interstates to replace US 66.

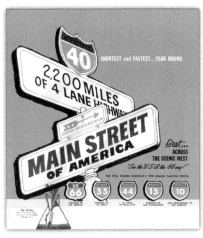

*Courtesy author*

## September 22, 1842

**James Shields and Abraham Lincoln met for a duel on an island on the Missouri side of the Mississippi River near Alton.** Shields, a Belleville attorney and state auditor, had accused Lincoln, then a state legislator, of writing a critical article about him. Lincoln wisely chose cavalry sabers as their weapons, and Shields could see Lincoln had a much longer reach. Lincoln said he didn't write the article, and the duel was called off. The site where the duel was to have taken place is no longer an island. It is now part of the Lincoln-Shields Recreation Area on the Missouri side of the river.

## September 23, 1806

**The Lewis and Clark Expedition returned to St. Louis.** Nearly the entire population of 1,000 met them on the riverbank. After two and a half years, most citizens had given them up for dead. The men would get double their promised pay and 320 acres of land as a reward. Lewis and Clark received 1,600 acres. Lewis would be named governor of the Louisiana Territory, and Clark would be named commander of the militia and agent of Indigenous Peoples affairs.

**The Lewis and Clark expedition returned to St. Louis.**

*Courtesy NPS, credit David Shane (CC 2.0)*

## September 24, 1912

**Tony Jannus flew four cases of Lemp's Beer from Kinloch Field to the St. Louis Fair on St. Charles Rock Road.** It was the very first consignment of freight to go by air. Jannus was the pilot when Albert Berry made the first parachute jump from a plane at Jefferson Barracks in 1912. In 1914, he became the first passenger airline pilot, pioneering "airboat" service between Tampa and St. Petersburg, Florida.

*Tony Jannus flew four cases of Lemp's Beer from Kinloch Field to the St. Louis Fair on St. Charles Rock Road.*

*Courtesy Wikipedia*

*Courtesy Missouri Historical Society, St. Louis*

## September 25, 1989

**St. Louis became a two-newspaper town again—briefly.** The *St. Louis Sun*, a tabloid-style paper, made its debut amid much fanfare. The paper folded in the spring of 1990.

**With a 6–4 win over the Giants in New York, the Cardinals clinched their very first pennant.** The *Post-Dispatch* compared the celebration to the end of the "Great War" as blizzards of paper enveloped the downtown area. A reception for the players was being planned for October 4, when they would return home following the first two World Series games in New York. The first game here was set for October 5.

### September 24, 1988

**José Oquendo put on the catcher's garb in the seventh inning in a game against New York.** "The Secret Weapon" became the first National League player in 70 years to play all nine positions in a single season. Eugene Paulette of the Cardinals had done it back in 1918. Oquendo later served as the third-base coach for the Redbirds.

### September 25, 1963

**The Cardinals announced that Stan Musial would become the first Cardinals player to have his number retired.** The Cardinals retired numbers are #1 Ozzie Smith, #2 Red Schoendienst, #6 Musial, #9 Enos Slaughter, #10 Tony La Russa, #14 Ken Boyer, #17 Dizzy Dean, #20 Lou Brock, #23 Ted Simmons, #24 Whitey Herzog, #42 Bruce Sutter, #45 Bob Gibson, and #85 for Gussie Busch, who was 85 when he was honored. Rogers Hornsby's name appears with these players, but he played before the uniforms were numbered. The initials JB also appear for broadcaster Jack Buck.

# SEPTEMBER

### September 26, 1950

**The first flight of the reborn Ozark Airlines left Lambert for Chicago—with one person on board.** Ozark started during World War II with a couple of flights a day between Springfield, Kansas City, and St. Louis. But the airline failed. This time, it took off, and the familiar green planes were serving 67 cities in 25 states when TWA took it over in 1986.

### September 27, 1806

**Eberhard Anheuser was born in Bad Kreuznach, Germany.** Anheuser was a successful owner of a St. Louis soap factory when he loaned money to the struggling Bavarian Brewery and later found himself in the beer business when the brewery failed in 1860. He changed the name to Eberhard Anheuser and Company. His daughter Lilly married Adolphus Busch, the owner of a brewery supply business, in 1861. Anheuser and Busch became partners in 1865.

### September 27, 1998

**Mark McGwire capped his amazing season with two more home runs against the Montreal Expos at Busch Stadium.** Number 69 came off Mike Thurman in the third inning. In the seventh, Big Mac lined the first pitch he had ever seen from rookie Carl Pavano over the left-field fence. McGwire had slammed two home runs the day before and ended the season four ahead of Sammy Sosa.

### September 28, 1963

**The first performance by a member of the Beatles in the US took place in Southern Illinois as George Harrison played with a local band called the "Four Vests" at the VFW Hall in Eldorado.** Harrison spent three weeks visiting his sister Louise in Benton. Louise had convinced a teenaged disc jockey named Marcia Raubach to play "From Me to You" back in June. WFRX in West Frankfort thus became the first US radio station to play a Beatles record.

### September 26, 1947

**The 66 Park-In on Watson Road opened with a showing of *Lady Luck* starring Frank Morgan and Barbara Hale.** That first night, vehicles made before 1915 were admitted free. Constructed by Flexer Drive-Ins, the 66 Park-In covered 18 acres of land, could accommodate up to 800 vehicles, and the screen was said to be five times larger than the average.

*Courtesy Missouri State Archives*

*Courtesy Missouri Historical Society, St. Louis*

### September 27, 1953

**The St. Louis Browns played their final game.** The team that made St. Louis "First in shoes, first in booze, and last in the American League" appropriately went out with a 2–1 loss in 10 innings to the Chicago White Sox at Sportsman's Park. Ed Mickelson drove in Johnny Groth in the fourth inning for the final run in the franchise's 52-year history. At 3:44 p.m., Jim Dyck flied to center for the final out. A crowd of 3,174 fans saw the game.

*Courtesy Wikipedia*

### September 28, 1953

**Bobby Greenlease, the six-year-old son of a wealthy Kansas City auto dealer, was kidnapped from his school by Carl Austin Hall and Bonnie Brown Heady.** A $600,000 ransom was paid, but the child had already been murdered. A cab driver who took Hall to the Coral Court Motel noticed him flashing money around and tipped off his boss, mobster Joe Costello.

Costello called police Lieutenant Louis Shoulders, who made the arrest with his driver, patrolman Elmer Dolan. But half of the ransom money never made it to the station.

Shoulders and Dolan were convicted of perjury, Hall and Heady went to the gas chamber on December 18, and the missing money was never found. The FBI believes Costello laundered the money through his mob connections.

## September 29, 1963

**Ceremonies at Busch Stadium I marked the last game for Stan "the Man" Musial.** Stan and his family circled the ballpark in convertibles while 27,576 fans cheered and tossed confetti. Stan was presented with a painting, *The Man and a Boy* by *Post-Dispatch* cartoonist Amadee; a ring from his teammates with the number 6 outlined in diamonds; and a Cub Scout neckerchief from scout Howard Lay. Musial smacked two hits off Jim Maloney, and the Cards beat the Reds, 3–2.

*Courtesy Missouri Historical Society, St. Louis*

## September 30, 2019

**The St. Louis Wheel opened at Union Station.** The observation wheel is 200 feet tall and features 42 gondolas that are climate controlled. They can hold up to eight people or six adults comfortably. The VIP gondola has glass floors, leather bucket seats, and other amenities. The rides last about 15 minutes.

*Courtesy Wikipedia, credit Retrodells*

## September 29, 1922

**The Chase Hotel, named after owner and builder Chase Ullman, opened to the public.** In 1929, Sam Koplar and his brothers began building the 27-story Park Plaza Hotel next door. Koplar later gained control of both and combined them to form the most glamorous hotel and night spot in the city. The Chase is now a Sonesta Hotel, and the Park Plaza has condos on the ninth through 27th floors. Floors eight and below combine executive suites and hotel rooms.

*Courtesy Missouri Historical Society, St. Louis*

## September 30, 1864

**It appeared that Kirkwood was about to become the scene of a major battle.** Two brigades of Union troops rushed in to head off the invasion by Confederates under Sterling Price. Price had been delayed by outnumbered federals at Pilot Knob. When he learned that reinforcements had arrived, Price abandoned his plans to march on the city, and the Battle of Kirkwood was never fought.

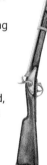

*Courtesy Freepik*

## September 30, 1883

**The Browns took out their frustration on the man they said caused them to finish second, one game behind the Philadelphia Athletics.** One by one, each man in the clubhouse lined up to beat up third baseman Arlie Latham. Latham offended teammates, opponents, and umpires with his pranks and insults. The "Freshest Man on Earth" also became the first Major League base line coach. The coach's box was developed to keep him from running up and down the line hurling insults.

# OCTOBER

## October 1, 1850

**David Rowland Francis was born in Richmond, Kentucky.** Francis served as the 30th mayor of St. Louis from 1885 to 1888. He then became the only St. Louis mayor to be elected governor of Missouri. Francis also served as secretary of the interior under President Cleveland. But Francis is best remembered for his tireless work as head of the 1904 World's Fair. He later became US ambassador to Russia.

## October 2, 1965

**St. Louisan Fontella Bass entered the Billboard chart with "Rescue Me."** The record went to number four on the Hot 100 pop chart, number one on the R&B chart, and number 11 in the UK. Minnie Ripperton ("Loving You") provided background vocals. According to Bass, the call-and-response moans heard in the song's fade were because she forgot the words.

## October 3, 1931

**Blues great Glenn Hall was born in Humboldt, Saskatchewan.** "Mister Goalie" came to the expansion club in the twilight of his great career, talked out of retirement. He led the team to the 1968 Stanley Cup finals in the team's first season. The combo of Hall and Jacques Plante also put the team in the finals the next two seasons. Hall hated playing goal, and he threw up before nearly every game.

*Courtesy Getty Images*

*Courtesy Wikipedia, credit Rick Dikeman*

## October 1, 1963

**Mark McGwire was born in Pomona, California.** The Montreal Expos drafted Big Mac right out of high school, as a pitcher! McGwire switched to first base at the urging of Ron Vaughn, an assistant coach in the Alaskan Summer League. Oakland used the 10th pick overall in the 1984 draft to take McGwire. Mark came to the Cardinals on July 31, 1997.

## October 2, 1968

**In the opening game of the 1968 World Series, Bob Gibson struck out a record 17 Detroit Tigers.** The Cardinals got to Detroit ace Denny McLain and won the game 4–0. Both McLain and Gibson would be named as their league's Most Valuable Players in "The Year of the Pitcher."

*Courtesy Missouri Historical Society, St. Louis*

## October 3, 1804

**The first St. Louis Post Office was established at Third and Elm, in the home of Rufus Easton.** Thomas Jefferson appointed Easton as the first postmaster. Rufus Easton also founded a town in Illinois he named after his son Alton. His daughter, Mary Easton Sibley, founded what is now Lindenwood University.

*Courtesy Wikipedia*

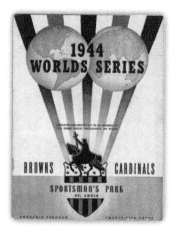

## October 4, 1944

**The first all–St. Louis World Series opened at Sportsman's Park.**
The city was buzzing and seemed to slightly favor the underdog Browns. Classes were cancelled at Saint Louis University and Washington University, and Mayor Aloys Kaufmann declared it "St. Louis Baseball Week." Mort Cooper of the Cardinals allowed just two hits, but the Browns took Game One, 2–1, on a home run by George McQuinn.

*Courtesy Missouri Historical Society, St. Louis*

## October 5, 1782

**Francois Dunegant received a tract of land from the Spanish to establish a government house and organize a village along Coldwater Creek**. The Spanish called the village San Fernando, later anglicized to St. Ferdinand, but the locals called it Florissant. The French had declared the area "Un vale Fluerissant" or "Valley of the Flowers."

*Courtesy State Historical Society of Missouri*

## October 6, 1926

**In Game Four of the World Series, Babe Ruth set a record.**
Babe Ruth became the first player to hit three home runs in a World Series game, including a shot that cleared the roof of Sportsman's Park and smashed through the window of the Wells Motor Company dealership across Grand. The Yankees won 10–5, tying the series at two games each.

Dizzy Dean, Babe Ruth, and Paul Dean (left to right)
*Courtesy Missouri Historical Society, St. Louis*

*Courtesy Wikipedia*

### October 4, 1906

**The statue of St. Louis on Art Hill was dedicated.** The statue became the symbol of the city, eclipsed only when the Arch was built in 1965. More than 7,000 people took part in the parade to mark the occasion. The statue was a bronze cast from an original at the 1904 World's Fair by Charles Niehaus.

*Courtesy Missouri Historical Society, St. Louis*

### October 5, 1916

**Ten people died, including seven firemen, in a fire at the Christian Brothers College at Kingshighway and Easton (now Dr. Martin Luther King Drive).** The other casualties were two of the brothers and the school watchman. The city bought the site of the college and turned it into Sherman Park.

### October 6, 1890

**Officer James Brady was shot to death outside Charles Starkes's saloon on 11th Street.** William Harrison, an African American, was charged with the murder. Starkes would confess that he had shot Brady, but the confession was not reported. Harrison was hanged from the "Bridge of Sighs" at the County Courthouse in Clayton in 1894. The folk song "Duncan and Brady" was written amid the racial tension that followed the trial.

### October 7, 1794

**"Villa a Robert" was laid out by the Spanish commander Francois Dunegant of San Fernando (later Florissant).** The French called the settlement "Marais des Liards" (*Cottonwood Swamp*). The Americans called it Owen's Station. It was known as Bridgeton long before the Missouri River Bridge, so the name probably referred to a span on Coldwater Creek.

### October 7, 1878

**Tony Faust's Restaurant became the first building in St. Louis to be lit by electricity.** The machinery was purchased in Paris, where it was reported that many buildings—and even some streets—were lit by electricity.

*Courtesy Wikipedia*

### October 8, 1878

**The first Veiled Prophet Ball and parade were held in St. Louis.** Merchant Charles Slayback dreamed up the Veiled Prophet. He saw the event as a way to drum up business during October fair week and build support for the Agricultural and Mechanical Exposition. In the wake of the 1877 general strike, the elite also saw it as a way to keep the masses under control and demonstrate their power.

### October 9, 1944

**The Cardinals won "the Streetcar Series," defeating the Browns four games to two.** The Brownies hit just .138 against the powerhouse pitching staff of the Cardinals, led by Mort Cooper, Max Lanier, and Ted Wilks. There was no celebration on the streets after the game, prompting J. Roy Stockton to write in the *Post-Dispatch* that there was one problem with having the World Series in the same city: "One of the teams has to lose."

*Courtesy Wikipedia*

### October 7, 1909

**Glenn Curtiss made the first airplane flight in St. Louis.** Albert Bond Lambert offered Curtiss $6,000 to bring his "Golden Flyer" for an aviation meet at Forest Park during the Centennial Week celebrations. Only a few people saw his first two early-morning flights. A crowd of over 300,000 waited for hours to see the third flight of about 60 yards in four seconds. Curtiss made seven flights during the meet, the longest lasting about 90 seconds.

### October 8, 2022

**Albert Pujols and Yadier Molina played in their final game as the Cardinals lost to the Phillies 2–0 in the last game of the NL Wild Card series.** Both Pujols and Yadi singled in their last at bats.

*Courtesy Getty Images*

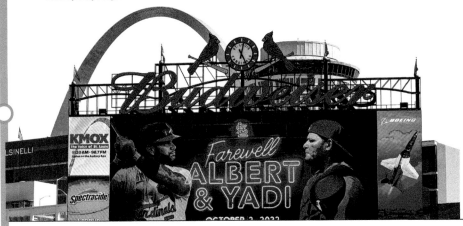

### October 9, 1954

**Actor Scott Bakula was born in St. Louis.** The 1973 graduate of Kirkwood High School starred as Sam Beckett in the NBC science-fiction series *Quantum Leap* from 1989 until 1993. He went on to play the role of Captain Jonathan Archer in *Enterprise*, the fifth incarnation of the *Star Trek* series. From 2014 to 2021, he portrayed Special Agent Dwayne Cassius "King" Pride on *NCIS: New Orleans*.

*Courtesy Wikipedia*

*Courtesy State Historical Society of Missouri*

## October 10, 1939

**Mayor Bernard Dickmann wielded a silver wrecking bar, prying out two bricks from a dilapidated building at 7 Market Street facing the Old Cathedral.** The first brick went to the city, and the second was sent to President Roosevelt. The ceremony marked the start of demolition work on the riverfront for the proposed riverfront memorial. Thirty-seven blocks would be cleared, but World War II and wrangling over the elevated railroad tracks on the riverfront delayed actual construction work until 1959.

*Courtesy Missouri Historical Society, St. Louis*

## October 11, 1910

**Former president Theodore Roosevelt became the first who ever held the office to ride in an airplane.** He flew in a biplane piloted by Archibald "Arch" Hoxsey, who was taking part in the International Aviation Meet at Kinloch Field (at present-day Graham and Frost). Roosevelt described the four-minute flight at an altitude of 50 feet as "bully," and said he wished they could have stayed in the air for an hour.

## October 12, 1967

**The Cardinals defeated the Boston Red Sox 7–2 in Game Seven of the 1967 World Series.** That morning, a Boston newspaper was confident the Sox would win, because ace Jim Lonborg would be on the mound. The headline read "Lonborg and Champagne." The headline angered and inspired the Cardinals. In 27 innings pitched during the series, Bob Gibson allowed just three runs and 14 hits. Lou Brock collected 12 hits for a .414 average and swiped a Series-record seven stolen bases.

*Courtesy Missouri Historical Society, St. Louis*

### October 10, 1700

**A French missionary, Father Gravier, noted in his journal: "Discovered the river Mirameguoua, where the very rich lead mine is situated, 12 or 13 leagues from its mouth."** Today we refer to that river as the Meramec. (It's an Indigenous word meaning catfish.)

### October 10, 1926

**Allegedly nursing a hangover and sleeping in the bullpen, Grover Cleveland Alexander was called in to relieve Jesse Haines in Game Seven of the 1926 World Series.** The bases were loaded with two outs in the seventh inning. Alexander struck out Tony Lazzeri to end the inning. He set the Yanks down in order until giving up a walk to Babe Ruth with two out in the ninth. Ruth was thrown out stealing, and the Cardinals were world champions for the first time.

### October 11, 1809

**Meriwether Lewis was found dead under mysterious circumstances at Grinder's Tavern on the Natchez Trace in Tennessee.** Ailing and in financial trouble, he was headed from St. Louis to Washington to ask the government for help with expenses from the famous expedition. Most historians believe it was a suicide.

### October 12, 1929

**C. L. Grigg of St. Louis was introducing his new soft drink.** Grigg had formed the Howdy Company to market his orange drink in 1920. His new product was called "Bib-Label Lithiated Lemon-Lime Soda." It sold well, despite the name and the fact that the new drink was more expensive than most of the 600 lemon-lime sodas already on the market. In 1931, Grigg changed the name to "7 Up."

*Courtesy Missouri Historical Society, St. Louis*

## October 13, 1834

**A road was laid out from the Village of Carondelet to the "LeMais" ferry on the Meramec River, named for the owner of the ferry at the time.** The ferry was originally built by Jean Baptiste de Gamache, so it could have been De Gamache Ferry. It was anglicized over the years to LEE-may.

## October 13, 1882

**The city was buzzing after a prominent attorney was shot to death by J. W. Cockrell, managing editor of the *St. Louis Post-Dispatch*.** Alonzo Slayback had gone to Cockrell's office to demand an apology for an editorial critical of his partner, a candidate for Congress. A mob tried to break down the door at the *Post* but Cockrell was not indicted.

## October 14, 1936

**President Franklin D. Roosevelt dedicated the Soldier's Memorial downtown.** As part of a 1923 bond issue, voters approved spending $6 million for a plaza and monument to commemorate St. Louisans who lost their lives in World War I. But all the money was spent to acquire the site, and voters had to approve money for the building 10 years later. The memorial and military museum reopened on November 3, 2018, after a multimillion-dollar renovation.

## October 15, 1899

**Frankie Baker shot her lover Albert Britt to death after an argument over another woman at 212 Targee Street.** Baker pleaded self-defense and was acquitted but pianist Bill Dooley wrote a song about the incident called "Frankie and Albert." Over the years, it became "Frankie and Johnny." Baker sued when a motion picture was based on the story, but the court ruled that it was a folk song. Baker died in a mental institution in 1950. The Enterprise Center stands on the site of Targee Street today.

*Courtesy State Historical Society of Missouri*

## October 13, 1809

**St. Charles was incorporated as a village under the laws of the territory.** Nathan Boone was named to make a new survey of the village. When Louis Blanchette settled on what is now Main Street, he called the village that sprang up around his post *Les Petites Cotes* or "Village of the Little Hills." The Spanish named it San Carlos, which was anglicized to St. Charles when the Americans took over.

*Courtesy Getty Images*

## October 14, 1985

**Ozzie Smith came to the plate in the bottom of the ninth in Game Five of the National League Championship Series with the game tied 2–2.** Tom Niedenfuer was on the mound for the Dodgers. The switch-hitting Wizard would hit left-handed. In over 3,000-career left-handed at bats, he had never hit a home run. But Smith corked one down the right-field line and over the wall. Describing the scene on KMOX, Jack Buck cried, "Go crazy folks, go crazy!"

## October 15, 1964

**The Cardinals won their first world championship in 18 years, as they beat the Yankees in Game Seven at Old Busch Stadium.** Bob Gibson tossed a complete game and struck out nine in the game. Lou Brock's home run sparked a three-run fifth

*Courtesy Getty Images*

inning and staked Gibson to a 6–0 lead. Mickey Mantle, Clete Boyer, and Phil Linz homered for New York, but it wasn't enough.

## October 16, 2000

**Missouri Governor Mel Carnahan, his son Randy, and top aide Chris Sifford died when their small plane crashed in Jefferson County.** The NTSB would find that pilot Randy Carnahan became disoriented when a key instrument failed in bad weather. Mel Carnahan was running against John Ashcroft for a US Senate seat. Carnahan won the November 2000 election posthumously, and his wife, Jean, was appointed to serve in his place.

*Courtesy Wikipedia*

## October 17, 1974

**Professional basketball returned to St. Louis as the Spirits of the old ABA lost to Memphis.** A crowd of 5,400 showed up at the Arena for the first game. The Spirits would last only two seasons before the ABA merged with the NBA, but the team included memorable characters such as Marvin Barnes and Fly Williams. The team's rookie announcer on KMOX was Bob Costas.

*Courtesy Missouri Historical Society, St. Louis*

## October 18, 1926

**Charles Edward Anderson "Chuck" Berry was born.** Berry attended Sumner High School and his family lived on Goode Street, which he would of course reference in the autobiographical song "Johnny B. Goode." Goode Street is now Annie Malone Drive. Berry trained as a hairdresser at the Poro Beauty School before he scored his first hit in 1955 with "Maybellene." Berry was a member of the inaugural class of the Rock & Roll Hall of Fame, inducted in 1986.

*Courtesy Wikipedia*

### October 16, 1941

**Tim McCarver was born in Memphis.** McCarver was an important part of the 1960s pennant-winning Cardinals teams. The catcher was traded to Philadelphia in 1969, returned here as a pinch hitter in 1973–74, and then ended up with the Phillies again. He was a part of three pennant winners before moving to the broadcast booth in 1980. McCarver called a record 24 World Series for ABC, CBS, and Fox. He died on February 16, 2023.

*Courtesy Wikipedia, credit Delaywaves*

### October 17, 1817

**Giuseppe (Joseph) Rosati arrived in St. Louis.** He became coadjutor to Bishop DuBourg and was named the first bishop of the newly created St. Louis diocese in 1827. He supervised construction of the cathedral and brought the Jesuits to establish Saint Louis University. The first Italian bishop in the US, he founded a Catholic newspaper and asked the Sisters of Charity to open the first hospital west of the Mississippi.

### October 18, 1904

**Helen Keller, "the celebrated blind and deaf signer," was the guest of honor on Helen Keller Day at the World's Fair.** Keller was the only living person to be honored with a special day at the fair. Keller said she "saw" the sights of the fair through the eyes of her companions.

### October 18, 1908

**The cornerstone was laid for the magnificent "new" cathedral on Lindell.** The first Mass to be held there would take place six years later to the day. The cathedral would not be formally dedicated until June 29, 1926.

## October 19, 1974

**Plaza Frontenac at Lindbergh and Highway 40 opened.** It was the first enclosed bi-level mall in the St. Louis area and is known for its luxury retailers, including Neiman Marcus and Saks Fifth Avenue, which relocated there from the Central West End. In "Ride Wit Me," Nelly raps, "Take you down to Frontenac, you don't know how to act."

## October 19, 1990

**The motion picture *White Palace* opened nationally.** James Spader plays a widowed 27-year-old yuppie. He falls for a 43-year-old waitress (portrayed by Susan Sarandon) at a hamburger joint. The film features many St. Louis locations, including the "White Palace" at 18th and Olive, Dogtown, Duff's Restaurant, the Hi-Pointe Cinema, and the Arch grounds. It also featured Jason Alexander, Kathy Bates, and Eileen Brennan.

## October 20, 1868

**Henry Shaw deeded his Tower Grove estate to the city to "be used as a park forever."** Shaw's estate was outside the city limits at the time, so the state legislature had to approve creation of the second-largest park in St. Louis. Shaw filled Tower Grove with statuary, lily ponds, and "ruins" salvaged from the Southern Hotel fire.

## October 20, 1953

**Keith Hernandez was born in San Francisco.** He played first base for the Cardinals from 1974 to 1983. In 1979, he led the National League in hitting and was named co-MVP with Willie Stargell. Hernandez was a key part of the 1982 World Championship team. Whitey Herzog dealt Hernandez to the Mets for pitchers Neil Allen and Rick Ownbey on June 15, 1983. Hernandez appeared on *Seinfeld* in "The Boyfriend: Part 1" and "The Boyfriend: Part 2," then came back for the series finale in 1998.

## October 19, 2005

*Courtesy author*

**At 10:22 p.m., Yadier Molina flied out to Astros right fielder Jason Lane, giving Houston the National League championship and bringing down the curtain on Busch Stadium II.** Demolition of the old ballpark began on November 7, 2005. The stadium was knocked down slowly rather than being imploded, in order to avoid damaging the nearby MetroLink line.

*Courtesy Missouri Historical Society, St. Louis*

## October 20, 1982

**Bruce Sutter blew a third strike past Gorman Thomas of the Milwaukee Brewers, and the Cardinals were the champions of the world.** The Cardinals overcame a 3–1 deficit to win Game Seven 6–3. Joaquín Andújar got the win and Bruce Sutter got the save. Darrell Porter was named as the World Series MVP.

## October 21, 1785

*Courtesy Wikipedia*

**Henry Miller Shreve was born in New Jersey.** The "Father of the Mississippi Steamboat" designed the now-familiar double-decked boat that made St. Louis a great city. He also invented a snag boat that cleared the 140-mile-long logjam on the Red River in Louisiana and founded a camp that became Shreveport. Shreve retired to his St. Louis estate near where Shreve Avenue runs today.

*Courtesy Wikipedia*

## October 22, 1734

**Daniel Boone was born in Pennsylvania. Boone rose to fame as a hunter and settler of what is now Kentucky.** The Spanish Governor at St. Louis offered Boone 1,000 arpents of land for bringing a group of settlers to the present-day St. Charles County in 1799. Boone died on September 26, 1820, and he left specific instructions that he was to be buried next to his wife in St. Charles County. But 25 years later, the state of Kentucky led a seemingly successful effort to move the remains there.

*Courtesy Wikipedia*

## October 23, 1826

**The army officially changed the name of its post south of St. Louis from Camp Adams to Jefferson Barracks.** It was established as a military post to replace Fort Belle Fontaine on the Missouri River north of St. Louis. Many of the greatest names in military history, including five presidents, spent part of their service at Jefferson Barracks before it was decommissioned as a military base in 1946.

## October 24, 1947

**Actor Kevin Kline was born in St. Louis.** Kline graduated from Priory High School in 1965, and the theater at Priory is named in his honor. He won two Tony Awards on Broadway before a role in *Sophie's Choice* made him a star in 1982. He is also known for films such as *The Big Chill*, *Dave*, and *The Ice Storm*. Kline won a best supporting actor Academy Award for *A Fish Called Wanda* in 1989.

*Courtesy Wikipedia, credit Chrisa Hickey*

## October 25, 1993

**Actor Vincent Price died at the age of 82.** The Country Day graduate originally planned to become an art historian before he turned to the theater. His first movie appearance came in *Service de Luxe* in 1938. He played many great historical figures but is best remembered for his roles in Roger Corman's adaptations of Edgar Allan Poe horror tales. He not only provided the "rap" on Michael Jackson's "Thriller" but also appeared in videos with Alice Cooper and Ringo Starr.

*Courtesy Getty Images*

## October 21, 1955

**Elvis Presley made his first concert appearance in St. Louis.** At the time, he had yet to have a national hit, so he was relegated to opening-act status for Roy Acuff at the Missouri Theatre. He also played shows on the 22nd and 23rd.

## October 22, 1876

**St. Louis City and County were officially separated, and the city boundaries were fixed permanently.** The "Great Divorce" is considered by many as one of the darkest days in the area's history as the lack of regional cooperation is to blame for many local problems. The population spread far beyond the city limits, and dozens of municipalities incorporated in the county.

## October 23, 1949

**SWITZER CANDY COMPANY MAIN PLANT EMPLOYEES ONLY**

*Courtesy Missouri Historical Society, St. Louis*

**Frederick Switzer died at his Clayton home of a pulmonary embolism at age 84.** In 1884, Frederick joined with his brother-in-law, a candymaker from Ireland, in a business called the Murphy and Switzer Candy Co. First he peddled candy from a cart on present-day Laclede's Landing, and then he started F.M. Switzer and Co. at 621 North First Street in 1888. The brand disappeared in the 1990s but was revived by Frederick's grandsons in 2005.

## October 24, 2022

**A 19-year-old former student walked into Central Visual and Performing Arts on South Kingshighway and opened fire with an assault rifle.** Alexzandria Bell, 15, and teacher Jean Kuckza were killed and four other students were wounded. Police cornered the shooter within minutes and fatally wounded him. The suspect's mother had told police she was worried about his mental condition and his gun but police said they could not seize the weapon.

## October 25, 1995

**Anheuser-Busch announced it was selling the St. Louis Cardinals.** The brewery had bought the team back in 1953. Fred Hanser formed a group to buy the club with his old Country Day School classmates, Bill DeWitt and Drew Bauer. Bill DeWitt's father had owned the Browns from 1949 to 1951. Tiny Eddie Gaedel wore Bill's batboy uniform when he made his pinch-hitting appearance in the most famous stunt in baseball history on August 19, 1951.

## October 25, 1997

**One of St. Louis's most offbeat attractions opened its doors.** The City Museum was the brainchild of Gail and Bob Cassilly, who brought an eclectic mix of hands-on exhibits and artwork for the young and old to the former International Shoe Building at 15th and Lucas.

*Courtesy Wikipedia, credit stefib230*

## October 26, 1834

**The "new" St. Louis cathedral was consecrated.** The night before, someone jammed some cannons that were to have been used in the ceremony. Some enraged Frenchmen thought it was the work of the Presbyterians. They wanted to turn the cannons on the Presbyterian Church, but cooler heads prevailed.

## October 27, 1914

**Barnes Hospital was dedicated.** The will of businessman Robert Barnes left $100,000 for construction and a $900,000 endowment for the hospital when he died in April 1892. Trustees postponed construction and invested the money until there were enough funds to build one of the most modern hospitals in the world. The trustees pledged to make Barnes the "Johns Hopkins of the West."

*Courtesy Getty Images*

## October 26, 1985

**Don Denkinger became public enemy number one in St. Louis.** With the Cardinals leading Game Six of the World Series 1–0 in the ninth, Denkinger called Jorge Orta safe at first, though replays showed he was clearly out. The Royals went on to win the game. Fans still blame Denkinger for the loss, even though Darrell Porter and Jack Clark misplayed a pop-up, and Porter allowed a passed ball that put the runners in scoring position for Dane Iorg. And there was a Game Seven.

## October 27, 2011

**The Cardinals were down to their last strike, trailing the Texas Rangers 7–5 and facing elimination in Game Six of the World Series.** With two men on and behind in the count 1–2, David Freese smacked a triple to tie the game. In the 10th inning, the Cards fell behind 10–7 and were down to the last strike again before Lance Berkman tied it. Freese came up in the 11th and blasted a 3–2 pitch from Mark Lowe over the wall in dead center to send the series to Game Seven.

*Courtesy Wikipedia, credit Herkie*

With two men on and behind in the count 1–2, David Freese smacked a triple to tie the game.

*Courtesy National Park Service*

## October 28, 1965

**At 9:26 a.m., a crane operated by William Quigley lifted the final section of the Gateway Arch into place.** Aline Saarinen was on hand. The widow of Arch designer Eero Saarinen was the art critic for the *Today* show and a commentator for NBC News. Other speakers included Mayor Alfonso Cervantes, Assistant Secretary of the Interior John Carver Jr., and LeRoy Brown of the National Park Service. Three fire department pumpers were used to cool down the south leg when it expanded due to the heat and threatened placement of the last section.

*Courtesy Missouri Historical Society, St. Louis*

## October 29, 1929

**Stock prices collapsed on "Black Tuesday."** Within four years, the unemployment rate in St. Louis would hit 35 percent, a staggering 80 percent among African Americans. A homeless shanty town or "Hooverville" would spring up on the Riverfront. But government relief programs would spend $50 million in St. Louis, funding riverfront clearance, road construction, Lambert Field expansion, construction of the Jewel Box in Forest Park, and many other projects.

## October 29, 1977

**The first issue of the *Riverfront Times* was published.** The alternative newspaper became a serious journalistic force and an important voice in the community, particularly after the demise of the *St. Louis Globe-Democrat*. Then there was the other side—the racy personals and phone-sex advertisements. The *Riverfront Times* was sold to a chain in 1998.

*Courtesy Missouri Historical Society, St. Louis*

## October 30, 1946

**Vincent Schoemehl was born in St. Louis.** The 46th mayor of the city served three terms, from 1981 to 1993. He worked for the renovation of Union Station, construction of the failed St. Louis Centre, and preservation of the Cupples Complex. Schoemehl got the daffodils planted along Highway 40, but his push for the ill-fated expansion of Lambert Field hampered his unsuccessful bid for governor in 1992.

## October 30, 1938

**A radio dramatization of *The War of the Worlds* put much of the nation in a panic.** The fictitious news bulletins in the broadcast over CBS by Orson Welles and the Mercury Theater on the Air reported that cylinders carrying Martians with death rays had landed in New Jersey, as well as in Chicago and St. Louis. It was reported that citizens in St. Louis residential neighborhoods gathered in the streets in a panic. Many had been listening to the more popular *Chase and Sanborn Hour* on KSD and had flipped to KMOX in the middle of the dramatization, missing the disclaimers.

*Courtesy Freepik*

## October 31, 1978

**The last regularly scheduled train pulled out of Union Station, once one of the busiest in the world.** Amtrak's Number 22 bound for Chicago ended 84 years of service to the grand old station. Amtrak moved operations to the forlorn "Amshak" east of the station. Union Station deteriorated and became a haven for the homeless until it was redeveloped in 1985.

*Courtesy Missouri Historical Society, St. Louis*

## October 31, 1999

**A St. Louis landmark closed its doors forever.** The Parkmoor Restaurant at Clayton Road and Big Bend opened in 1930 and was the first restaurant in the area to offer curb service. At one time there were five Parkmoor locations.

# NOVEMBER

## November 1, 1855

A special train carrying dignitaries to celebrate the completion of the Pacific Railroad to Jefferson City plunged into the Gasconade River as a bridge gave way. Thirty-four people died and 100 were injured. St. Louis Mayor Washington King was seriously hurt. The president of the city council was killed, and former Mayor John Wimer was injured. Kate Chopin's father and Sara Teasdale's grandfather were also killed.

## November 2, 1971

Amid demonstrations both pro and con, the musical *Hair* opened at the American Theatre. After flying to Kansas City to see the show, Circuit Judge Lackland Bloom issued an order preventing the city from using an anti-obscenity ordinance to stop the show. Plainclothes policemen were on hand anyway to make sure the show didn't violate the ordinance. There were no arrests, and the crowd gave the show a standing ovation even before it began.

## November 3, 1968

Camille "the Eel" Henry became the first Blues player to ever score a "hat trick," or three goals in a game. The first Blues hat trick came against the Red Wings in Detroit. The 1954 Rookie of the Year played two seasons with the Blues before he retired.

## November 3, 1968

Bob Gibson was named as the National League Cy Young Award winner for 1968, the "Year of the Pitcher." All Gibby had done that year was go 22 and nine, with 28 complete games and 13 shutouts. His earned run average was an astounding 1.12.

## November 1, 1930

*Courtesy Missouri Historical Society, St. Louis*

**The Octagon Building in University City was dedicated as city hall by Governor Henry Caulfield.** U-City founder Edward G. Lewis constructed the building just before the World's Fair to house his publishing empire. The 250-million-candlepower searchlight on top of the building was relit.

*Courtesy Wikipedia, credit AfricanGeo*

## November 2, 1991

**The St. Louis Science Center opened in a brand-new building connected to the McDonnell Planetarium by a bridge over Highway 40.** The Academy of Science of St. Louis founded the forerunner of the Science Center, the Museum of Science and Industry in Clayton's Oak Knoll Park, in 1959. The center was located at the planetarium from 1985 to 1991.

## November 3, 2018

**The Soldier's Memorial downtown reopened after a complete restoration undertaken by the Missouri History Museum and largely funded by the Taylor family of Enterprise Rent-A-Car.** The History Museum took over management of the memorial, constructed in 1938.

*Courtesy Missouri Historical Society, St. Louis*

*Courtesy Library of Congress*

## November 4, 1948

**President-elect Harry S Truman's special train from Independence to Washington, DC, pulled onto Track 35 at Union Station for a brief stop, and the victor was handed a 48-hour-old copy of the** *Chicago Tribune.* Forced to go to press early on election night due in part to a printer's strike, the *Tribune* had printed the erroneous headline "DEWEY DEFEATS TRUMAN." Exclaiming, "This one is for the books," Truman held up the paper as photographers snapped away. All three of the St. Louis newspapers had endorsed Dewey.

## November 4, 1953

**Radar was used for the first time to nab speeders in St. Louis.** The cumbersome transmitter unit weighed 45 pounds. Placed along the shoulder of the Express Highway at Forest Park, it sent a signal to a recording device in the trunk of the police car. Four people were nailed for exceeding the 40-miles-per-hour speed limit.

## November 4, 1979

**Militant Iranian students seized the US embassy in Tehran.** They took 52 American hostages, including Marine Sergeant Rocky Sickman of Krakow, Missouri. His parents, Virgil and Toni, and his girlfriend, Jill Ditch, would become media celebrities over the next 444 days and a huge yellow ribbon was tied around the McDonnell Planetarium in honor of the hostages. They were released on January 20, 1981, and Rocky arrived home to a tumultuous welcome at Lambert Field eight days later.

## November 5, 1955

**The St. Louis Hawks made their NBA regular season debut.** The Hawks defeated the Minneapolis Lakers 101–89 before a crowd of over 7,000 at Kiel Auditorium. Frank Selvy and Bob Pettit scored 21 points each. Coached by Red Holzman, the Hawks lost the division finals after finishing the regular season in third place in the Western Division with a 33–39 record.

*Courtesy Missouri Historical Society, St. Louis*

## November 5, 1931

**Izear Luster Turner Jr. was born in Clarksdale, Mississippi.** He moved to St. Louis in 1954 and re-formed his band, the Kings of Rhythm. In 1956, Ike met a teenage singer named Anna Mae Bullock at the Club Manhattan in East St. Louis. They were married in 1958, and Ike gave her the stage name Tina. Ike was an abusive drug addict and Tina walked out on him in 1975. But together they scored hits such as "A Fool in Love" and, of course, "Proud Mary." Ike died on December 12, 2007.

## November 6, 1924

**Ellis Wainwright died a recluse at his suite in the Buckingham Hotel.** In 1890, the brewing magnate hired Louis Sullivan to design the 10-story Wainwright Building at Chestnut and Seventh Streets, considered the first skyscraper. When his wife, Charlotte, died suddenly at age 34, he commissioned Sullivan's firm to design the tomb in Bellefontaine Cemetery known as the "Taj Mahal of St. Louis."

*Courtesy Flickr, credit joseph a*

## November 6, 1925

**The new $1,350,000 Union Market on Broadway was dedicated.** It was the first project completed under the $87 million 1922 bond issue. Part of it later became a bus station, and it is now a hotel. Because of the bond issue, downtown St. Louis was undergoing a facelift like never before. The biggest project was the leveling of the saloons and brothels along Market Street to create Memorial Plaza.

## November 7, 1837

**Elijah Lovejoy became a martyr for freedom of the press.** Lovejoy had moved his Presbyterian paper, the *Observer*, from St. Louis to Alton after his antislavery stance made him the target of violence. He continued to speak out, angering the citizens of Alton, who tossed three of his presses into the river. Lovejoy was shot while helping supporters defend a fourth press at the Godfrey and Gilham warehouse. Recovered from the river, part of one press is preserved today at the Alton Telegraph building.

## November 7, 1967

**"White Rabbit" by Jefferson Airplane was broadcast over 94.7 FM, marking the debut of the rock format on KSHE.** The station had signed on in 1961, playing soft music aimed at a female audience, which explains the K-SHE call letters.

## November 8, 1989

**Solána Imani Rowe, the singer known as SZA, was born in St. Louis.** Her debut studio album *Ctrl* was released in 2017; it went triple platinum and garnered four Grammy nominations. Her second album

spent nine straight weeks at number one.

*Courtesy Wikipedia Commons, credit Erin Cazes; The Come Up Show from Canada*

## November 9, 1967

**After seven years of planning and construction, the Poplar Street Bridge opened with little fanfare.** The barricades were removed at noon. Traffic was very light on the first day, but officials said that would change once motorists became accustomed to the maze of on- and off-ramps. The bridge carried US 66 from 1967 to 1977.

*Courtesy Don Korte*

## November 7, 1968

**It was an unbelievable night for Red Berenson of the Blues.** Red scored six goals in one game as the Blues beat the Flyers 8–0 at the Spectrum in Philadelphia. His sixth goal came with 5:56 left in the game, but Berenson stayed on the bench rather than attempt to score again and possibly cost the goaltender a shutout. Darryl Sittler of Toronto is the only player to have equaled Berenson's feat since, and no other player has scored six in a road game. Berenson also picked up an assist that night on a goal by Camille Henry.

*Courtesy Getty Images*

*Courtesy Barbara Northcott*

## November 8, 2008

**The takeover of Anheuser-Busch by Belgian brewer InBev took effect.** The $52 billion deal created the world's largest brewery. InBev promised to keep the St. Louis base as the company's North American headquarters, but the takeover ended 150 years of family rule at Anheuser-Busch. The brewery employs about 3,300 workers in St. Louis today, down from about 5,200 at the end of 2007.

## November 9, 1935

**Robert Gibson was born in Omaha, Nebraska.** He overcame childhood health problems to become a star basketball player for Creighton and for the Harlem Globetrotters. The Cardinals signed him in 1957. Gibson would become the greatest pitcher in Redbird history. In 1968, he won the National League Cy Young and Most Valuable Player honors with an ERA of 1.12. The Major Leagues decided to lower the pitcher's mound starting the following season to help out the hitters.

*Courtesy Wikipedia*

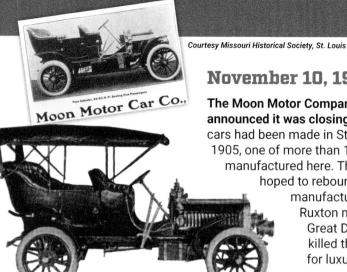

*Courtesy Missouri Historical Society, St. Louis*

## November 10, 1930

**The Moon Motor Company of St. Louis announced it was closing its doors.** Moon cars had been made in St. Louis since 1905, one of more than 100 makes once manufactured here. The company had hoped to rebound by agreeing to manufacture the luxury Ruxton model, but the Great Depression killed the demand for luxury cars.

*Courtesy Wikipedia*

## November 11, 1926

**The numbering for the proposed federal highway system was officially adopted, making today the birthday of Route 66, Route 40, and all the other US routes.** At the time, Route 66 crossed the McKinley Bridge to Salisbury, Natural Bridge, Grand, Delmar, Sarah, Lindell, Skinker, and McCausland to Manchester.

## November 12, 1995

**The Trans World Dome made its debut.** A crowd of 65,598 watched as the Rams beat the Carolina Panthers 28–17. Some painting and electrical work remained to be done on the $280 million facility. Fans said the sound system needed some work, too.

*Courtesy Wikipedia*

## November 10, 1910

**The McKinley Bridge officially opened.** The bridge is not named for President William McKinley but for Congressman William McKinley, then president of the Illinois Traction Company, later the Illinois Terminal System. His firm built the bridge to carry its interurban trains. The bridge carried US 66 traffic from 1926 until 1932 and Optional 66 until 1938. The bridge fell into disrepair and was closed in 2001, reopening in 2007 after renovation.

## November 10, 2005

**Chris Carpenter became only the second Cardinal to win the National League Cy Young Award.** Carp had gone 21–5 with a 2.83 ERA. Two years earlier, Carpenter had been ready to give up on baseball. Bob Gibson was the only other Cardinal to win the award, and he won it twice.

*Courtesy Wikipedia*

## November 11, 1918

**Factory whistles here blew at 2:30 a.m. upon the news from Europe that World War I was over.** The streets were filled with people celebrating. Mayor Henry Kiel declared it a public holiday. Most business had been suspended, and schools were closed anyway in an effort to halt the deadly flu epidemic. A total of 1,057 St. Louisans died in World War I.

## November 12, 1947

**The city of Crestwood was formally incorporated by a county court.** The residents of the Crestwood subdivision sought incorporation to avoid annexation by the adjacent town of Oakland. The name came from an old white oak tree on Diversey Drive.

# NOVEMBER

### November 13, 1967

**Dwight D. Eisenhower became the only president or ex-president to ride to the top of the Arch.** Eisenhower authorized construction of the memorial on May 17, 1954. The Secret Service has never allowed a sitting president to ride to the top, because of security concerns over the limited space.

### November 14, 1836

**William Carr Lane announced he was building an "addition" (what we would call a "subdivision" today).** He named the streets in his addition after his sons and daughters, which is why we have thoroughfares named for Sidney, Victor, and Ann today. Lane was the first mayor of St. Louis and was reelected seven times.

### November 15, 1877

**A measure was introduced in the city council to tear down city-owned Lucas Market and make 12th Street a grand boulevard between Market and Washington.** That's why the street is so wide today. Opponents denounced the plan as a disaster for merchants who owned stalls in the market.

### November 15, 1932

**Robert Brookings died at the age of 82.** He rose from a shipping clerk at the Cupples Woodware plant to dominate the shipping industry. The designer of the track system at the Cupples Complex gave his own money and raised more to help Washington University obtain its new site across from Forest Park. He also gave money for construction of an administration building (now Brookings Hall) to be used for the 1904 World's Fair.

*Courtesy Missouri Historical Society, St. Louis*

### November 13, 1997

**After 93 years, the old highway bridge at St. Charles was history.** Explosive charges sent the fourth and final span of the bridge crashing into the Missouri River. The bridge closed on December 17, 1992, a day after the Discovery Bridge carrying Route 370 opened.

*Courtesy Wikipedia*

*Courtesy Don Korte*

### November 14, 1936

**The Jewel Box in Forest Park was dedicated.** William Becker, an engineer for the St. Louis Board of Public Service, came up with the radical Art Deco design featuring cantilevered 50-foot-tall vertical glass walls. The *Post-Dispatch* said the Jewel Box was the "latest word in display greenhouses." On December 11, 2002, the Jewel Box reopened after a $3.5 million, 11-month restoration.

### November 15, 1953

**Construction began on what was billed as the "first automobile-age shopping center in the area."** Northland shopping center was built on what were then the fringes of suburbia, at Lucas and Hunt and West Florissant. Northland faded quickly after Famous-Barr moved out in 1994. In 2005 it was demolished for the $50 million Buzz Westfall Plaza on the Boulevard, at that time with Target and a Schnuck's as major tenants.

*Courtesy Missouri Historical Society, St. Louis*

*Courtesy State Historical Society of Missouri*

## November 16, 1795

**Antoine Pierre Soulard married Julia Cérre, the daughter of St. Louis merchant Gabriel Cérre.** Cérre gave his son-in-law 64 acres of land south of the city. The land was the subject of a legal battle after the Louisiana Purchase, and Julia finally won the title in 1836, 11 years after her husband's death. The city annexed the Soulard farm in 1841. When Julia died in 1845, her will left two acres to the city, on the condition that the land would be used for a market.

## November 17, 1965

**St. Louisans heard their first airborne radio traffic report.** Police Captain Don Miller reported from the KSD traffic copter. Robert Hyland wooed Miller over to KMOX in 1972. Miller had served in the marines, was wounded during World War II, and earned a second Purple Heart in Korea. He retired from KMOX in 1992 and died on December 21, 2009 at age 84.

*Courtesy St. Louis Media History Foundation Archive*

## November 18, 1852

**Today is the feast day of St. Rose Philippine Duchesne.** Mother Duchesne died at the convent she founded at St. Charles on this date in 1852. She came here with four other nuns in 1818 to establish a seminary and school for girls, the first in the United States founded by the Society of the Sacred Heart. The brick convent school building, erected in 1835, still stands today. The pioneer educator was canonized in 1988.

*Courtesy Wikipedia*

### November 16, 1818

**This is the birthday of Saint Louis University.** Bishop William DuBourg founded the forerunner of SLU, St. Louis Academy, in a private home. Tuition was free. The college failed in 1827 but was revived as St. Louis College under Jesuit administration in 1829. Father Peter Verhaegen served as the first Jesuit president. The school received its charter from the state in 1832, making SLU the oldest university west of the Mississippi.

### November 17, 1791

**John O'Fallon was born in Louisville.** O'Fallon made a fortune as a merchant, banker, and president of two railroads. He gave much of his money away and donated huge tracts of land to the city, Saint Louis University, and Washington University. His estate was acquired by the city and is now O'Fallon Park. Two railroad towns were named for him: O'Fallon, Missouri, and O'Fallon, Illinois.

### November 17, 1796

**Joseph Chartrand of St. Charles received a land grant to operate a Missouri River ferry.** It was to be bordered by "a passage for inhabitants crossing into St. Charles," which developed into the St. Charles Road. It was rocked in 1865 and has been known as the St. Charles Rock Road ever since, even though it has been a paved highway since 1921.

### November 18, 1949

**Vice President Alben Barkley married a St. Louis widow, the former Mrs. Carlton Hadley, at St. John's Methodist Church.** The vice president's many trips to St. Louis had made headlines before the engagement was announced in October. The wedding marked the first time a vice president had married while in office. Barkley was the first to refer to his office as "Veep."

# NOVEMBER

### November 19, 1976

**Jack Dorsey was born in St. Louis.** The computer programmer and businessman cofounded Twitter in 2006. The graduate of Bishop DuBourg served as CEO, chairman of the board, and executive chairman of Twitter. He also launched the successful online payment platform Square in 2010. In 2015, Dorsey returned to Twitter. He first served as an interim CEO and then became its CEO. Twitter was sold to Elon Musk in October 2022.

### November 20, 1967

**Lynn Patrick resigned as coach of the Blues.** His assistant, Scotty Bowman, was named the new coach. Bowman would lead the Blues to the Stanley Cup finals in their first three seasons.

### November 20, 2005

**Rusty Wallace of St. Louis ended his 22-year NASCAR career with a 13th-place finish in the Ford 400 at Homestead-Miami.** When Wallace retired, he had 55 NASCAR Cup wins under his belt, which tied him for eighth place on the NASCAR's all-time win list. He also established an all-time record for short-track wins with a total of 34.

*Wikimedia commons/James Phelps*

### November 21, 1795

**William Beaumont was born in Connecticut.** Doctor Beaumont was the post surgeon at Fort Mackinac in Michigan when he treated trapper Alexis St. Martin for a gunshot wound in the chest. The wound healed in such a way that it left a hole through which Beaumont studied the digestive system. Beaumont became a renowned frontier doctor in St. Louis. Beaumont Street and Beaumont High School are named in his honor.

*Courtesy Getty Images*

### November 19, 2018

**The Blues fired coach Mike Yeo and replaced him with Craig Berube.** (At the time, Berube was given the title interim coach.) The Blues had struggled to a 7–8–3 record through 18 games, last place in the Central Division. Yeo, who took over for Ken Hitchcock behind the Blues bench in 2017, had a 73–48–11 record over parts of three seasons here. Berube would lead the Blues to their first Stanley Cup. He was fired on December 12, 2023.

### November 20, 1855

**Kate Brewington Bennett died suddenly at the age of 37.** She was the toast of society and considered the most beautiful woman in St. Louis. Other women envied her lily-white complexion. It turned out she had been taking small doses of arsenic in order to keep her pale complexion, not knowing arsenic is a poison that accumulates in the bloodstream. She is buried in Bellefontaine Cemetery.

*Courtesy author*

*Courtesy Wikipedia*

### November 21, 1920

**Stanley Frank Musial was born in Donora, Pennsylvania.** Musial consistently teed off on Dodger pitching, and fans at Ebbets Field were heard to murmur "Here comes the man again" as he came to bat. Writer Bob Broeg was soon referring to him as "Stan the Man." Musial played for the Cardinals for a record 22 years. After he retired in 1963, he served as GM and senior vice president of the team and became the team's number one ambassador.

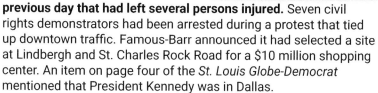

## November 22, 1963

**The big news that rainy and chilly morning was a train collision in North St. Louis the previous day that had left several persons injured.** Seven civil rights demonstrators had been arrested during a protest that tied up downtown traffic. Famous-Barr announced it had selected a site at Lindbergh and St. Charles Rock Road for a $10 million shopping center. An item on page four of the *St. Louis Globe-Democrat* mentioned that President Kennedy was in Dallas.

On KMOX, Rex Davis was conducting an interview about a mass polio immunization set for that weekend when newsman John Sabin rushed in with the bulletin from Dallas. A banner proclaiming "Beat Kennedy" was taken down from the lobby of the Sheraton-Jefferson Hotel, where a GOP leadership conference was underway. Southwestern Bell reported call volume was two times the normal level. Phyllis Diller cancelled her performance at Gaslight Square.

## November 23, 1958

**Red Bird Lanes at Gravois and Hampton opened.** Joe Garagiola, Stan Musial, and J. "Biggie" Garagnani were among the partners in the 32-lane facility along with Tom Carbone, Sam Caputa, and Carl Scioto. The last 24-hour bowling alley in St. Louis closed on May 7, 1996, and it was demolished for a Walgreens. Joe Garagiola filed a lawsuit against Musial over the business in 1986. It was settled out of court, but Musial never forgave him.

*Courtesy Lauren Garrick*

## November 24, 1868

**According to several sources, Scott Joplin was born in Linden, Texas.** (Others put the date sometime between June 1867 and January 1868.) He began his musical career in Sedalia but wrote some of his best-known

*Courtesy Wikipedia, credit Kevin Saff*

compositions, including "The Entertainer," while living at 265B Morgan, now Delmar. Joplin moved to New York City in 1911 and composed the opera *Treemonisha*, often cited as the first opera by an African American, though it was not produced during his lifetime. The first production was in 1972.

## November 22, 1729

**Pierre Laclède Liguest was born in Bedous, near the French Pyrenees.** He would come to New Orleans and form a company to trade with the "savages" of the Mississippi. In 1763, he led an expedition upriver to choose a site for a trading post, and the following year he sent young Auguste Chouteau to oversee construction on the site that would become the city of St. Louis.

## November 23, 1925

**The St. Louis Theater opened.** Opening night included "Drusilla with a Million" and "Orpheum vaudeville acts headlined by the famous Singer's Midgets." The last movie shown in the old theater was *The Sound of Music* in 1966. After a $2 million renovation, it reopened in 1968 as the new home of the St. Louis Symphony. It was named after Walter S. Powell, a businessman whose widow donated $1 million toward the purchase.

"Drusilla with a Million"
*Courtesy Wikipedia*

## November 24, 2014

**Violence erupted following the announcement that police officer Darren Wilson would not be indicted in the shooting death of robbery suspect Michael Brown.** More than 25 businesses burned or were badly damaged in Ferguson, Dellwood, and St. Louis. Protestors blocked off I-44 downtown for 30 minutes. Governor Jay Nixon faced fierce criticism for waiting to send in the National Guard even though he had been pressured to demilitarize the response.

## November 25, 1820

**Governor Alexander McNair signed a bill making St. Charles the capital of Missouri upon admission to the union.** On June 4, 1821, legislators met for the first time on the second floor of adjoining buildings at 206 Main. (Charles and Ruluff Peck ran a dry-goods store on the first floor of one of the buildings and Chauncy Shepard ran a carpentry shop on the first floor of the other.) Jefferson City became the capital in 1826.

## November 26, 1828

**The Sisters of Charity of St. Vincent DePaul opened the first hospital west of the Mississippi.** Bishop Rosati had asked the sisters to come here, and John Mullanphy donated a tract of land at Fourth and Spruce for the three-room log cabin. The hospital moved several times and has been known by several names. Today, DePaul Hospital stands in Bridgeton.

## November 26, 1908

**St. Francis de Sales Church at Gravois and Ohio was dedicated.** The imposing "Cathedral of the South Side," with its 300-foot-tall steeple, is the sixth-tallest church in the nation. It was modeled after St. Paul's in Berlin and the Cathedral in Frankfurt. The church was dedicated in November 1908 and served a parish until 2005. It is now the St. Francis de Sales Oratory where Catholics celebrate the traditional Latin mass.

## November 27, 1979

**The new Interstate 70 bridge at St. Charles opened to traffic.** The first Interstate 70 bridge had opened in 1958 and was immediately overloaded. When the second bridge to carry the eastbound lanes was completed, both were named for Louis Blanchette, who first established the trading post that became St. Charles.

## November 25, 1987

**The movie *Planes, Trains and Automobiles*, starring John Candy and Steve Martin, premiered.** Much of the film was shot in and around Lambert Field. In one scene, the two characters are supposedly driving from Jefferson City to St. Louis, but the shot shows them crossing into St. Louis from Illinois.

## November 26, 1939

**Anna Mae Bullock was born in Brownsville, Tennessee.** She grew up in nearby Nutbush and then moved to St. Louis in 1955, attending Sumner High School. She met Ike Turner at the Club Manhattan in East St. Louis when Ike's group the Kings of Rhythm were mainstays on the area R & B scene. When a session singer failed to show, Bullock stepped in to handle vocals on "A Fool in Love." Released in 1960, it would be the first hit for Ike & Tina Turner. Tina was inducted into the Rock & Roll Hall of Fame in 1991. She died on May 24, 2023.

## November 27, 1985

**Vince Coleman of the Cardinals became only the fourth player in Major League history to be unanimously elected as Rookie of the Year.** (The others were Frank Robinson, Orlando Cepeda, and Willie McCovey.)

*Courtesy Missouri Historical Society, St. Louis*

## November 28, 1939

**"Black Tuesday" changed St. Louis forever.** A cloud of black smoke covered downtown. The streetlights were on at noon, traffic was snarled, and visibility was near zero. Mayor Dickmann's secretary, Raymond Tucker, fought coal interests to put together a coalition of businesses and city leaders to tackle the problem. A tough anti-smoke ordinance was passed in 1940. Tucker earned a reputation for tackling the city's problems head-on and would be elected mayor in 1953.

## November 29, 1967

**Two Blues legends came to the club in a trade with the New York Rangers.** The Blues picked up Barclay Plager and Red Berenson for Ron Atwell and Ron Stewart.

Red Berenson
*Courtesy Getty Images*

## November 30, 1835

**Samuel Langhorne Clemens was born in Florida, Missouri.** His father moved the family to Hannibal in 1839. Clemens came to St. Louis in 1853 to work as a typesetter. Horace Bixby hired him as an apprentice steamboat pilot, and Clemens received his pilot license in 1859. It was while working on the river that he picked up a term used to measure the water's depth, "Mark Twain." His last visit to St. Louis was in 1902, when he dedicated a tablet at the Eugene Field home.

*Courtesy Wikipedia*

### November 28, 1945

**Dwight Davis died at his home in Washington.** Davis was a former St. Louisan who served as secretary of war under Calvin Coolidge and governor general of the Philippines under Herbert Hoover. As St. Louis parks director, he donated his salary to ensure the success of the public tennis courts at Forest Park. He donated the Davis Cup for a match between the US and Britain in 1901.

### November 28, 1964

**The Big Red used the 12th pick in the NFL draft to select quarterback Joe Namath of Alabama.** But the Cardinals lost a bidding war to the New York Jets of the AFL. Namath signed a three-year deal for an unheard of $427,000. St. Louis fans complained that the Bidwill family, which owned the Big Red, was cheap.

### November 29, 1808

**Robert A. Barnes was born in Washington, DC.** The St. Louis merchant died on April 2, 1892. He left his estate to establish a Methodist hospital to care for all patients, regardless of race. The executors of his will shrewdly invested the money and waited until his $940,000 estate had grown to $2 million. Barnes Hospital opened on December 7, 1914, with 26 patients.

### November 30, 1927

**Robert Guillaume was born Robert Williams in St. Louis.** He stole the show in the comedy series *Soap* in the 1970s in his role as the butler, Benson. He was rewarded with a best supporting actor in a comedy Emmy in 1979 and his own spin-off series, *Benson*. He won the best actor in a comedy series Emmy in 1985. He also appeared in the ABC series *Sports Night*, returning to the show following a stroke in 1999.

*Courtesy Wikipedia*

## December 1, 1936

**The three villages of McKnight, Deer Creek, and Ladue joined together to form the City of Ladue.** The road had come first, running to the land owned by Revolutionary War veteran Peter Albert LaDue. Other family names in the area included Conway, McCutcheon, McKnight, Litzsinger, Spoede, Warson, Lay, and Price.

## December 1, 1958

**"Phil the Gorilla," one of the largest gorillas on record and a beloved resident of the Saint Louis Zoo since 1941, died of ulcerative colitis.** Phil weighed 776 pounds. Schwarz Studios did the taxidermy, and the mounted figure of Phil was on display for many years. He is now in the Educational Outpost.

## December 2, 1823

**Erastus Wells was born in New York.** Orphaned at 14, he arrived in St. Louis with just $140 to his name. He became a congressman and leader in Western settlement, but he is best remembered as the founder of the St. Louis streetcar system. He also founded the narrow-gauge railroad between St. Louis and Florissant, which ran past his country estate, Wellston.

## December 2, 1913

**Mayor Henry Kiel signed an ordinance setting aside 77 acres in Forest Park for a zoo.** Park Commissioner Dwight Davis objected, because park employees would have to cut the grass. Kiel told Davis that "What the people want is a lot of elephants, lions, tigers, and monkeys and they don't care how the grass is cut." A modest collection of animals had been housed at Forest Park since 1891.

*Courtesy Missouri Historical Society, St. Louis*

## December 1, 1904

**The greatest period in St. Louis history came to an end, as the World's Fair closed.** A crowd of 100,000 watched as David Francis, president of the exposition, said, "Farewell to all thy splendor," and threw the switch. The band played "Auld Lang Syne" as the lights went down and the grounds fell silent. More than 20 million people had come to the fair.

The lasting appeal of the fair is probably due in part to the fact that it was temporary, for the most part a dream city constructed just for a bright and special year. The birdcage and the art museum remain, and the Grand Basin can still be seen. But the giant palaces were reduced to scrap lumber and dust, and the great Observation Wheel was destroyed.

*Courtesy Missouri State Archives*

## December 2, 1966

**The Board of Aldermen renamed the bridge under construction at the foot of Poplar Street in honor of Bernard Dickmann.** As mayor of St. Louis from 1933 until 1941, Dickmann fought to secure funds for the Jefferson Expansion Memorial and battled to clean up the smoke-filled air. The media and the public preferred to call it the Poplar Street Bridge, and in October 2013, the bridge was officially renamed for another politician, but that name also failed to catch on with the public.

*Courtesy Wikipedia*

## December 3, 1990

**Schools in four states were closed, people stocked up on supplies, and emergency-response personnel stood on alert.** It was all because of Doctor Iben Browning. Based on some dubious theories about the tides and the pull of the moon, the New Mexico climatologist and business consultant predicted a major earthquake along the New Madrid Fault on this date. Browning died shortly after the hysteria.

## December 4, 1948

**Gus and Edith Belt opened the first Steak 'n Shake in St. Louis at 6622 Chippewa.** Gus had owned a struggling Shell station and restaurant in Normal, Illinois. In 1934, he turned it into the White House Steak and Shake and adopted the slogan "In Sight It Must Be Right," because the meat was ground in front of the customers. The St. Louis location was the 26th in the chain.

*Courtesy Missouri Historical Society, St. Louis*

*Courtesy Wikipedia*

## December 5, 2000

**The *Admiral* was moved from its berth near the Eads Bridge, its home for 60 years.** The owners of the President Casino on the *Admiral* said the move north to Laclede's Landing would increase revenue and provide protection from wayward barges. More than 70 gamblers had been injured when a runaway barge struck the casino in 1998.

### December 3, 1818

**President Monroe signed the congressional resolution making Illinois the 21st state of the Union.** At the time, the capital was located at Kaskaskia; it was moved to Vandalia two years later and moved to Springfield in 1837. Shadrach Bond served as the first governor. Bond County was named in his honor.

*Courtesy Wikipedia*

### December 3, 1967

**The riverboat restaurant *River Queen* suddenly sank on the riverfront.** No one was injured, but officials were mystified as to the cause. The *River Queen* was one of the last "Texas-deck" stern-wheelers left on the river. The boat was once known as the *Gordon C. Greene* and appeared in *Gone with the Wind*. John Groffel of St. Louis and Arthur Krato of Hannibal brought her to St. Louis in 1964.

### December 4, 1904

**Frank "Buster" Wortman was born in St. Louis.** He led the Capone Gang interests in St. Louis and Southern Illinois. During the 1940s and '50s, Wortman and his associates controlled the nightclubs, taverns, and gambling, along with a racing news service and a trucking line. He lived in a home near Collinsville that was surrounded by a moat.

### December 5, 1871

**The most successful madam in St. Louis died at the age of 51.** Eliza Haycraft owned five brothels when the Civil War ended and was known for offering financial aid and help to the poor of the city. She left an estate of $250,000, and more than 5,000 people attended her funeral. But her grave site in Bellefontaine Cemetery is unmarked.

# DECEMBER

## December 6, 1875

**Albert Bond Lambert was born. In 1881, his father founded Lambert Pharmaceuticals, producers of Listerine.** The young millionaire took his first airplane ride with Orville Wright and was the first person in St. Louis to receive a pilot's license. Beginning in 1920, Major Lambert developed the flying field at his own expense and sold it to the city at cost to promote St. Louis as an aviation center.

## December 7, 1947

**Garry Unger was born in Calgary.** In nine seasons with the Blues, the golden-haired Number Seven set several team records that still stand. He played 662 games with the Blues, part of an "Iron Man" streak of 914 consecutive games. That streak still ranks fourth all-time in the NHL.

## December 8, 1939

Courtesy Wikimedia Commons

**Red Berenson was born in Regina, Saskatchewan.** The Blues star scored six goals in one game against the Philadelphia Flyers on November 7, 1968. The "Red Baron" played in six NHL All-Star games. He was traded to Detroit in 1972 but later rejoined the Blues and coached the team from December 1979 to March of 1982.

## December 8, 1941

**Nervous guards at Jefferson Barracks opened fire on a milk truck that failed to obey a command to halt at four in the morning.** No one was hurt. Police rounded up 22 Germans and one Italian alien deemed "dangerous to the welfare of the city." Over 600 men swarmed the army, navy, marine corps, and coast guard recruiting stations in the Federal Building.

## December 6, 1900

**Agnes Moorehead was born in Clinton, Massachusetts.** She moved to St. Louis as a child, spent four seasons as a dancer at the Muny Opera, and made her debut as a singer on KMOX. Her first big-screen role was in *Citizen Kane*, and she went on to appear in more than 60 films. She is best remembered as Endora on *Bewitched* from 1964 to 1972. Moorehead was one of several stars of *The Conqueror* who died of cancer. The movie was filmed near St. George, Utah, downwind from the Nevada nuclear test site.

Courtesy Wikipedia

## December 7, 1941

Courtesy Wikipedia

**Missouri Governor Phil Donnelly and St. Louis Mayor Dee Becker wasted no time in reacting to the news from Hawaii.** More than 65,000 soldiers on leave from Fort Leonard Wood, Scott Field, and Jefferson Barracks were told to report for duty immediately. Detachments from Jefferson Barracks rushed to guard the bridges and the 12 largest private industrial plants. Mayor Becker said the city would immediately begin to set up agencies to accelerate production, promote civil defense, and prevent sabotage. There were about 140 St. Louisans at Pearl Harbor. Most were members of a naval reserve unit called to active duty in 1940. They served mostly on the destroyers *Schley*, *Allen*, and *Chew*, all World War I–vintage four-stackers. Twelve St. Louisans died aboard the battleship *Arizona*.

## December 8, 2005

**At 12:24 a.m., a wrecking ball brought down the final section of Busch Stadium II downtown.** A handful of fans braved the freezing temperatures to watch the end of the demolition, which was marked by a brief fireworks display.

Courtesy Wikipedia

## December 9, 1922

**John Elroy Sanford was born in St. Louis.** He dropped out of school at age 13 to break into show business and became known as "Redd" because of his complexion. He also took the name of baseball player Jimmy Foxx. The groundbreaking comedian made his movie debut in *Cotton Comes to Harlem* in 1972. That same year, Norman Lear signed him to star in the American version of the British show, *Steptoe and Son*. *Sanford and Son* ran on NBC from 1972 to 1977.

*Courtesy Wikipedia*

*Courtesy Missouri Historical Society, St. Louis*

## December 10, 1904

**Washington University officials explained their opposition to making "the Pike" on the World's Fair grounds a permanent amusement park.** In the *St. Louis Globe-Democrat*, they expressed the hope that the city might one day see the area north of Forest Park "filled with the homes of multimillionaires" and an atmosphere of "solitude and gentility."

## December 11, 1944

*Life* **magazine featured** *Meet Me in St. Louis* **as its movie of the week.** The film was based on Sally Benson's autobiographical stories in the *New Yorker*. *Life* said, "This simple story gives Judy Garland an opportunity to sing the current hit, 'The Trolley Song,' and two numbers resurrected from the past, 'Meet Me in St. Louis' and 'Under the Bamboo Tree.' Margaret O'Brien it gives a chance to enact with naturalness and enchantment the experience of childhood in a friendly city."

*Courtesy Wikipedia*

## December 9, 1822

**The Missouri Legislature granted St. Louis a town charter, incorporating the town government with a mayor and a board of aldermen.** At the time, the population was about 1,200. The charter expanded the boundaries of the town to Seventh Street on the west, Ashley and Biddle on the north, and Convent Street on the south.

## December 9, 1852

**The first passenger train ever to run west of the Mississippi traveled over the five miles of completed track on the Pacific Railroad.** A trial run with cars hauling rail ties and iron had been made a few days earlier. The line began at 14th and Chouteau and ended at the community of Sulphur Springs at today's Manchester and Hampton. The rails reached Kirkwood in May 1853 and Jefferson City in 1855.

## December 10, 1873

**Construction superintendent Theodore Cooper became the first person to cross the Eads Bridge.** In a hurry to cross, he had workmen throw narrow planks across the two remaining gaps, one 12 feet wide and the other 24 feet across. As the stunned workmen watched, he nonchalantly crossed, 90 feet above the river.

*Courtesy State Historical Society of Missouri*

## December 11, 1862

**William Marion Reedy was born in St. Louis.** For nearly 25 years he was one of the leading figures of American literature. Through his *Reedy's Mirror* publication, he discovered or was instrumental in bringing to the public such writers as Zoe Akins, Sara Teasdale, and Carl Sandburg.

# DECEMBER

## December 12, 1944

**A crowd jammed the Old Courthouse rotunda to honor Black aviator Wendell Pruitt of St. Louis.** Pruitt won the Distinguished Flying Cross for shooting down three German planes, destroying 70 on the ground and helping sink an enemy destroyer. Four months later he was killed while training pilots for the "Tuskegee Airmen." In 1955, the city would name its gleaming new public housing project after Pruitt.

## December 12, 2001

**After 107 years, Ralston Purina was no longer an independent company.** Nestlé SA completed its acquisition of the St. Louis–based pet-food maker in an $11.2 billion deal. Nestlé Purina PetCare Company would keep its headquarters in St. Louis, where Ralston employed about 2,000 people at the time.

## December 13, 1987

**The football Cardinals played their last game at Busch Stadium.** They beat the Giants 27–24 before 29,623 die-hard fans. Vai Sikahema's 76-yard punt return for a touchdown highlighted the game.

## December 14, 1979

**More than 18,000 fans came to the Arena for the home debut of the new Major Indoor Soccer League team, the St. Louis Steamers.** By 1982, the Steamers were averaging more than 17,000 fans per home game. But it was all over by 1988.

*Courtesy Missouri Historical Museum, St. Louis*

## December 14, 1992

**Blues superstar Brett Hull fired a symbolic puck into a net.** The goal began demolition work on the old Kiel Auditorium to make room for the new Kiel Center.

## December 12, 1878

**The first issue of the *St. Louis Post and Dispatch* hit the streets, just days after Joseph Pulitzer bought the bankrupt *Dispatch* at an auction.** The four-page first issue had a press run of 4,020 and was distributed by wheelbarrow. The name was shortened to the *Post-Dispatch* on March 10, 1879.

POST-DISPATCH BUILDING.
515 & 517 Market St., St. Louis.

*Courtesy Missouri Historical Society, St. Louis*

*Courtesy Landmarks Association of St. Louis Collection*

## December 13, 1926

**The oldest major auto manufacturer in St. Louis announced it was closing.** Officials with the Dorris Motor Car Company said they could no longer compete with the financial giants dominating the auto industry. The plant, which was located at 4100 Laclede, was renovated in the 1980s and turned into loft condominiums.

## December 14, 1939

**The first modern shopping center in St. Louis opened.** Hampton Village at Chippewa (US 66) and Hampton Avenue was developed by Harold Brinkop, who foresaw the changes the automobile would bring. Bettendorf's opened a supermarket at

*Courtesy Missouri Historical Society, St. Louis*

the Colonial-style development in 1940, and in 1946, Brinkop added Colonial-style buildings on the west side of Hampton Avenue. The buildings on the west side were torn down in 1962 for construction of a discount store.

## December 15, 1919

**The City of Brentwood was incorporated in a hurried attempt to avoid being annexed by Maplewood.** The incorporation papers were filed about 24 hours before the election on the proposed annexation. The community was originally known as Maddenville.

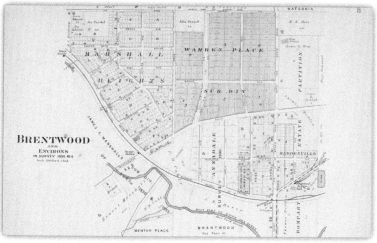

*Courtesy Missouri Historical Society, St. Louis*

## December 16, 1811

**The great New Madrid earthquake rocked nearly half of the continent.** The Mississippi flowed backward, islands appeared and disappeared, and Reelfoot Lake was formed by a change in the river's course. The quake was clearly felt in St. Louis and rang church bells as far away as Philadelphia, but there were few deaths because the area was sparsely populated. Hundreds of aftershocks rattled the area all winter long, and another massive quake struck in February.

*Courtesy Missouri Historical Society, St. Louis*

## December 17, 1992

**It was a great day for commuters.** The new Discovery Bridge carrying Highway 370 across the Missouri north of St. Charles was opened. It replaced the old 115 bridge, built in 1903. Almost immediately, the daily backups headed for the Blanchette Bridge on Interstate 70 began to ease.

*Courtesy Wikipedia, credit Americasroof*

## December 15, 1961

**The Missouri Pacific Railroad ended service on the last commuter line out of Union Station.** At one time, Missouri Pacific had 16 trains daily between St. Louis and Pacific. At the line's peak, as many as 20,000 people rode the commuter trains daily.

*Courtesy Wikipedia*

## December 15, 1996

**Boeing announced a buyout of its archrival, St. Louis–based McDonnell Douglas.** The deal created the world's largest aerospace company. Boeing CEO Phil Condit and McDonnell Douglas President and CEO Harry Stonecipher said the merger represented more job security at the largest employer in the St. Louis area.

## December 16, 1941

**The first cartridges began rolling off the line at the St. Louis Ordnance Plant on Goodfellow.** By 1943, there were almost 35,000 people working in 300 buildings at the 276-acre complex. The plant made 6.7 billion cartridges during World War II and also produced ordnance during the Korean and Vietnam conflicts. The forge building demolished in 2007 is remembered for its clamshell-type roof, designed to draw the heat upward and out.

## December 17, 1979

**The *Admiral* left for a New Orleans dry dock for repairs to its hull.** The repairs were expected to take just a few weeks, but it turned out that the *Admiral* had made her last cruise. Streckfus Steamers would sell her to Pittsburgh businessman John Connelly for $600,000. Connelly made repairs, stripped her of her engines, and sold the *Admiral* to a group of St. Louis investors for a profit. In 1987, the *Admiral* would reopen as an entertainment venue that failed spectacularly. It was a casino from 1994 to 2010 before the ship was scrapped in 2011.

## December 17, 2015

**The Rams played their last home game in St. Louis.** That night they beat the Tampa Bay Buccaneers 31–23 on *Thursday Night Football* at what was then known as the Edward Jones Dome. About 40,000 fans were on hand, many chanting angrily at owner Stan Kroenke. The Rams would finish the season 7–9.

## December 18, 1936

**The Eugene Field home at 634 South Broadway opened as a children's museum.** The home was once part of a line of 12 adjoining homes known as Walsh's Row. It was barely saved from the wrecking ball by two St. Louis businessmen.

*Courtesy Missouri Historical Society, St. Louis*

## December 19, 1972

**Interstate 44 was opened to traffic between Interstate 55 and Laclede Station Road, becoming a four-lane highway across Missouri.** Route 66 was now mostly obsolete, although the last section (in Pulaski County) was not bypassed until 1981. Officials were predicting a bottleneck at I-55 because only one exit was complete.

## December 20, 1904

**The first recorded auto theft in St. Louis took place.** H. M. Noel, of 3654 Delmar, left his 1904 Oldsmobile running as he visited a friend at 3635 Washington Avenue. Police were uncertain just where to look for the machine bearing license number 49.

## December 18, 1916

**Ruth Elizabeth Grable was born in St. Louis.** Her mother was determined to get her daughter into show business and brought her to Hollywood in 1929. At 13, Betty lied about her age and appeared in a blackface chorus line in *Let's Go Places*. She went on to appear in more than 40 films and became the most popular of all the pinup girls during World War II. In 1943, Lloyd's of London insured her legs for $1 million.

*Courtesy Wikipedia*

## December 19, 1973

**The smallest crowd ever to see a Blues game at the Arena braved a foot of snow to watch the Blues beat the Los Angeles Kings, 3–1.** The 4,1115 fans who made it in were allowed to sit in the empty seats, and concessions were on the house. The snowstorm was the worst in St. Louis since 1890. The Blues had asked the NHL for permission to cancel the game, but the request was denied.

*Courtesy State Historical Society of Missouri*

*Courtesy Missouri Historical Society, St. Louis*

## December 20, 1901

**Formal groundbreaking ceremonies were held for the World's Fair.** There were five inches of snow on the ground, and the bitter cold forced the postponement of the huge parade planned to mark the occasion. A bonfire was kept burning to thaw the ground.

*Courtesy Missouri Historical Society, St. Louis*

## December 21, 1949

**Creve Coeur was incorporated.** The name means "broken heart" or "cleft heart" in French. Legend says an Indigenous girl named Me-Me-Ton-Wish was heartbroken over her unrequited love for a French-Canadian trapper and jumped from the bluffs. It actually probably refers to the shape of what is now Creve Coeur Lake. When the area was settled it was actually two lakes, resembling a broken heart.

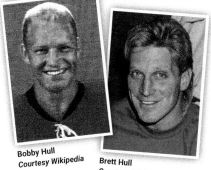

Bobby Hull
*Courtesy Wikipedia*

Brett Hull
*Courtesy Wikipedia, credit Johnmaxmena2*

## December 22, 1996

**Brett Hull became the 24th player in NHL history to score 500 goals, notching a hat trick in a game here against the Los Angeles Kings.** Brett and his father, Bobby, became the first father and son to join the 500-goal club.

## December 23, 1867

**Sarah Breedlove was born on a plantation in Louisiana.** She moved to St. Louis in 1887 and worked as a washerwoman. A scalp ailment caused her to lose much of her hair, and she sold Annie Malone's hair-care products before developing her own line in 1906. She moved to Denver, married, and changed her name to Madam C. J. Walker. Madam Walker became one of the first female African American millionaires and a great philanthropist.

## December 21, 1934

**The film *Zouzou* premiered in Paris.** It featured Josephine Baker of St. Louis, the first African American woman to play the leading role in a major motion picture. Baker went on to work for the French Resistance during World War II and became a civil rights leader in the US. On November 30, 2021, she was inducted into the Pantheon mausoleum in Paris, France's highest honor.

## December 22, 1944

**Steven Norman Carlton was born in Miami.** "Lefty" came up with the Cardinals in 1965. He was a key part of the 1967 and 1968 pennant winners and posted a 2.17 ERA in 1969. But Gussie Busch ordered him traded to Philadelphia following a contract dispute in 1971. The Cardinals picked up Rick Wise, and Carlton went on win four Cy Young Awards. He was elected to the Hall of Fame in 1996.

## December 23, 1929

**Dick Weber was born in Indianapolis.** He moved to Florissant in 1955 and joined the famous Budweiser bowling team. Weber went on to win 26 PBA tournaments and six senior titles, winning Bowler of the Year honors in 1961, 1963, and 1965. Weber was the sport's first television star and was the first to win a PBA title in six different decades. He died on February 13, 2005, at the age of 75.

*Courtesy Pixabay*

## December 23, 1982

**The Centers for Disease Control and the Missouri Division of Health recommended that the town of Times Beach be evacuated.** Just two months earlier, residents had learned the town could be contaminated with deadly dioxin contained in waste oil sprayed to keep the dust down on the streets years ago. A devastating flood along the Meramec River followed the news.

## December 24, 1774

**Work began on the first church in St. Louis.** The small log church was built on the same site where the Old Cathedral stands today, the only property in St. Louis that has never changed hands. Father Valentin blessed the first church bell on Christmas Eve in front of the assembled inhabitants of the village.

## December 24, 1925

**At 7 p.m., KMOX signed on the air with a word from announcer Nate Caldwell.** That was followed by a performance of the national anthem and "Hail to the Chief" by the Little Symphony Orchestra, an address by Mayor Victor Miller, and speeches by the businessmen who founded the station to promote the city. At the time, KMOX broadcast from the Mayfair Hotel at 1070 kilocycles.

## December 25, 1927

***The Jazz Singer*, the first full-length talking picture, had its St. Louis premiere.** The film at the Grand Central Theatre wowed a capacity invitation-only audience. The Grand Central at Grand and Lucas was the first theater in St. Louis specifically built for first-run motion pictures. It opened in 1913, closed in 1931, and was torn down for a parking lot in 1948.

## December 25, 1983

**The coldest Christmas Day ever was recorded in St. Louis.** The temperature hit 13 below. The record for the whitest Christmas is 9.5 inches of snow on December 25, 1913.

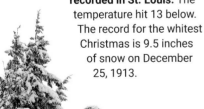

## December 24, 1892

**William Danforth opened a small feed store.** In January 1894, he incorporated the business as the Robinson-Danforth Commission Company. The store was wiped out by the 1896 tornado, and he put up a new building on Gratiot. In 1902, the company name was changed to Ralston Purina. Danforth fondly remembered the checkerboard pattern he chose to symbolize the company, something he used to illustrate his belief that a man must balance his physical, mental, social, and religious lives.

## December 25, 1895

**William Lyons and his friend Lee "Stag' Lee" or "Stack Lee" Sheldon argued inside Bill Curtiss's saloon at 11th and Morgan (now Convention Plaza).** Lyons grabbed Sheldon's lucky hat, and Sheldon shot him. The incident became the basis for the folk song "Stagger Lee," recorded by Lloyd Price, James Brown, Cab Calloway, Bob Dylan, and many others. Sheldon once lived in the lone row home on 12th Street (now Tucker) that still stands across from the former *Post-Dispatch* Building.

## December 26, 1954

**Osborne Earl Smith was born in Mobile, Alabama.** Ozzie made his big-league debut with the San Diego Padres. He came to St. Louis in a trade for Garry Templeton in 1982. "The Wizard" won 13 Gold Glove Awards and set six defensive records for shortstops. He racked up 2,460 career hits, stole 580 bases, and was named to 15 All-Star teams. His first career home run batting left-handed won Game Five of the 1985 National League Championship Series.

*Courtesy Getty Images*

### December 26, 1864

**Major James Morgan Utz was hanged as a spy.** He was arrested at Clayton and Ballas in September 1864 with Paul Fusz and five others for bringing letters and supplies to the rebels. President Lincoln issued a pardon for Utz, but it arrived too late. Fusz was only 17, so he was paroled after six months of hard labor, and the Fusz family later was known for their auto dealerships. The Utz family home was moved from Utz Lane to Brookes Park in Hazelwood in September 2003.

## December 27, 1992

**For the first time, an Asian elephant was born at the Saint Louis Zoo.** He was named Raja. He fathered four daughters: Maliha (2006), Jade (2007), Kenzi (2011–2018), and Priya (2013). As few as 35,000 Asian elephants remain in the wild according to the Saint Louis Zoo.

*Courtesy Missouri Historical Society, St. Louis*

### December 26, 1939

**W. C. Handy of Memphis, one of the legendary blues composers of all time, recorded the classic "St. Louis Blues."** Handy and his band recorded in New York for Varsity Records, and Handy was one of the first to use the flat third and seventh notes in his compositions, known in the music world as "blue" notes.

### December 27, 1983

**Walther Nothies disappeared from his St. Charles County home.** Under the name Walter Scott, he sang lead on the 1965 Bob Kuban and the In-Men hit "The Cheater." His body was found in a cistern on April 10, 1987. James Williams, who was having an affair with Scott's wife, was convicted of the crime. Williams had also murdered his own wife.

## December 28, 2015

**The National Weather Service declared 2015 as the wettest year on record in the St. Louis region to that date.** Rain was still falling. Interstate 44 between Highway 109 and I-270 was closed, and parts of Interstate 70 in St. Charles County flooded that day as the area's total rainfall had reached 58.14 inches to that point. The old record was 57.96, set in 2008. The total for 2015 would reach 61.82 inches.

### December 28, 1832

**Missouri Governor Daniel Dunklin signed the charter for Saint Louis University, the first university west of the Mississippi.** The school that became SLU opened in 1818 and was fading by 1826. Bishop Rosati revived the school and invited the Jesuits to teach in 1829. According to Jesuit tradition, no tuition could be charged, but Bishop Rosati obtained a dispensation from Pope Gregory XVI to allow the university to charge tuition.

*Courtesy Getty Images*

## December 29, 1913

**The city of Richmond Heights was incorporated.** At the time, the population was about 500. The city got its start because of a wandering quail hunter. Frederick Nelson, a wealthy Realtor, strayed onto part of the Old Spanish land grants while hunting, and he was so impressed, he promised to live there one day.

## December 30, 1964

**Some say Gaslight Square began to die on this date, when Lillian Heller was murdered at an apartment building at 4254 Gaslight Square.** Area businessmen said it was an isolated incident, but the media soon began to focus on crimes that occurred anywhere near the square, or the area and the go-go joints took over. The area is now suburban-style homes.

## December 31, 1911

**Plans were announced for the tallest building in the city at the time.** The Railway Exchange Building would occupy the entire block bounded by Olive, Locust, Sixth, and Seventh Streets, at that time occupied by the William Barr Dry Goods Company. Plans called for the first six floors of the 21-story structure to be occupied by the department store and completion was expected by January 1, 1913. Macy's vacated the building in 2013.

## December 31, 1999

**The St. Louis area braced for the worst in case the "Y2K" bug caused havoc.** Ninety percent of the city's police officers were on duty, along with 24 extra firefighters and six additional ambulances. TWA cut its schedule by a third, and hospitals brought in extra workers. The *St. Louis Business Journal* reported that 36 area companies spent $317 million preparing for the date change.

*Courtesy Wikimedia*

## December 29, 1865

**August Busch Sr. was born. He took over the brewery upon the death of Adolphus Busch in 1913.** He built the Bevo Mill to prove that beer was a beverage for respectable restaurants. August led the brewery through the dark days of Prohibition, as the brewery made yeast, corn, and syrups for the baking industry. AB even built truck bodies and refrigerated cabinets. Ailing and in intense pain, August Sr. shot himself in 1934.

## December 30, 1944

*Courtesy Wikipedia*

**The minesweeper *Inaugural* was launched at Winslow, Washington.** It earned two battle stars in the Pacific during World War II. St. Louisans Eugene Slay and Robert O'Brien brought it here as a tourist attraction in 1968, but the *Inaugural* sank after being torn from its moorings during the flood of 1993. It ended up on its side and is still visible when the river is low, although portions have been cut up for scrap.

## December 31, 1922

Planter's Hotel
*Courtesy Library of Congress*

**The landmark Planter's Hotel closed.** The various incarnations of the hotel on the west side of Fourth Street between Chestnut and Pine had hosted such dignitaries as Charles Dickens, Ulysses S. Grant, Grover Cleveland, William Howard Taft, and Theodore Roosevelt. The story that the Tom Collins was invented there is a myth. The Planter's became the Cotton Belt Building, which was torn down for the Boatman's Tower (Bank of America today).

# BIBLIOGRAPHY

Amsler, Kevin. *Final Resting Place*. St. Louis: Virginia Publishing, 1997

Bartley, Mary. *St. Louis Lost*. St. Louis: Virginia Publishing, 1994

Broeg, Bob. *The 100 Greatest Moments in St. Louis Sports*. St. Louis: Missouri Historical Society Press, 2000

Burnett, Betty. *St. Louis at War*. St. Louis: Patrice Press, 1987

Butterworth, Molly and Eyssell, Thomas. *They Will Run The Golden Age of the Automobile in St. Louis*. St. Louis: Reedy Press, 2019

Charlton, James. *The Baseball Chronology*. New York: MacMillan Publishing, 1991

Christenson, Lawrence O, Foley, William E, Kremer, Gary R and Winn, Kenneth H. *The Dictionary of Missouri Biography*. Columbia MO: University of Missouri Press, 1999

Couch, Ernie. *Missouri Trivia*. Nashville TN: Rutledge Hill Press, 1992.

Curtis, Skip. *The Route 66 Tour Book*. Lake St. Louis: Curtis Enterprises, 1994

Dahl, June Wilkerson. *A History of Kirkwood, Missouri*. Kirkwood Historical Society, 1965

Dickson, Terry. *Clayton – A History*. Von Hoffman Press, 1976

Dickson, Terry. "The Story of the Arch" in *Cherry Diamond*. St. Louis: Missouri Athletic Club, 1964

Edwards, Joe. *St. Louis Walk of Fame. 140 Great St. Louisans*. St. Louis Walk of Fame, 2013

Eisenbath, Mike. *The Cardinals Encyclopedia*. Philadelphia. Temple University Press, 1999

Everson, Linda. *St. Louis Rams Facts and Trivia*. South Bend IN: E.B. Houchin, 1995

Faherty, William Barnaby, S.J. *St. Louis – A Concise History*. St. Louis. Masonry Institute of St. Louis, 1989

Fox Tim. *Where We Live*. St. Louis. Missouri Historical Society Press 1995

Graham, Shellee. *Tales From the Coral Court*. St. Louis. Virginia Publishing 2000

Grant, H. Roger, Hosommer, Don L. and Overby, Osmund. *St. Louis Union Station*. St. Louis Mercantile Library Association, 1994

Hannon, Robert E. *St. Louis: Its Neighborhoods and Neighbors, Landmarks and Milestones*. St. Louis. Regional Commerce and Growth Association, 1986

Harris, Nini. *A Legacy of Lions, a History of University City*. University City: University City Historical Society, 1981

Hernon Peter and Ganey, Terry. *Under the Influence, the Unauthorized Story of the Anheuser-Busch Dynasty*. New York: Simon and Schuster, 1991

Horgan, James J. *City of Flight*. St. Louis. Patrice Press 1984

Jackson, Pattti Smith. *St. Louis Arena Memories*. St. Charles: GBH Publishers, 2000

Jenson, Billie Snell in *Louisiana Purchase Exposition*. St. Louis: Missouri Historical Society, 1979

Kirsten, Ernest. *Catfish and Crystal*. Garden City, NY: Doubleday, 1960

Leptich, John and Barnowski Dave. *This Date in St. Louis Cardinal History*. New York: Stein and Day, 1983

Linzee, Davis. *St. Louis Crimes and Mysteries*. St. Louis: Palmerston and Reed, 2001

Loughlin, Caroline and Anderson, Catherine. *Forest Park*. St. Louis: Junior League of St. Louis and University of Missouri Press, 1986

Magnan, William B. and Marcella C. *The Streets of St. Louis*. St. Louis. Virginia Publishing, 1986

Malone, Ross. *This Day in Missouri History*. Union, MO. Ross Malone

Miksicek, Barbara; McElreath, David and Pollihan, Steven. *In the Line of Duty*. St. Louis: Metropolitan Police Department, 1991

Nunes, Bill. *Southern Illinois an Illustrated History*. Glen Carbon, IL: Bill Nunes, 2001

Nunes, Bill. *The Big Book of St. Louis Nostalgia*. Glen Carbon, IL. Bill Nunes, 2009

Potter, McClure. *Missouri: Its Geography, History and Government*. Chicago. Laidlaw Publishers, 1940.

Powell, Jim. "Route 66 Timeline" in *Show Me Route 66 Magazine*. Route 66 Association of Missouri Fall 2001

Priddy, Bob. *Across Our Wide Missouri* (3 Volumes). Independence, MO: Herald House/Independence Press, 1982

Primm, James. *Lion of the Valley*. Boulder, CO: Pruett Publising, 1981

Scharf, John Thomas. *History of St. Louis City and County*. Philadelphia. Louis Everts and Co. 1883

*St. Louis Globe-Democrat*

*St. Louis Post-Dispatch*

*St. Louis Republic*

*St. Louis Star-Times*

Stadler, Frances Hurd. *St. Louis Day by Day*. St. Louis: Patrice Press, 1989

Stage, William. *Mound City Chronicles*. St. Louis: Hartman Publishing, 1991

Start, Clarissa. *Webster Groves*. City of Webster Groves, 1975

Steele, Tim. *The Cardinals Chronology*. St. Louis. Palmerston and Reed. 2001

Wacker, Stephen P. Lemp. *The Haunting History*. St. Louis: Lemp Preservation Society, 1988

Wayman, Norbury L. *St. Louis Union Station and Its Railroads*. St. Louis: The Evelyn E. Newman Group, 1987

Whitburn, Joel. *The Billboard Book of Top 40 Hits*. New York: Billboard Publications, 1987.

Winter, William C. *The Civil War in St. Louis*. St. Louis: Missouri Historical Society Press, 1994.

Works Progress Administation. *Missouri: The WPA Guide to the Show Me State*. Jefferson City, Missouri State Highway Department, 1941

Wright, John. *Discovering African-American St. Louis: A Guide to Historic Sites*. St. Louis: Missouri Historical Society Press, 1994.

Boyer, Clete, 110
Boyer, Ken, 56, 63, 103
Bozek, Steve, 27
Bradley, William Warren, 80
Brady, James, 107
Brantford, Ontario, 9
Breckenridge, Donald, 43
Breedlove, Sarah, 133
Brennan, Eileen, 112
Brentwood, Missouri, 131
Bridgestone Winter Classic, 1
Bridgeton, 13, 22, 108
Bridgeton Station Road, 28
Brinkop, Harold, 130
British Empire, 17
Britt, Albert, 110
Britton, James, 55
Broadhead, William, 41
Broadway, 43, 70, 95
Broadway Drive-In, 59
Brock, Lou, 3, 65, 66, 80, 86, 92, 97, 103, 109, 110
Broeg, Bob, 101, 122
Broglio, Ernie, 3, 65
Bronx, New York, 98
Bronx Zoo, 70
Brookes Park in Hazelwood, 135
Brookings, Robert, 120
Brooklyn, New York, 11, 76
Brooks, Hugh M., 38
Brown, Charles, 73
Brown, James, 134
Brown, LeRoy, 114
Brown, Michael, 84, 85, 123
Brown, Rose, 96
Brown, Sterling Kelby, 38
Browning, Iben, 127
Brownsville, Tennessee, 124
Bruce, Isaac, 11, 84
Bruce, Lenny, 34
Brunswick, 49
Buchek, Jerry, 52
Buck, Joe, 45
Buck, John Francis "Jack," 16, 22, 45, 46, 60, 66, 67, 83, 89, 100, 103, 110
Buckingham Hotel, 117
Buder building, 90
Budovice, Ceske, 8
Budweiser, 8, 11, 35, 39, 133
Budweiser Brew House, 35
Buffalo Zoo, 35
Builders Square, 90
Bullock, Anna Mae, 117, 124
Bullock, James, 99
Bunce, Elsworth W., 18
Burger King, 82
Burlington, Iowa, 67
Burroughs, William, 13
Burroughs Adding Machine Company, 13
Busch, Adolphus, 8, 27, 53, 136
Busch, August "Gussie," Jr.,16, 21, 30, 35, 39, 51, 133
Busch, August, Sr., 15, 61, 136
Busch Estate, 61
Busch family, 75
Busch Stadium, 1, 35, 40, 44, 51, 83
Busch Stadium II, 42
Bush, Captain Prescott, 64
Bush, George Herbert Walker, 64
Bush, George Walker, 64
Buzz Westfall Plaza, 120
Byzantine coin, 16
Cabanne, Charles, 92
Cahokia, Illinois, 35, 43, 58, 69, 87
Cain, Bob, 88

Caldwell, Nate, 134
Calgary, 27, 128
Calloway, Cab, 134
Camp Adams, 113
Camp DuBois, 53
Camp Jackson, 35
Campbell Conference Finals, 5
Canada, 74
Candy, John, 124
Canfield Drive, 84
Cannon, Captain John, 72
Canton, Ohio, 69, 84
Capone, Al, 101
Capone Gang, 127
Caputa, Sam, 123
Carabina, Harry Christopher, 25
Caray, Harry, 16, 18, 25, 46, 66, 89
Carbone, Tom, 123
Cardinals Hall of Fame Museum, 35
Cardinals Nation restaurant, 35
Carlton, Steve, 21, 133
Carnahan, Mel, 63, 111
Carnahan, Randy, 111
Carnegie, Andrew, 3
Carolina Panthers, 119
Carondelet, 25, 50
Carpathia, 43
Carpenter, Chris, 119
Carpenter, John, 68
Carr, Connie, 14
Carroll, Phil, 98
Carroll College, 96
Carson, Johnny, 62, 66
Carter, Al, 78
Carthage, Missouri, 35
Carver High School, 21
Carver, John, Jr., 114
Cassilly, Bob, 114
Cathedral Basilica, 9, 64, 68, 70
Cats, 2
Caulfield, Henry, 11, 102, 116
CBS Radio Network, 39
CBS Television, 21
Cecil Place, 49
Cedar Rapids, Iowa, 67
Centennial Week, 108
Centers for Disease Control, 133
Centerville, Missouri, 43
Central Division, 122
Central Hardware, The, 102
Central Visual and Performing Arts High School, 113
Central West End, 35, 112
Century Electric Foundry, 85
Ceries, Mr. and Mrs. Ed, 15
Cérre, Gabriel, 121
Cervantes, Alfonso J., 35, 38, 57, 69, 91, 92, 114
Chain of Rocks, 34, 51
Chain of Rocks Bridge, 38, 60, 68, 76
Chain of Rocks Canal, 51
Chain of Rocks Fun Fair, 41
Chamber of Commerce, 82
Champ Dairy Farm, 41
Channel Nine, 101
Channel Two, 15
Chapter of the Congress of Racial Equality, 36
Chartrand, Joseph, 121
Chase and Sanborn Hour, 115
Chase Hotel, 32, 66, 93, 105
Chase, Chevy, 80
Chatsworth, 78
Checkerboard Square, 4
Checkerdome, 79
Chess Records of Chicago, 49

Chess, Leonard, 49
Chesterfield, Missouri, 60
Chesterfield Mercantile, 60
Chesterfield Valley, 81, 82
Chew, 128
Chicago Cardinals, 29
Chicago Cubs, 3, 21, 25, 53, 65, 67, 86, 96, 97
Chicago, Illinois, 4, 10, 12, 29, 39, 40, 44, 52, 55, 58, 67, 78, 88, 101, 104, 115
Chicago Tribune, 117
Chicago White Sox, 18, 25, 79, 104, 107
Chicago White Stockings, 50
Chief Pontiac, 43
Chippewa, 6, 18, 90, 127, 130
Cholera epidemic, 19, 20, 27
Chouteau Avenue, 1, 129
Chouteau, René-Auguste, 17, 21, 82, 95, 97, 123
Christian Brothers College High School (CBC), 73, 75, 107
Christmas Day, 134
Christmas Eve, 134
Cincinnati, Ohio, 12, 40, 89
Cincinnati Reds, 46, 76, 105
Citizen Kane, 128
City 66, 7, 83
City Bathhouse #6, 53
City Council, 15, 72, 116, 120
City Foundry, 85
City Museum, The, 114
City Route 66, 50, 90
City Sanitarium, 44
City Workhouse, 59
Citygarden, 71
Civic Center Redevelopment, 30
Civil Courts Building, 67, 90
Civil rights, 9, 32, 57, 67, 123, 133
Civil War, 13
Clark, Brady, 40
Clark, George Rogers, 58
Clark, Jack, 114
Clark, Vonda, 51
Clark, William, 27, 53, 88
Clark Bridge, 2
Clarksdale, Mississippi, 117
Clay, Henry 37
Clay, William L., 36
Clayco Construction, The, 26
Clayton, Missouri, 41, 107, 113, 116
Clayton Road, 75, 115, 135
Clayton, Ohio, 78
Clayton, Ralph, 20
Clayton's Oak Knoll Park, 116
Clean Room, 50
Clemens, Doug, 65
Clemens, Samuel, 12, 39, 125
Clemons, Reginald, 38
Cleveland Spiders, 29
Cleveland, Grover, 106, 136
Climatron, 88
Clinton, Bill, 9
Clinton, Massachusetts, 128
Club Imperial, 50
Club Manhattan, 50, 117, 124
Clydesdales, The, 11, 39
Coast Guard, 54
Cobb, Ty, 2, 92
Coca-Cola Santa Claus, 35
Cockrell, J. W., 110
Col. John D. Hopkins' vaudeville theater, 57
Colbert, Nate, 49
Coldwater Creek, 53, 107, 108
Cole, Nat King, 32

Cole Street, 73
Coleman, Vince, 124
Collins, Tom, 136
Collinsville, Illinois, 127
Colorado Rockies, 37
Columbia Poetry Society of America Prize, 84
Columbia, Illinois, 82
Columbian Exposition, 52
Columbo, Charles, 69
Comfort Printing and Stationery Company, 57
Compton, Arthur Holly, 101
Compton, William, 4
Compton Hill, 35
Condit, Phil, 131
Confederacy, 39, 105
Conn Smythe Trophy, 64
Connecticut, 8, 122
Connelly, John, 131
Connor, Jeremiah, 31
Connors, The, 66
Conqueror, The, 128
Conrad, Carl, 8
Conrad Properties, 49
Continental Building, 77, 99
Continental Insurance Company, 77
Convent Street, 129
Coolidge, Calvin, 125
Cooper, Alice, 113
Cooper, Mort, 107, 108
Cooper, Theodore, 129
Coors Field, 37
Coral Court Motel, 49
CORE, 36
Corky the Clown, 26
Corman, Roger, 58
Corps of Engineers, 7
Corregidor, 59
Corvette Assembly Plant, 34
Corvettes, 34, 81
Costas, Bob, 33, 111
Costello, Joe, 104
Cotton Belt Building, 136
Cotton Comes to Harlem, 129
Couch, William H., 95
Country Grammar, 69
Court of Honor, 39, 59
COVID-19, 30, 84, 88
Cray, Robert, 64
Crestwood, Missouri, 15, 32, 63, 119
Crestwood Plaza, 63
Creve Coeur Lake, 68, 133
Creve Coeur, Missouri, 89, 133
Crockett, Davy, 37
Crow, Sheryl, 75
Crowe, R. T., 54
Crow's Nest Loop, 68
Cruz, José, 86
Crystal City, Missouri, 80
Crystal Palace, 76
Cuba, 99
Cunningham, Charles, 82
Cupples Complex, 115, 120
Cupples Woodware, 120
Curtiss, Bill, 134
Curtiss, Glenn, 108
Curtiss-Parks Airport, 69
Curtiss-Steinberg Airport, 69
Curtiss-Wright, 69
Custer, George, 34
Cy Young Awards, 21, 133
Cyrkle, The, 89
Dallas, Texas, 123
Danforth, John Claggett, 96
Danforth, William, 3, 134

St. Ann, Missouri, 41, 102
St. Charles, Missouri, 28
St. Charles County, 40, 65, 81
St. Charles Rock Road, 102, 103, 121, 123
St. Clair County, 35, 77
St. Ferdinand, 107
St. Francis de Sales Church, 124
St. George, Utah, 128
St. James, Clif, 26
St. John's Mercy Medical Center, 11
St. John's Methodist Church, 121
St. Louis Advertising Club, 42
St. Louis Air Exposition, 18
St. Louis Aquarium, 92
St. Louis Avenue, 53
St. Louis Blues, 1, 3, 5, 9, 13, 21, 22, 27, 28, 34, 37, 43, 52, 59, 61, 62, 64, 79, 83, 95, 106, 116, 118, 122, 125, 128, 130, 132
St. Louis Board of Alderman, 34, 37
St. Louis Board of Public Service, 120
St. Louis Bombers, 33
St. Louis Brown Stockings, The, 12, 50
St. Louis Browns, 14
*St. Louis Business Journal*, 136
St. Louis Cardinals, 3, 4, 5, 6, 7, 8, 10, 12, 16, 17, 18, 19, 21, 22, 25, 35, 37, 40, 41, 44, 45, 56, 49, 50, 51, 52, 53, 56, 57, 61, 62, 63, 65, 66, 67, 69, 71, 73, 75, 76, 78, 79, 84, 85, 86, 89, 92, 96, 97, 98, 99, 100, 101, 103, 106, 107, 108, 109, 110, 111, 112, 114, 118, 122, 124, 125, 133
St. Louis Circuit Court, 70
St. Louis City, 56
St. Louis City and County, 89
St. Louis City Hall, 40, 55, 65
St. Louis City Insane Asylum, 44
St. Louis Coliseum, 79
St. Louis Colored Orphans Home, 52
St. Louis Community College at Forest Park, 77
St. Louis County Court, 41, 82, 97
St. Louis County Lunatic Asylum, 44
*St. Louis Globe-Democrat*, 2, 17, 26, 36, 77, 102, 115, 123, 129
"St. Louis Has It All from A to Z," 45
St. Louis Hawks, 33, 49
St. Louis National League, 40
St. Louis Ordnance Plant, 131
St. Louis Perfectos, 29
St. Louis Police Department, 74
*St. Louis Post-Dispatch*, 10, 16, 17, 21, 36, 40, 41, 43, 53, 55, 60, 61, 95, 101, 103, 105, 108, 110, 120, 130
St. Louis Psychiatric Rehabilitation Center, 44
St. Louis Rams, 8, 10, 11, 12, 13, 15, 21, 67, 83, 84, 90, 91, 119, 132
St. Louis Regional Commerce and Growth Association, 45
St. Louis Republic, 29, 57
St. Louis Science Center, 116
St. Louis soccer team, 44
St. Louis Spirits of the ABA, 33
*St. Louis Star-Times*, 59

St. Louis State Hospital, 44
St. Louis Steamers, 130
St. Louis Superintendent of Schools, 62
St. Louis Symphony Orchestra, The, 9
St. Louis Theatre, 9
St. Louis Walk of Fame on Delmar, 68
St. Louis Wheel, 92
St. Louis World's Fair, 10
St. Louis. Beaumont Street, 122
St. Louisans, 39
St. Mary's High School, 31
St. Patrick's Day, 31
St. Paul Foundry Company, 96
St. Petersburg, Florida, 103
St. Rose Philippine Duchesne, 121
St. Vincent DePaul, 124
St. Vincent DePaul Church, 15
St. Vincent DePaul Hospital, 100
Stadium East Garage, 43
*Stalag*, 42
Stan Musial Veterans Memorial Bridge, 14
Standells, The, 74
Stanford, 38
Stanley Cup Finals, 34
Stanwyck, Barbara, 42
*Star Trek*, 108
Starkes, Charles, 107
Starr, Ringo, 113
State Department of Education, 17
State Highway Department, 76
State Hospital, 58
Station 9YK, 45
Steak 'n Shake, 59, 127
Steely Dan, 16
Stein farm, 41
Steinberg, Mark, 69
Stengel, Casey, 74
Stephen and Peter Sachs Museum, 65
*Steptoe and Son*, 129
Sterling, Andrew B., 12
Stewart, Ron, 125
Stifel Theatre, 83
Stix, John, 10, 44
Stocksick, Bill, 51
Stockton, J. Roy, 108
Stoddard, Captain Amos, 28
Stole, 49
Stone, Edward Durell, 29
Stonecipher, Harry, 131
Stratford, Virginia, 7
Strauss, Leon and Mary, 97
Streckfus Steamers, 131
Streckfuss Lines, 54
Street Angel, 11
Streetcar Series, The, 108
Streisand, Barbra, 34
Stromberg, Germany, 74
Sublette Avenue, 44, 72
Sullivan, Louis, 59, 117
Sulphur Springs, 129
Sumner High School, 111
Sunset Boulevard, 42
Sunset Hills Country Club, 61
Sunset Hills, Missouri, 61
Sunset Inn, 61
Super Bowl, 11, 67
Super Bowl XXXIV, 11, 13, 15, 83, 84
Super Bridge, 2
Super Sports, 61
Superdome, 21, 100
Sutherland, John H., 38

Sutter, Brian, 13
Sutter, Bruce, 4, 103, 112
Switzer, Frederick, 113
Switzer Candy Co., 113
Swoboda, Mike, 14
Sycamore, 71
Symphony Orchestra, 134
T-38 jet, 22
Taft, William Howard, 46, 136
Taillon, Joseph, 95
"Take Me Out to the Ball Game," 18
"Takin' It to the Streets," 16
Tampa Bay Buccaneers, 132
Tampa, Florida, 8, 107
Tarasenko, Vladimir, 1
Tarawa, 29, 101
Tardif, Patrice, 9, 22
Targee, Thomas, 55
Targee Street, 55, 110
Tatis, Fernando, 44
Taylor, Zach, 88
Taylor family, 116
TD Garden, 64
Teasdale, Sara, 53, 84, 116, 129
Tehran, 117
Temple, Oklahoma, 22
Templeton, Garry, 135
Tenbrook, 101
Tennessee, 5, 39
Tennessee Titans, 11
Terminal Hotel, 91
Territorial Enterprise, 12
Tesson Ferry, 20
Texas Rangers, 114
Thierry, August, 12
*This Is Us*, 38
Thomas, Gorman, 112
Thompson, Floyd, 3
Thornton, Charles "Cookie," 14
Thurman, Mike, 104
*Thursday Night Football*, 132
Tibbe, Henry, 73
Tilden, Samuel, 99
Timberlake, Mary, 90
Times Beach, 59, 133
*Titanic*, 41, 43
*Today Show, The*, 16, 114
Tokyo, 43
*Tonight Show, The*, 62
Tony Awards, 113
Tony Faust's Oyster House and Restaurant, 1, 70, 108
Toronto Maple Leafs, 21, 61
Torre, Joe, 73, 76
Toth, Paul, 65
Tower Grove, 29, 50, 65, 78
Tower Grove House, 65
Tower Grove Park, 29
Trachsel, Steve, 97
Track 35, 117
Trade Winds, The, 74
Trampe, Stephen, 77
Trans World Dome, 9, 119
Trapnell, Thomas, 67
Travelers Aid Society, 100
*Treemonisha*, 123
Trigen Energy Corporation, 37
Triple Crown, 33
*Trouble with Girls, The*, 58
Trudeau, Zenon, 87
Truman, Harry, 56, 63
Tucker, Raymond, 22, 28, 59, 73, 84
Tunis, 45
Tunisia, 90
Turner, Ike, 50, 84, 117, 124
Turner, James Milton, 17
Turner, Tina, 6, 50, 84, 124

Tuxedo Park, 37
TWA, 4, 9, 19, 35
Twain, Mark, 12, 39, 95
Uhrig's Cave, 79
Ullman, Chase, 105
Unger, Garry, 21, 59, 128
Union Electric powerhouse, The, 37
Union Pacific, 82
Union Station, 52
United States, 16, 66
University City, 41, 43, 68, 96
University of Missouri, 78
Upper Louisiana, 28
Upson, Walter P., 17
US 66, 60, 102
US Census Bureau, 39
US Justice Department, 84
US Marine, 67
US Men's National Soccer team, 69
US Secretary, 57
US Senate, 26
US Supreme Court, 27, 49
US War Department, 60, 77
USS *Lexington*, 29
Utz, James Morgan, 135
Valentin, Father, 134
Varsity Records, 135
Varsity Theater, The, 2
Vatican, 64
Vatterott, Charles F., 41
Vaughn, Ron, 106
VE Day, 51
Veeck, Bill, 19, 71, 73, 88, 90
Veiled Prophet Ball, 108
Venture, 6
Verhaegen, Father Peter, 121
Vermeil, Dick, 11, 12, 15, 84
Versing, Von, 49
Veterans Bridge, 5
Veterans Committee, 22
Veterans Linoleum and Rug Company, 12
Veterans Memorial Bridge, 32
Vezina Trophy, 5
VFW Hall in Eldorado, 104
Viacom, 73
Vierheller Station, 92
Vietnam, 62
Villa a Robert, 22, 108
Village of Carondelet, 110
Village of Hazelwood, 97
Village of Madison, Illinois, 60
Village of St. Peters, The, 18
Vincent, John C., 99
Vintage Vinyl, 2
Virginia, 20, 32, 54
Virginia City, Nevada, 12
Vito, Frank, 44
Von der Ahe, Chris, 53
Vopat, Roman, 9, 22
VP Fair, 32
Wabash Transit Company, 97
Wadlow, Robert Pershing, 20
Wagner, Honus, 55
Wainwright Building, 59, 117
Wainwright, Adam, 96, 99, 101
Wainwright, Ellis, 59, 117
Wainwright, General Jonathan, 59
Walgreens, 1, 6
*Walk Hard: The Dewey Cox Story*, 27
Walker, Eli, 64
Walker, George Herbert, 64
Walker, Harry, 45
Walker, Madam C. J., 133
Wallace, Bobby, 45